OFFENSIVE LITERATURE

Decensorship in Britain, 1960–1982

OFFENSIVE LITERATURE

Decensorship in Britain, 1960–1982

John Sutherland

BARNES & NOBLE BOOKS
TOTOWA, NEW JERSEY

© 1982 John Sutherland

First published in Great Britain by
Junction Books Ltd
15 St John's Hill
London SW11

First published in the USA 1983 by
Barnes & Noble Books
81 Adams Drive
Totowa, New Jersey, 07512

Library of Congress Cataloguing in Publication Data

Sutherland, John   1938–
  Offensive literature.

  Includes index.
  1.   Censorship–Great Britain–history.
  I.   Title.
Z658.G7S87   1983   323,44′5   82-22758

ISBN 0 389 20354 8

Contents

Preface and Acknowledgements

In organisation, this book is a calendar following a series of events (mainly trials) from 1960 to the present day. The aim is to investigate how Britain's 'permissive' society has come to terms with 'prohibited' books, or 'offensive literature'. I have had a personal motive for writing and for the chronological layout. I was an undergraduate, flushed with liberal enthusiasm, at the time of the *Chatterley* trial. Everything seemed clear in November 1960: 'literature' had won, repression (or the 'custodians' as one of my lecturers, Richard Hoggart, called them) had lost. After this date, although a lot always seemed to be happening on the obscenity–pornography front, things were never clear again. This book is an attempt to set the subject in order. The pattern which has emerged is not straightforward; indeed at times it is crazy. Nor does the struggle seem as noble to me as it once did. But the sequential exercise has been useful to me, and I hope it will be so for others.

Particular books have been very useful to me. In the section on *Lady Chatterley's Lover* I have drawn on Hugh Ford's *Published in Paris* (1975), C.H. Rolph's *The Trial of Lady Chatterley* (1961) and Charles Rembar's *The End of Obscenity* (1968); in the section on 'The End of the Lord Chamberlain' I have drawn on *Bond: A Study of his Plays* by Philip Roberts and Malcolm Hay; in the section on *OZ* 28, I have drawn on Tony Palmer's *The Trials of OZ* (1971); in the section on 'The Fall of the Dirty Squad' I have drawn on Barry Cox's *The Fall of Scotland Yard* (1978); in the section on the *Gay News* blasphemy trial, I have drawn on the account given by Nicolas Walter, as a pamphlet for the Rationalist Press Association.

I thank my colleague and publisher, Michael Mason for encouragement, Stephen Fender for advice and Geoffrey Soare for help with the University College library's collection of underground publications.

Introduction

Historically, this book is mainly concerned with the career of the 1959 Obscene Publications Act – sometimes called the 'Jenkins Act' after the backbencher (later Home Secretary) who sponsored it. As it was first formulated, this piece of law was two pronged. It was designed to 'provide for the protection of literature and to strengthen the law concerning pornography'. Optimists may have thought the victory for 'literature' decisively won in November 1960 with the liberation of *Lady Chatterley*. The forces of reaction were, however, tenacious and ingenious. They staged a notable counter-attack with *Fanny Hill* in 1964 – putting that innocent novel into bowdlerised limbo for six years. And they almost put the clock right back with the *Last Exit to Brooklyn* trial of 1967 when, against all expectation and judicial direction, a jury ignored the 'experts' and found a manifestly literary (if hardboiled) novel from a respectable (if chance-taking) publisher, obscene. Only the Court of Appeal saved the authorities from the embarrassment of a new dark age. But with eventual clearance of Selby's novel, the trials of 'literature' (that is to say, critically approved texts with identifiable single authors) were over. The liberals had won their battle.

Meanwhile the longer-term drive against 'pornography' continued. For a while, it seemed as if authority's main target was to be the burgeoning mass-market paperback. Some custodians had been alarmed less at the four-letter words and 'bouts' in *Lady Chatterley's Lover* than at the fact that they were available to all in a 3s.6d book. Part of the motivation of the Mayflower–*Fanny Hill* trial was that John Cleland's chaste (linguistically) erotic picaresque fiction had the temerity also to appear in a 3s.6d. version. An expensive *édition de luxe* was tolerated. John Calder found mitigating favour with the authorities in that he invariably brought out

1

his most explosive items (e.g., Alexander Trocchi's *Cain's Book*, Henry Miller's *Tropics*, William Burroughs's *The Naked Lunch*) in small hardback editions at a higher price than the going rate for new novels. The firm was certainly persecuted (over *Last Exit*, for instance), but not as much as they would have been had they, like their equivalent Grove Press in the US, put out books which were strong in content and cheap in price.

The paperback revolution was not to be denied, however, and with the eruption of new, aggressive firms (Pan, Panther, Sphere, etc.) the attempt to stem mass-market books was given up. Hence the all-time bestsellers of the 1960s and 1970s are dominated by novels which would have been unpublishable, in Britain or America, before 1960 (e.g., Erica Jong's *Fear of Flying*, Philip Roth's *Portnoy's Complaint*, Harold Robbins's *The Carpetbaggers*).

The law, and its enforcers, had other, more alarming problems than the man in the street's deplorable taste in reading matter. The 1960s released all sorts of new energies and dissidence. Television, stage and film chafed against restriction. There was a new charter for the BBC in 1964 and liberal direction under Hugh Carleton Greene (a truly demonic figure, according to Mrs Whitehouse). At the British Board of Film Censors, John Trevelyan liberalised film licensing. It was a gradual process, but in terms of the milestones by which such things are measured, 1966-68 would seem to have been the critical threshold. In November 1966, Kenneth Tynan used the word 'fuck' in a television studio discussion. There was immediate uproar, but the monosyllable could not be unsaid. Threatened prosecution of Edward Bond's *Saved* in 1967 mobilised Parliament at last to get rid of the ludicrous Lord Chamberlain's censorship. And Lindsay Anderson's film *If* (1968) got through to general release with a tuft of female pubic hair visible to the 18-plus British population. As Roy Jenkins put it in a phrase which the *Daily Telegraph* will throw back in his face for ever more – the permissive society was the civilized society. Liberalisation was fought every inch, but its tide in the 1960s was irresistible.

The struggle was not pitched simply on the grounds of morality, aesthetics and standards of artistic permissibility. Ideology crept in. Youth revolutionaries of 1960 onwards employed sexual radicalism of a kind their elders easily mistook for old-fashioned filth. (*Fuck You!* was the title of one internationally circulated underground magazine, *Suck* another, *Nasty Tales* a third). After 1964-5 (see my later discussions of *Cain's Book* and *The Golden Convulvulus*) censorious attention was increasingly directed at the counter-culture. Drugs, rock music, tough talk and ostentatiously relished sex were absorbed into a cloudy new definition of 'obscenity'. A number of legal auxiliaries to the 1959 Act were recruited for the crackdown: conspiracy to corrupt public morals (a charge conveniently 'invented' in 1961); the 1953 Postal Act (underground magazines were dependent on the mails); even the antique vagrancy acts.

This drive against youth radicalism was conducted with ruthlessness and frequent illegality by the police. Manifest and unfair 'political' persecution on spurious grounds of obscenity had the effect of keeping the liberals, who might otherwise have hung up their guns in 1968, in a state of militant opposition to censorship. John Mortimer defending Richard Neville (or later in the day, Johnny Rotten of the Sex Pistols) represented a potent alliance between Hampstead and the counter-culture. The crunch year was undoubtedly 1971, with the *IT*, *Little Red Schoolbook*, *OZ* and *The Mouth* trials – all of which were scored (initially at least) to the authorities and the censorious populists headed by Mrs Whitehouse. Effectively, this battle ended with the *Nasty Tales* acquittal in 1973. It cannot be said that either side won, merely that the issue was no longer historically relevant. For the youth–radical press of the middle and late 1970s, sexual offensiveness was not any more a legitimate weapon. Indeed, the new opinion-formers like *Time Out*, the *Leveller* or *City Limits* took a severely puritanical line against 'sexist' pornography.

The period 1973-77 is confused and shabby. 'Liberal' pressure (embodied in what Mrs Whitehouse contemptuously called 'Mortimer's travelling circus') was apparently prepared to defend anything, however insignificant or seamy. As Mortimer himself put it, after the *OZ* verdict, 'there cannot be a limit on the writer.' Therefore, any limit must be over-thrown, even if it meant going to the stake for the most exploitative of skin mags. This inglorious phase ended with the tacky *Linda Lovelace* defence in 1976. A tawdry ghost-written book of confessions was defended by a panel of experts and distinguished counsel who could scarcely have been more righteously passionate had they been defending *Anna Karenina* against the Czar's censors.

After *Lovelace*, it seems tacitly to have been agreed that nothing printed could be obscene. Phonetic transcriptions printed on a page could no more be obscene (though they could still be racially offensive, or betrayals of state secrecy) than music. This understanding was confirmed by the *Williams Report* in 1979.

The road to freedom from censorship over the period 1960-77 is best conceived as a series of rushing advances, encountered by stubborn rearguard and backlash actions. The permissives would gain a couple of points, Mrs Whitehouse (or Lord Longford, Raymond Blackburn, David Holbrook, The Festival of Light) would regain one. To follow a typical sequence: the socialist Attorney-General in the mid 1960s evidently resolved not to prosecute any book which had a vouched-for claim to be 'literary'. Illiberal (and Tory) opponents of this policy therefore brought a private prosecution against *Last Exit*. After that affair was rather messily concluded, the authorities closed the private prosecution option within the 1959 law. In order to force trials, Mrs Whitehouse resourcefully dug up blasphemy, gross indecency and vagrancy pretexts for private action. In one of these far-fetched cases (that of *Gay News*), she won; the others she lost on technicalities, having 'made her point'.

Meanwhile, in the shadows behind these spotlighted censorship spectacles, 'pornography' was growing steadily from a hole-in-corner specialist supply service to a multi-million pound, efficiently organised industry. The 1959 law had created, at a stroke of the drafter's pen, a vast new 'legitimate' market – but no geared-up British mass production to exploit it. This new market would not be satisfied with *Lady Chatterley's Lover* (which sold over two million copies in its first year) once the novelty of seeing 'fuck' in print was passed. There was, accordingly, a huge suction into Britain of material from abroad. Up to 1964, the main source of supply was America; thereafter, newly emancipated Europe and Scandinavia. The import surge is reflected in customs seizures of pornographic materials, which between the late 1950s and mid 1960s rose from 2,000 items annually to a million or more.

For most of the 1960s, the British domestic production of pornography was on a cottage-industrial scale. Where the business thrived, it imported. Even the very softest, and most respectably laundered porn was felt to be un-English. In December 1964, Anne Kerr MP asked questions in the House about *Penthouse*, a copy of which had been sent her by a constituent. It was, she declared: 'perverted muck . . . the

House should be on record as opposing the dissemination of this type of vicious literature.' It marks some kind of revolution to note that thirteen years later, Enoch Powell was happy to give the monthly star-interview in Mr Guccione's congenially Tory journal.

By the end of the 1960s, three factors were combining to give the British a firm base in their own porn market, and even a useful export capacity. First of these was the 'boutique' revolution in shop styles. All over the country, as the 1960s swung, retailing became trendier; less assistance from pin-striped assistants with 'lines of goods', more self-service and gaiety. Porn in Britain had traditionally retailed through dubious 'herbalists', 'novelty shops' and the seedier newsagents. Now there were established in London 'sex shops' whose demeanour was wholesome and hedonistic. There was no shame, no furtiveness. It was 'normal' to buy vibrators, sexy underwear and a magazine or two to pep up one's love life. These shops had nice, affirmative names (Ann Summers, Aquarius, The Joy of Sex) and pretty young ladies at the till. Men *and* women were invited to browse. It was all respectable and commercially legal. For, as the 1970 American *Report on Pornography* revealed, the typical user was not the legendary pervert in his dirty mackintosh, but 'predominantly white, middle class, married males, dressed in a business suit or neat casual attire'. Sex shops were also middle class, casual and neat.

Sex shops gave a legitimate front to pornography from which it benefited enormously (although mail order and 'specialist' suppliers continued operating less visibly). A second, and perhaps more significant factor in the industry's expansion was the emergence on the scene of a generation of young, entrepreneurial publishers (Paul Raymond was probably the most dynamic). These businessmen were determined to cash in on the market opened up by *Playboy*. Hugh Hefner's magazine (which started obscurely in 1953) was a miscellany which exploited post-1959 freedoms. It used new and visually imaginative pictorial techniques (the famous centrefolds, for instance). Hefner, like the sex shops, was in the absolution business. According to the 'Playboy philosophy', promiscuous hedonistic sex was normal. *Playboy* also projected an intensely consumerist lifestyle: the real pin-ups sometimes seemed the Lamborghini cars or Sony hi-fis. Hefner took no 'inadequacy ads' (e.g., dealing with baldness, acne, impotence). The way of life valued by *Playboy* was unblemished, physically and morally.

Avis to Hefner's Hertz was Bob Guccione, with *Penthouse*. It was similar in style and layout to *Playboy* but had a more rightist political attitude. Like *Playboy*, the *Penthouse* operation diversified into clubs, films, books. Downmarket (after 1974), was Larry Flynt with *Hustler*; an all out 'raunchy' magazine, it constantly nudged against the permissible in its pictures and projected tough, machismo attitudes. It was less concerned with sophisticated living than its competitors.

It was the *Penthouse* and *Hustler* styles which were principally adopted in Britain with magazines like *Men Only*, *Knave*, *Rustler*, *Club* and the insolently named *Whitehouse*. They used legitimate distribution systems (*Mayfair* was even carried by W.H. Smith) and their success was extraordinary. As a depressed David Holbrook put it (*Spectator*, 13 April 1974): 'if *Mayfair* sells half a million, we must be a nation of masturbators.' Circulations of 300,000 or more were routine for the market leaders, which pushed their tamer American originals well into the second division. These home-grown skin mags were multiply profitable in that not only were they 'stronger', they could also carry London advertisements for saunas, massage parlours, private shops, 'models' and classified 'contact' advertisements. Following *Playboy*, they had the equivalent of 'agony columns' which in many cases (following *Forum*'s success) were hived off into small format 'advice' and 'sexual research' magazines.

A third factor fostering the late 1960s–early 1970s boom was the corruption of the Metropolitan Police's Obscene Publications Squad. Until Robert Mark undertook the Augean task of cleansing his force, the 'dirty squad' ran Soho like a fiefdom, and with a business efficiency which the Kray gang might have envied. While straight or 'soft' porn boomed country-wide via conventional newsagents, hard or 'bent' porn (e.g., that dealing with flagellation, pederasty, excretion, sodomy, bondage) was given free range in Soho. Providing, that is, payoffs were made. The OPS was finally purged in 1977, culminating in the most embarrassing series of trials Scotland Yard had ever had to live through. But the infrastructure or industrial base for the pornography market was laid down. The producers subsequently organised themselves (via such self-regulating organisations as BAPA – the British Adult Publications Association) and the boom went on.

In 1980, the national press realised with a jolt that the country had a fully grown sex industry, and that it was transforming a whole section of the capital. The figures of 164

Soho sex shops and 70 cinema 'clubs' were talismanically repeated and complained about. From *Private Eye* and the *Leveller* to *The Times*, the issue was taken up and worried over. There had not been such consensus since 1960. But now there was no single piece of legislation or decisive trial that could put things straight. What the country got instead was two very inadequate 'control' laws. One was the 1981 Indecent Display Bill: a piece of law which promised never to be effectively used because no one in 1981 was sure what 'indecent' meant. The other was a clause introduced into the Local Government (Miscellaneous Provisions) Bill due to come into force in 1982. This would licence 'sex establishments', and notionally restrict their number. Its prospects were not hopeful if one remembered the botch which the GLC made early in the 1970s over film censorship (which led to *Oh! Calcutta!* being banned as a film while the show was running in the West End). Also the GLC had shown themselves absolutely paralysed over the question of offensive shop signs in Soho, an area where they already had powers.

In 1964, amending the 1959 Act, the Solicitor-General had declared the Government's firm intention of 'striking hard' at the pornographer. Eighteen years later, a pornographer might well think that if he kept within the well-known thresholds (to do with erection, penetration, deviant practices, age of models) the law existed to help him prosper, like any other businessman.

Thematically, this book is about 'decensorship'. The process has been anything but smooth or linear. Unevenness can be put down to a number of causes. There was a jerkiness or tardiness in the introduction of new law. (It would, for instance, have been logical to harmonise legislation on theatre and film together with that for print.) Another factor has been the variable resistance of the people and their legislators to change: at one moment the popular mood has been progressive, as in 1959, at another deeply reactionary, as in 1970-2. A third factor is that reading matter is rarely delivered to the consumer directly. It usually requires the intermediate services of various middle-men and distribution systems. Especially in the 1960s, these intermediaries tended to be cautious and censorious. W.H. Smith, for example, were unwilling in 1968 to carry Paul Ableman's *Vac* (an entirely respectable 'literary' novel, published by Gollancz). In the same year, the same firm refused to handle the 'new wave', and again all too literary, *New Worlds* science-fiction magazine, because it carried a story by Norman Spinrad (an eminent science-fiction writer, whose work was termed 'degenerate' by an irate backbencher in Parliament). In 1968, again, Smith's would apparently wholesale, but not retail, *Last Exit* – even after its exoneration in court. Things change. In 1975 the same company were prepared to fight 'all the way' for Alex Comfort and the *Joy of Sex*: a manual which certain provincial authorities found pornographic.

Like W.H. Smith in the 1960s, many British public libraries were timid and had 'poison shelves', or secret cataloguing, or 'X certificates' for their hotter items. Throughout the 1960s, Edinburgh public library had an 'annexe' whose sole purpose was to stop citizens from getting access to 'strong' fiction which their rates had gone to purchase. Such ruses gradually disappeared in the 1970s. But in the 1960s, even the country's premier library was hidebound in its censoriousness. In 1966, Peter Fryer wrote a book *Private Case: Public Scandal*, complaining at the British Museum's scandalously restrictive practice where the 'Cupboard' (i.e., pornography store) was concerned. From the middle 1970s onwards, however, the official Bloomsbury attitude softened. In 1981, a full catalogue was published, and card-carrying members of the reading public could expect to be fobbed off no longer. (Although the British Library – as it now is – still has its special table of shame, at the head of the North Gallery, for 'readers of special books'; special, of course, has the same connotation as with hospital wards.)

In all these cases liberalisation was held back by the conservative habits and instincts of British institutions. *Cain's Book* for instance, could not have been bought in any W.H. Smith's shop in 1966, nor could it have been found open-shelved in most public libraries, and getting it from the British Museum would have required infinite patience and gall in the face of bureaucratic venom. Yet the book was, in itself, entirely 'legal'.

There was of course in the 1960s a bypass route via the 'underground' press. Underground magazines had troubles with printers from time to time (more, ironically, than 'straight' authors had with their publishers), but being able to circumvent orthodox distribution and retail networks (by, for instance, street sales) meant that they enjoyed freedom from institutional censorship. Many things killed the underground press in the 1970s: but one, certainly, was that an emancipated W.H. Smith would have probably stocked

OZ - had it survived the success of its 1971 trials. And if 'W.H. Smut' had consigned 1970s *OZ*, together with *Private Eye*, into the realm of the unstockable, then myriad news-agents would have been only too keen to display it, together with the ubiquitous: *Mayfair, Men Only, Knave, Private, Whitehouse, Playbirds, Club, Fiesta, Rustler, Over 21, Quest, Sting, Swish* and *Oui*.

A number of reflections arise from the legal changes and trials followed in this book. The most persistent is that Parliament - and still more courts - are bad places in which to analyse and evaluate literature. The critic ('expert' when he appears in the stand) respects ambiguity, complexity, undertone. Like the psychiatrist, his mission seems to be to weave Gordian knots too intricate for forensic single-minded-ness to sever. Too often, the critic-as-witness is obliged to talk down, to oversimplify, to lie.

If the subject of pornography perplexes the professional discourses it touches another general observation is that as a commodity it is hideously destructive of the environment. It is possible to browse with equanimity through Foyles and congratulate one's country on the degree of literary freedom it tolerates. Walk a hundred yards west, through Soho, and I, for one, feel a Kurtzian exterminatory rage. If the cost of *Lady Chatterley's Lover* in the bookshops is the reduction of a formerly pleasant quarter of London into a 'combat zone' (as Boston's sex-ghetto is proudly termed), it seems a high price to pay. Nor would the Williams proposals (buttressed by the 1981 Indecent Display Act) improve things. Row upon row of shuttered shops all containing wares of matching uniform ugliness, is not the urban renewal one would wish on central London.

Historical predictions are chancy where censorship is con-cerned. Did not the Festival of Light, in 1971, predict the end of civilisation in five years unless Britain were cleaned up? Did not permissive thinkers like Maurice Girodias in the 1960s predict that pornography would wither away once it was tolerated? But it seems that just as the forces of 'en-lightenment' started the whole thing off in 1959-60 so their more politicised descendants (notably the environmental lobby and the woman's movement) will be the focus of necessary future reforms.

November 1960:

Lady Chatterley's Lover

D.H. Lawrence wrote three versions of *Lady Chatterley's Lover*, the last of which was freest with the awkwardly termed 'four-letter words'. This final draft could not then legally be published in Britain (nor easily printed; printers are notoriously strait-laced – even Penguin in 1960 had trouble on this score). Nevertheless, Lawrence tried Cape, Secker and Chatto with his new novel. Their rejections he took as hypocritical, and he sarcastically pictured them 'trying to cover their nakedness with "great patches of beauty" and sighing, "It's a great pity".' In fact, their negativity was entirely prudent. No one but a fool or a martyr would have tried to bring out the untrimmed *Chatterley* in England. As late as 1955, an English magistrate sentenced a Hornsey retailer to two-months imprisonment for handling the novel. In 1930, a similarly reckless businessman would have been breaking stones for years.

It is interesting, in view of the book's later record-breaking popularity, that Lawrence thought it 'far too good for the public . . . for the gross public' and that he suggested that his agent send order forms 'to the right people. You can reach a lot of the right sort of people in the Universities.' Ironically enough, these right sort of people, by giving testimony at the Old Bailey, secured for *Lady Chatterley's Lover* the grossest public that any novel has ever enjoyed in Britain (six million Penguin copies sold by the end of the 1970s).

Lawrence was bookwise after twenty years in authorship, and intended to make money for himself (as much as £1,000 he hoped) rather than for his posthumous estate. In the 1920s, there were often good chances for books published on the continent by Britons and Americans, denied legitimate distribution in their home markets. (The examples of *Ulysses* and *The Well of Loneliness* were probably in Lawrence's mind.) Lawrence personally supervised a first printing of 1,000 copies of *Chatterley* in Florence, to sell at two guineas apiece. There were advantages to self-publishing in this fashion – notably the high return to the author on every copy sold (the Florentine edition sold out promptly, despite the sky-high price). There was also professional satisfaction to Lawrence, who hated literary 'middle men'. The main disadvantage in the system was that an author–publisher had difficulty protecting his work; and if it caught on – as *Chatterley* did – he lacked a distribution system to supply the market quickly enough to forestall piracy.

Lady Chatterley's Lover was sadly plundered. In April 1929, Lawrence noted, 'and still *another* – the fifth – pirated edition of Lady Chatterley! Makes one ill.' To preserve his literary property, he therefore sought some 'decent bookseller or publisher'. He found the man in the Paris publisher Edward Titus. In Titus's 'Popular' edition, the novelist inserted a preface describing his 'skirmishes with Jolly Roger', i.e., the censors and the pirates – *Chatterley's* unfailing persecutors. By December 1930, shortly after Lawrence's death, Titus had nearly 10,000 copies in hand, and the author's share of the profits already earned stood at 89,150 francs.

In its subsequent career with various Parisian publishers, *Chatterley* was always an offshore bestseller. And a main market was the English, largely in the form of tourists who either timidly left their copies in hotel rooms or bravely smuggled them past HM customs. Reading *Lady Chatterley's Lover* seems to have been a pre-1960 rite of passage for anyone professing literary sophistication. One of the more surprising things to emerge at the Old Bailey trial was that all the 'experts' had apparently contrived to read the ostensibly banned novel without any difficulty at all. A perverse construction was put on this by Colin MacInnes who argued that the trial was evidently redundant. Anyone who wanted to, and was clever enough to appreciate it, could get *Chatterley* in England already.

The process of above-ground, or legitimate publication of the undoctored *Chatterley* in the English-speaking world began in 1944, in America, when *The First Lady Chatterley* was brought out. This is milder than Lawrence's preferred third version, but still offensive by pre-1960 UK standards. Parkin, for instance, instructs Connie to call him 'my fucker' rather than 'my lover'. (This first try was not published in the UK until 1972.) *The First Lady Chatterley* was published in America by Dial Press, who had a suit brought against them by the veteran campaigner John S. Sumner, secretary of the

New York Society for the Suppression of Vice. The Staten Island Court found the book 'clearly obscene' on the usual *mens rea* grounds that Lawrence was advocating adultery. The Court of Special Sessions later narrowly voted the book not obscene, but even though finally exonerated, this text never went into general production – partly because of the uncertain legal climate, partly because of problems with Lawrence's executors.

Attention switched to an expurgated version of the final *Chatterley*, approved by Frieda in 1932, two years after Lawrence's death. This was published by Knopf in America, and Secker in the UK in high price, small edition hardback form. NAL (New American Library) leased this abridged version, as it was euphemistically called, from Knopf and it was in mass-market American paperback form from 1946 onwards. In the next ten years this 'mutilated and emasculated drugstore paperback', sold 1.5 million copies. It was not, however, paperbacked in the always more nervous UK until 1958.

The abridged *Chatterley*, in its address to the purchaser, glossed over the excisions and bowdlerisations, and proclaimed itself 'authorized' without indicating that it was Lawrence's estate which had apparently done the authorising. The novelist's proclaimed view was that his novel must be swallowed whole; as for abridging, 'I might as well try to clip my own nose into shape with scissors, the book bleeds.' A more honest compromise would have been what Richard Aldington did with his 1929 novel, *Death of a Hero*, and use fig-leaf asterisks. As it was, the majority of the 1.5 million American copies must have gone to conveniently gullible thrill-seekers. But disappointed purchasers of dirty books are as unlikely to demand their money back as infected customers of a prostitute.

In order to follow the career of *Chatterley* to its eventual emancipation in the late 1950s, it is necessary to explain the American Comstock Law. Anthony Comstock was an evangelical crusader against filth, especially filthy novels, in the last decades of the nineteenth century. In 1873 he was, simultaneously, First Secretary of the New York Society for the Suppression of Vice, a special agent of the Post Office and an accredited lobbyist in Washington (fancifully, this is the equivalent of Mrs Whitehouse being appointed honorary comptroller of the BBC). With his unique combination of authority, Comstock succeeded in imposing censorship of literary materials by the criterion of 'mailability' – hence the greater importance of the US Post Office in obscenity matters than its British counterpart.

The other major difference in literary censorship between the two countries is that quarrels are usually sharper and clearer in America by virtue of the first amendment to its constitution, which guarantees freedom of speech. This constitutional right took on new significance with the Samuel Roth case in 1955-57, which opened the way for more liberal interpretations of what literary freedom might mean. Essentially, the Roth case determined that literary material which was *prima facie* 'obscene' might still be published if it could argue 'redeeming social importance'. (The pornographer Roth did not benefit and went to prison for a long time.) Just how this mitigating quality might be ascertained was shown by the 1957 trial of Allen Ginsberg's 'Howl', in San Francisco immediately post-Roth. The defence assembled nine 'expert' literary–critical (not forensically expert) witnesses to testify that their poet's celebration of the holiness of 'the tongue and cock and hand and asshole' had the necessary 'literary merit'.

Among the regiment of literary critics assembled on 'Howl's behalf was Mark Schorer. This distinguished man of letters was immediately recruited by Grove Press, who logically intended to test the implications of the Roth case by bringing out the first unexpurgated *Chatterley*. Schorer was despatched to New Mexico, to look at Lawrence's manuscripts. Also recruited by Grove was the internationally famous poet and critic, Archibald MacLeish. He was to write a preface. This prophylactic use of weighty littérateurs to validate the 'redeeming value' of the text in question was to be a feature of the next round of *Chatterley* and related obscenity trials.

Grove Press's unexpurgated edition of *Lady Chatterley's Lover* appeared in 1959. It cost $6 – a high price at least partly designed to keep it as caviare to the general and turn away official wrath. (In the subsequent prosecutions, price and availability were to be almost as much an issue as incendiary Lawrentian content.) Grove Press is often compared with Calder and Boyars, the English publishing house which brought out many of the same titles, and likewise took risks with prohibited books. But despite the frequent similarity of their lists, there are significant differences. Grove's proprietor, Barney Rosset, was more frankly mercenary in his publishing programme. He published *Lady Chatterley's Lover*, as he candidly admitted, 'to make money'. Two factors promised the prosperity he desired. He had secured a big book-club deal for the novel with Readers' Subscription. Secondly, the Lawrence estate had refused to accept royalties, out of misplaced loyalty to the authorised Knopf-NAL abridged *Chatterley*. This meant 10 per cent more for Grove. On the other hand, both these factors could be worrisome. A book-club edition would involve a lot of budget price copies of the book being sent through the mails. And the fact that Lawrence's book was not protected by legal agreement with an American publishing house meant that it was, effectively, in the public domain. Grove could not claim copyright in their edition, which might be duplicated by anyone, without Rosset having any comeback.

Shortly after publication, the Post Office struck. Twenty-four cartons of *Chatterley* were seized. There was a trial in the Post Office Department (without jury, but with the expert testimony of Malcolm Cowley and Alfred Kazin) in May 1959. 'If this book is not filth,' asked the Postmaster-General, 'pray tell me what filth is.' Under the Comstock statute, the novel was determined indeed filthy, and deemed non-mailable. This was a mortal blow to Rosset's book-club deal, and (given America's continent-wide distances) to any normal book distribution.

Grove Press retaliated by bringing a suit to restrain the Postmaster from banning carriage of their book. On 21 July 1959, Judge Fred van Pelt Bryan of the US District Court, Southern District of New York, judged *Chatterley* not obscene and mailable. He was largely swayed by the literary–historical context in which Schorer and MacLeish situated the work. The Government continued the intricately shifting battle by appealing against Bryan's decision. But on 26 March 1960, the US Court of Appeals upheld Bryan with the verdict 'this is a major and distinguished novel, and Lawrence one of the great writers of the age.' It accompanied its vindication with an extended critical explication of the book which would not have dishonoured a learned journal.

By comparison with the Old Bailey affair which lasted five days and was ridden with cant, the American trials of *Chatterley* were brisk and to the point (constitutionality and mailability). For one thing, there was no jury to talk down to, or bamboozle. The first Post Office investigation lasted two days, and Grove's two experts still had longer to flex their critical muscles than their 35 British counterparts. They were uninhibited by the ruling that defence could rest on the whole of the book, not selected passages and still

less on four-letter words. This forestalled some of the idiocies
of the British trial where, for instance, the prosecutor produced as significant the statistic that the novel contained:
30 'fucks' or 'fuckings', 14 'cunts', 13 'balls', 6 each of 'shit'
and 'arse', 4 'cocks' and 3 'piss'.

The proceedings were further enhanced by the fact that
the prosecution was – apparently – a more intelligent reader
of Lawrence than its British counterpart. In America they
realised the 'unhealthy' significance of the final buggery
episode between Connie and Mellors and would have made
persuasive use of it – had they not been headed off by
Grove's lawyer who objected to its close examination on the
'whole book' principle. This is not to say that the American
proceedings did not produce some balderdash: Rosset's
claim, for instance, that his publishing *Chatterley* ('pirating'
from the Lawrence estate's point of view) was 'an important
public service' or Cowley's confident exchange with his cross-
questioning judicial officer that went:

> Q. Are you familiar with the works of D.H. Lawrence?
> A. I am.
> Q. Can you tell us about the place he occupies in English
> literature?
> A. Very briefly, he is considered to be the most signifi-
> cant English novelist after Joseph Conrad.
> Q. Are literary critics and literary historians in general in
> agreement with this estimate?
> A. We are in such agreement on that point that eight
> hundred books have been written about D.H. Lawrence.

At this date, eighteen would have been a generous estimate.

Rosset had made a huge investment in *Chatterley*. At the
time of the first trial, he had 75,000 copies in print and had
laid out $ 35,000 on advertising. But the Lawrence estate
refused his offer of royalties and would make no agreement
with him, which meant that his involvement in a high-price,
de luxe $ 6 edition was not protected. Since Lawrence was an
'alien', no contract meant no copyright. *Lady Chatterley* was
anyone's for the taking, despite Grove's gallant defence of
her in court. It was too good an opportunity for the sharpers
in the American book trade to pass over.

Four paperback firms got in on the *Chatterley* act following Judge Bryan's ruling in July that the book was not

obscene. Most aggressive was Pocket Books – the pioneer of American mass-market soft cover publishing. In a crash production campaign, they got an unexpurgated edition of *Chatterley* out in eight days from the Bryan ruling. It sold at 35 cents (undercutting the Dell and Pyramid competition paperbacks by a full 15 cents). Pocket Books sold a million copies of 'their' *Chatterley* in six days. Even they could be undercut, however. In New England the 'Tabloid Publishing Company' brought out a newspaper format edition of Lawrence's novel, selling on street corners at 25 cents.

It was, as Grove said in a plaintive advertisement in the 10 August *Publishers Weekly*, 'publishing ethics of the wolfpack . . . throwing decent publishing practice into the ashcan'. The concern was echoed in an editorial in the journal a week later: 'the questions that arise pertain to the ethics of the publishing industry . . . the public image of the whole book trade has been cheapened by the *Chatterley* sweepstake.' Rosset could not move against the pirates since legally they were no more pirates than he was. He could, however, take legal action against NAL who were still bringing out the 'mutilated' *Chatterley*. In July alone, NAL sold 650,000 copies of their paperback which did not, to say the least, obtrude on the purchaser the fact that 'abridged' means 'no dirty words'. Rosset angrily denounced this as 'commercial hitch-hiking'. NAL were taking advantage of a legal triumph which Grove undertook at their sole expense and risk. Of course, people were buying the NAL paperback under the misapprehension that it was the unvarnished thing for whose publication Rosset had risked jail. The publisher's blurb connived at the misapprehension, presenting the contents as 'A complete reprint of the authorised American edition.' Grove took NAL to court in the busy month of July, alleging infringement and misrepresentation. At the trial, NAL offered to insert the word 'expurgated' banking probably that the general public would be as fooled by that term as by abridged. There was a long statement offered by Lawrence's agents, asserting that Lawrence had authorised the abridged version for the English firm Secker (although NAL's rights were derived from Knopf). It was an incredibly tangled business, and the court came down in favour of NAL, dismissing Grove's suit. NAL promptly brought out an *unexpurgated* version, rushing a million copies into print in six days, neck and neck with Pocket Books, and several dollars cheaper than Grove.

In early August Rosset was forced to mix it with his

undercutting competitors. He brought out his own paperback version. But his problems were not yet over. NAL now took *him* to court, with a $500,000 countersuit, claiming that his advertisement 'the only authorised and unexpurgated edition of Lady Chatterley in America' was a lie. They had sole 'authorization' (but, of course, only for the abridged edition). On 12 September Grove issued another sorry-for-themselves 'Memo to the Publishing Industry', in which they protested that 'it is probably without precedent in publishing history that a publisher has dragged competitive rivalry down to the level of a street brawl by hawking a fellow publisher into court on a misdemeanour charge.' NAL issued an answering statement 'to the literary community of the Trade' in which they pointed out 'we pay a royalty to Knopf . . . Grove first proceeded to publishing in hardcover edition *without asking for the approval of the Lawrence estate . . .* we have such a contract while Grove does not.' On 17 October, the parties compromised mutually agreed to drop this dog-eat-dog litigation. They would, henceforward, both issue 'complete' *Chatterleys* and would both remit royalties to the Lawrence estate. This, however, was a voluntary act; technically the book remained in the public domain.

The 1959 *Chatterley* gold rush did not, as everyone agreed, reflect well on the American publishing profession. But from all the commercial brawling one fact emerged: there was a quick fortune to be made from a paperback version of *Lady Chatterley's Lover* for whoever could bring it out first in Britain.

The American legal processes and sales bonanza are part of the context to the British liberation of Lawrence's novel. The other important precondition occurred the day after the Bryan judgment, 21 July 1959, when the Obscene Publications Act (Jenkins Act as it was called after its backbench sponsor, then a socialist) passed into law. This took over the Roth 'redeeming social importance' consideration, rephrased for British law as 'public good'. As in America, this vindicating merit was to be vouched for by experts.

Penguin's publication of an unexpurgated *Lady Chatterley's Lover* was announced in the *Bookseller* on 9 January 1960. It was to come out with seven other Lawrence titles. The mass issue would mark the thirtieth anniversary of Lawrence's death, and the twenty-fifth of Penguin's birth. There were auspicious signs for Penguin – other than the

liberalising 1959 Jenkins Act. In January 1960, the British
Museum released Oscar Wilde's *De Profundis* manuscript
– amnesty for wicked authors was in the air. And largely due
to the efforts of F.R. Leavis, many now thought of Lawrence
not as an immoralist but as our greatest novelist. Apropos of
an imminent film of *Sons and Lovers*, *The Times* (9 January
1960) declared: 'If anyone is making a list of authors who
will come into their own in 1960, then D.H. Lawrence
claims to be the favourite.' Even Parliament seemed well
disposed to the writer. In a question to the Government in
December 1959, Alan Thompson asked why a Swedish lady
had had her luggage searched at customs and her American
copy of *Chatterley* confiscated. 'Lawrence', Thompson told
his fellow MPs, 'is now recognised as a major English novelist
. . . His works are prescribed reading in every reputable
Department of English Literature in this country and America.'
On 30 January 1960, Roy Jenkins himself addressed the
Society of Young Publishers on the subject of *Lolita*. According to Jenkins (whose party was out of power) the Director
of Public Prosecutions was sounding out literary–critical
opinion on both Vladimir Nabokov's novel and *Lady Chatterley's Lover* – so as 'not to make a fool of himself'.

Lolita got through, but in spite of Jenkins's confidence in
the new enlightenment, the DPP determined to make a fool
of himself over *Chatterley*. His motives were probably two-
fold. First Lawrence's novel had a profusion of four-letter
words (*Lolita* was chaste stylistically) and a jury would more
easily apprehend the obscenity of, say, Mellors's encomiastic
'Tha's got the nicest arse of anybody . . . An' if tha shits an'
if tha pisses, I'm glad' than the first pederastic bout in *Lolita*,
written as it is in Nabokov's euphuistic baroque:

> I have reserved for the conclusion of my 'Annabel' phase
> the account of our unsuccessful first tryst. One night, she
> managed to deceive the vicious vigilance of her family. In a
> nervous and slender-leaved mimosa grove at the back of
> their villa we found a perch on the ruins of a low stone
> wall. Through the darkness and the tender trees we could
> see the arabesques of lighted windows which, touched up
> by the coloured inks of sensitive memory, appear to me now
> like playing cards – presumably because a bridge game was
> keeping the enemy busy. She trembled and twitched as I
> kissed the corner of her parted lips and the hot lobe of her
> ear. A cluster of stars palely glowed above us, between the
> silhouettes of long thin leaves; that vibrant sky seemed as

naked as she was under her light frock. I saw her face in
the sky, strangely distinct, as if it emitted a faint radiance
of its own. Her legs, her lovely live legs, were not too close
together, and when my hand located what it sought, a
dreamy and eerie expression, half-pleasure, half-pain, came
over those childish features. She sat a little higher than I,
and whenever in her solitary ecstasy she was led to kiss me,
her head would bend with a sleepy, soft, drooping movement that was almost woeful, and her bare knees caught
and compressed my wrist, and slackened again; and her
quivering mouth, distorted by the acridity of some myster-
ious potion, with a sibilant intake of breath came near to
my face. She would try to relieve the pain of love by first
roughly rubbing her dry lips against mine; then my darling
would draw away with a nervous toss of her hair, and then
again come darkly near and let me feed on her open mouth,
while with a generosity that was ready to offer her everything, my heart, my throat, my entrails, I gave her to hold
in her awkward fist the sceptre of my passion.

The DPP's other motive was astutely surmised by C.H.
Rolph, writing in the *New Statesman* (12 November 1960):
'The Penguin *Lady Chatterley* was prosecuted, one supposes,
because the Law Officers, learning that it was to come out
at 3s.6d. instead of about 25s., read it again and decided that
it must be kept from the hoi polloi.' It was a suspicion which
was to recur frequently over the subsequent years and trials;
the authorities could tolerate obscenity, erotica and even
pornography – so long as it wasn't in paperback.

But whatever the motive was for prosecuting *Chatterley*,
it was signally wrongheaded. The situation in which a major
work of English literature was published in America but
banned from its cis-Atlantic readers could not be long sustained (*Ulysses* had shown this). And if *Lady Chatterley's
Lover* was to be published in the UK, a Penguin edition
would at least diminish the 'wolfpack' behaviour which had
been so grossly evident in the US. Penguin could claim to be
not just the most prestigious British paperback publisher,
but most prestigious British publisher *tout court*. They also
had a distinguished relationship with Lawrence. In 1948 they
had published *Sons and Lovers*, in 1949 *The Rainbow* and
in 1950 they brought out a collective batch of no less than
ten of his novels simultaneously: honorific treatment reserved for writers of Shakespearian status. Penguin style was
ultra-respectable. This was the more significant since less

scrupulous firms would doubtless be interested in cashing in on the Lawrence boom. In 1958, a downmarket British paperbacker, Ace, brought out the abridged *Chatterley* (it went through four editions in twelve months). In 1959 this firm brought out *Women in Love* (the only major Lawrence item missing from the Penguin catalogue) with a *Titbits* or *Reveille* lovely up front. When asked in the *Bookseller* (26 September 1959) about their cover, Ace blandly confessed: 'We think . . . people are quite willing to plough through a lot of intellectual stuff for two or three lines of what-not. We get a great many appreciative letters – mostly from prisons.' Only a cultural Canute would think that Lawrence could be kept out of Britain, and if he had to be published then best it was done as 'intellectual stuff' in Penguin's sober, non-pictorial covers, than as 'what-not' with Ace's naked cuties.

Penguin put *Lady Chatterley's Lover* into production early in 1960, and had a first impression of 200,000 in their Harmondsworth warehouse when they 'published' the work – in a merely technical sense – by releasing a dozen copies to the DPP. Thus invited, the DPP announced that he would prosecute. The trial was originally set for August 1960, then moved to November. Unprovocatively, Penguin froze their stocks of the novel.

The trial, whatever it did for Lawrence, would be a first test of the 1959 Jenkins Act. For this inauguration the defence counsel, Rubinstein Nash and Co. mustered a troupe of witnesses to testify to the 'public good' of the novel. They wrote initially to 300 and finally got together 70, of whom 35 were eventually called to the stand. (F.R. Leavis, the leading Lawrence critic in the world, declined to appear for reasons which he was to make public after the trial.) The 35 were, to say the least, motley. There was a hard-core of eight Eng. Lit. academics; an educational psychologist; Dilys Powell the film critic; a headmaster and a headmistress; Anne Scott-James, a popular journalist; Mr Noel Annan – undefinably grand; a young lady whose only qualification was that she had recently been an even younger schoolgirl, had read *Lady Chatterley's Lover* and claimed not to be corrupted. There were various clerics, headed by the Bishop of Woolwich; there were publishers, politicians (Roy Jenkins himself); Grand Old Men and Women of Letters, like E.M. Forster and Rebecca West. Stephen Spender and T.S. Eliot were in the corridors outside the court; they were not called to testify, but Eliot thought sufficiently well of his deposition to have it placed in the archives at Nottingham University for posterity to consult.

Charles Rembar, the lawyer who had successfully seen *Chatterley* through the American courts in 1959, regarded the Old Bailey proceedings as

> low parody . . . a caricature . . . Our trial took one day; theirs took five. We called two witnesses (other than the publishers); the Penguin defence called thirty-five (and announced that there were another thirty-five suited up and ready to take the field).

His witnesses were literary critics, and permitted to acquit themselves as such. But, according to Rembar the Old Bailey witnesses were in no sense experts, they were

> lobbyists . . . the defence was grounded on (a) associations with religion and respectability and (b) the weight of numbers. The witnesses were not so much offering evidence as putting prestige into the claim that the book was innocent.

It's a severe judgment on what is fondly thought of in Britain as a milestone of enlightenment. But comparing the two sets of trials, it is hard not to agree with Rembar. The witnesses could as well have come on as a chorus line and chanted 'Lawrence is pure, Lawrence is good.'

The prosecution, led by Mervyn Griffith-Jones had a simple strategy. They called no witnesses and seemed prepared to let the book speak for itself; their view of Lawrence seemed untempered by any of the critical assessments and reassessments which had been going on since *John Bull*, in 1928, declared that 'the sewers of French pornography would be dragged in vain to find a parallel in beastliness. The creations of muddy minded perverts, peddled in the back-street bookstalls of Paris, are prudish by comparison.' If not quoted, this was largely the sentiment and rhetoric of Griffith-Jones.

The defence, by contrast, had a well-articulated strategy depending on a number of interlocking theses. First, the book itself was 'hygienic'. Lawrence's aim was to purify language, and to restore the holiness of the love relationship. Time and again, the discarded title 'Tenderness' was referred to. (The bawdy other title, 'John Thomas and Lady Jane' was decently glossed over.) This theme was enunciated with polemic force by Richard Hoggart in his introduction to the post-trial edition: '*Lady Chatterley's Lover* is *not* a dirty book. It is clean and serious and beautiful.' (Hoggart also flummoxed Griffith-Jones completely during his testimony by contending that Lawrence was a 'puritan'.) The furthest extreme of the 'Lawrence is wholesome' assertion was reached by the clerical witnesses who declared (on an oath which they surely took more seriously than their fellows) that *Chatterley* was a book 'Christians ought to read', that it was a 'guide to young people about to get married' and – from the Bishop of Woolwich – that Connie and Mellors's adultery 'is an act of holy communion'.

Looking over the testimony, it is evident that the literary critics were happier eulogising Lawrence and Lawrentian morality than in praising this particular book. Most avoided direct praise; only Richard Hoggart (who declared it one of the best novels written since 1930) and Walter Allen (who thought it a work of genius) came out unequivocally for the text. The prosecution could have exploited this unwillingness to talk about the wholeness of the book, rather than the wholeness of Lawrence. As it was, Griffith-Jones hammered away at the 'purple passages', the seven 'bouts', the 'four-letter words' and was easily sidestepped.

A stronger plank for the defence was that Penguin were not pornographers – they were a fine English institution, like the Navy, Parliament, the Queen. This was accepted without question by the court. Unlike Frederic Warburg in the case of the *Philanderer* three years earlier, Allen Lane was not required to stand in the dock, but sat in the well of the court – a spectator to his trial, not an accused man. This, and the fact that there were no prosecution witnesses, must have had a powerful effect on the jury.

The most effective emphasis in the defence presentation was that the trial was essentially a class battle. They stressed, for instance, Allen Lane's demotic origins:

Of course, there were those who thought he [Lane] was mad. They said it's no good giving the working classes good books, they wouldn't understand them if they read them. The next year he formed this company, Penguin Books Limited, to publish good books at the price of ten cigarettes . . . Whether he was right or wrong in thinking the average person would buy good books is perhaps shown by the fact that since then this company has made and sold 250 million – perhaps I might repeat that, 250 million books . . . It was not their intention to seek to publish new books, but substantially to republish, in a form and at a price which the ordinary people could afford to buy, all the great books in our literature.

The contents of Lawrence's novel reinforced this line of argument. Mellors embodies proletarian energy and authenticity against aristocratic paralysis, personified in the paraplegic Sir Clifford. 'It's a bit of a revolution . . . a bit of a bomb' said Lawrence of his book. The defence was helped when, in a lapse so grotesque it has gone into folklore, Griffith-Jones cast himself as Marie Antoinette to the opposition's sansculottes:

> You may think [he told the jury in his opening address] that one of the ways in which you can read this book, and test it from the most liberal outlook, is to ask yourselves the question, when you have read it through, would you approve of your young sons, young daughters – because girls can read as well as boys – reading this book. Is it a book that you would have lying around in your own house? Is it a book that you would even wish your wife or your servants to read?

Servants! Five of the jury apparently had difficulty in reading the oath.

Given the defence's populist stress, it is not surprising that star of the Old Bailey proceedings was not, as might have been anticipated, E.M. Forster (a contemporary of Lawrence's, and England's greatest living novelist) nor Graham Hough (who alone of the witnesses had written a book on Lawrence) nor Helen Gardner (the most stately literary critic) but Richard Hoggart. Hoggart was a mere senior lecturer, educated at one provincial university (Leeds) and now teaching at another (Leicester).

As his semi-autobiographical *The Uses of Literacy* records, he was brought up 'copper-bottomed' working class, in a back-to-back terrace. Added to this, Hoggart was (and is) a brilliant public performer capable of projecting immense sincerity while exercising sophisticated critical intelligence. For observers, it was almost as if Lawrence had been reincarnated to defend himself. As C.H. Rolph put it in the *New Statesman* (5 November 1960) 'the highlight of the trial was Mr Richard Hoggart's passionate defence speaking himself as a son of the working class.' The following week, another article in the journal elaborated the tribute:

One important aspect of the *Lady Chatterley* verdict is that it is a triumph for a working class writer defended with masterly clear headedness by (among others) a working class critic. Mr Hoggart's speech exposed with real authority that the solid centre of British philistinism is in the establishment . . .

As Penguin's blurb was to put it, with all the strident excitement typical of the cultural moment: 'it was not just a legal tussle, but a conflict of generation and class.' This was a period of insurgence. National Service, with all its hated conformity, was finished. Footballers – those other working-class heroes – had successfully broken the terms of contract that kept them to a maximum £20 a week (how bizarre that serfdom appears, from the standpoint of the 1980s). While the *Chatterley* circus was running at the Old Bailey, the film hit of the season was Woodfall's *Saturday Night and Sunday Morning*. The tag that the bestselling Pan paperback edition of Alan Sillitoe's novel carried was apposite: 'Thirty years have passed since D.H. Lawrence's proletarian hero – Lady Chatterley's Lover – shook the bookshops. Now, from the Lawrence country, comes a new author with a hero who might have startled Lawrence himself.' John Arden's bolshy-pacifist, regional–vernacular *Serjeant Musgrave's Dance* was the thinking man's favourite play of the period. Centre 42 had just been formed by Arnold Wesker (of *Roots* fame) to bring art, through the trade unions, to the working man.

The jury of nine men and three women would no more stand against this than they could stand against history or the Beatles (just emerging from the Cavern to the limelight). They did their cultural duty and duly cleared *Lady Chatterley's Lover*. Penguin returned the compliment by dedicating the next edition of the novel to them – and the next, and the next. Two-million copies were sold in the year. Penguin were very happy, and Roy Jenkins was very happy: the acquittal of *Lady Chatterley* and the defeat of Harold Wilson's leadership attempt had made it, he declared, a week 'almost too good to be true'. But both Wilson and the book-burners would make a come back.

Not everyone was happy. Probably most of the two million purchasers were disappointed at what they got for their 3s.6d. In a House of Lords debate on the trial, many of the gamekeeper-employing class expressed themselves very unhappy – was not Sir Clifford one of their number? A more persuasive dissent from the popular jubilation was struck by F.R. Leavis. In a review of the book of the trial, published three months after in the *Spectator* (not his usual platform, but he wanted maximum publicity) Leavis denounced the Old Bailey proceedings. He had been asked to testify, but had sternly refused. At the time of his death in 1978, when the quarrel blew up again, his wife, Q.D. Leavis, reiterated the public reasons, and revealed his private misgivings:

> Besides refusing to countenance the case that *Lady Chatterley* is great literature and a good novel, Dr Leavis deplored, above all, that the trial, whatever the outcome, could only harm Lawrence since the novelist would become identified with this most unrepresentative work, a deplorable state of affairs. Moreover, though he refrained from disclosing this reason in print, he was suspicious of the motives for inviting the prosecution; he said to the solicitor: 'I can see no reason for Sir Allan's knight errantry unless he has a golden fleece in view' – in fact, it was subsequently revealed that this smart commercial venture had brought such immense sales to the Penguin reprint of *Lady Chatterley* as to make its publisher a millionaire.

Leavis entitled his 1961 piece 'The New Orthodoxy', and when reprinted, 'The Orthodoxy of Enlightenment.' He remembered that as a pioneer of Lawrence criticism he had been bitterly attacked. Now, in 1960, it was so fashionable to support Lawrence that even anti-Lawrentians (he was thinking particularly of T.S. Eliot) found it convenient to turn their coats. Herd instinct now totemised Lawrence just as herd instinct had once reviled him. This new orthodoxy had no critical rigour in it, and was the dupe of money-men who wanted nothing more than to cash in on Lawrence. They had rallied round the work that was least representative and least worthy – a novel which Leavis himself had studiously relegated from discussion in *D.H. Lawrence: Novelist*.

Leavis's objection received support from what was (from his point of view) an uncongenial quarter. The magazine *Encounter* published a number of pieces before and after the trial which sounded sour notes. They included Katherine Anne Porter's polemic 'A Wreath for the Gamekeeper' (February 1960) which poured opprobrium on American publishing 'gangsterism' and the *conformisme des clercs* which accompanied the *Chatterley* disinhibition:

for the past several months [in America] there has been a
steady flood of extremely well managed publicity in
defence of Lawrence's motives and the purity of his novel,
into which not only critics, but newspaper and magazine
reporters, editorial writers, ministers of various religious
beliefs, women's clubs, the police, postal authorities,
educators have been drawn, clamorously. I do not object
to censorship being so roundly defeated again for the
present. I merely do not approve of the way it was done.

Encounter carried various other anti-*Chatterley* articles.
But the most powerful counter-punch was delivered by John
Sparrow, Warden of All Souls, in an article a month after the
trial. Vast and undisguised distaste was evident from Sparrow's
first sentence: 'Now the case is over and the shareholders are
in enjoyment of their profits . . .' He went on to examine in
detail the seventh love encounter between Connie and
Mellors, pointing out what none of the 'experts' or the
defence lawyers had allowed to emerge at the trial, that the
gamekeeper manifestly sodomises the aristocrat's wife:

> It was a night of sensual passion, in which she was a
> little startled and almost unwilling: yet pierced again with
> piercing thrills of sensuality, different, sharper, more
> terrible than the thrills of tenderness, but, at the moment,
> more desirable. Though a little frightened, she let him have
> his way, and the reckless, shameless sensuality shook her
> to her foundations, stripped her to the very last, and made
> a different woman of her. It was not really love. It was not
> voluptuousness. It was sensuality sharp and searing as fire,
> burning the soul to tinder.
>   Burning out the shames, the deepest, oldest shames, in
> the most secret places. It cost her an effort to let him have
> his way and his will of her. She had to be a passive, con-
> senting thing, like a slave, a physical slave. Yet the passion
> licked round her, consuming, and when the sensual flame
> of it pressed through her bowels and breast, she really
> thought she was dying: yet a poignant, marvellous death.
>   She had often wondered what Abélard meant, when he
> said that in their year of love he and Héloïse had passed
> through all the stages and refinements of passion. The
> same thing, a thousand years ago: ten thousand years ago!
> The same on the Greek vases, everywhere! The refinements
> of passion, the extravagances of sensuality! And necessary,
> forever necessary, to burn out false shames and smelt out

the heaviest ore of the body into purity. With the fire of sheer sensuality.

In the short summer night she learnt so much. She would have thought a woman would have died of shame. Instead of which, the shame died. Shame, which is fear: the deep organic shame, the old, old physical fear which crouches in the bodily roots of us, and can only be chased away by the sensual fire, at last it was roused up and routed by the phallic hunt of the man, and she came to the very heart of the jungle of herself. She felt, now, she had come to the real bed-rock of her nature, and was essentially shameless.

Sparrow's interpretation of this episode has been universally accepted by Lawrence critics. But would the jury have been so ready to acquit, had they been told that Lawrence's 'hygienic' programme extended to the inclusion of buggery in the lovers' repertoire? Sparrow thought not. He also thought that a book with these sexual–moral doctrines should not be generally available: 'it seems to me from every point of view a pity that Penguin Books should have launched it on the public at 3*s*.6*d*. a copy.' Sparrow evidently would not want the servants at Oxford's richest college to read it.

The main damage of Sparrow's article (whose contentions were widely ventilated) was its allegation that the defence counsel and the literary–critical witnesses had been disingenuous. They knew all about the implications of the seventh bout but they weren't going to tell – not the jury, at any rate. It all 'reeked of humbug', thought Sparrow. Would the Bishop of Woolwich have termed *penetratio in ano* 'an act of Holy Communion'? Odd theology if he did. 'Reverence for a man's balls?' asked Griffith-Jones incredulously – 'Indeed yes', replied Hoggart famously. Would he have been so confident if pressed on reverence and the 'sensual hunting out'? Worst of all, Lawrence came through as something of a humbug – at least by the false lights of the defence. They had insisted that *Lady Chatterley's Lover* was an attempt at hygienic 'straight talking' about sex. He avoided prurient circumlocution, that was the whole *raison d'être* of the book. And yet, Mellors is not made to say something along the lines of 'Eeh, ah laks a bit o' arse fucking.' Instead we have descriptive circuitousness as dense (though admittedly more skilful) as anything to be found in Radclyffe Hall. Lawrence, all this is to say, is a more complex writer than defence tactics chose to present him.

In November 1960, onlookers generally were prepared to give the defence and the witnesses all credit. They were partisan Lawrentians, but honest. After the Sparrow attack (and the unconnected, but potent Leavis anathema) the suspicion of 'humbug' was never fully purged. Diplomatists are hired to lie abroad for their country; so do 'experts' lie in court for literature .

1961: Lady Chatterley and the Paperback Revolution

The trial had been ostensibly about Lawrence, literature and censorship. But the article in question was a cheap paperback reprint of a venerable 'classic' text. Following this lead, the primary liberating effect seems not to have benefited practising authors. Most mid-career English novelists continued for some years in the belief that to use four-letter words, or post-*Chatterley* frankness, was an admission of artistic defeat. (Such a decorous view was put forcibly by Kingsley Amis and Elizabeth Jane Howard in their submission to the 1971 *Longford Report*. But by this late date a new generation of writers, including Amis's son Martin, had grown up and were taking full advantage of the new range of fictional vocabulary.)

Viewed historically, the main breakthrough was in the area of paperback 'updating'. Works which had previously been available in expensive, or foreign and expensive editions, were now democratically on sale for the price of Allen Lane's ten cigarettes in every corner shop. Take, for instance, James Baldwin – a novelist who in England had hitherto had a very touch-and-go relationship with censorship. Before 1960 his work was more often than not kept on public library 'poison shelves', where it was kept at all. Baldwin's *Go Tell it on the Mountain* (the story of a black childhood with frank sex scenes) was published in hardback by Michael Joseph in 1954, in paperback by Corgi in 1963. His *Giovanni's Room* (an unromantic novel of homosexual relationships) was published in hardback by Michael Joseph in 1957, and as a Corgi paperback in 1963.

The same pattern is evident with J.P. Donleavy's scandalous *The Ginger Man*. It was published unexpurgated by Girodias in France 1955, in expurgated hardback in the UK by Neville Spearman in 1956 and as a 'complete and unexpurgated' Corgi paperback in 1963. Nor was it just fiction that benefited. A notable hit was Simone de Beauvoir's *The*

Second Sex - a crucial text for the later women's liberation movement. It was first published in France in 1949. Cape brought out a hardback in 1953. The Four Square paperback (the name, incidentally, reflected the firm's other interest: tobacco; their books aimed mainly to sell in newsagents) came out in 1960, and went through no less than twelve editions in a year. Between 1962 and 1965, various previously hardback only, or absolutely prohibited, sex-manuals were paperbacked: *The Kama Sutra, The Perfumed Garden, The ABZ of Love.* Yoni and lingam became common terms of speech and judging by sales, couples all over the country were practising the congress of the bee and the ant.

Consider, for instance, the *Merry Muses of Caledonia*: this volume originated with the repertoire of bawdy songs known to the Crocahallan Fencibles club of Edinburgh. Robert Burns collected and printed them; the collection survived as a strictly prohibited book until 1959, when it was printed for private distribution to another Edinburgh club, the Auk Society. By 1965, the collection was available unbowdlerised in mass-market paperback giving for the first time the definitive texts of such still current ballads as *The Ball of Kirrie-muir* with its rousing chorus, 'If you canna get fucked on a Saturday night/Ye'll never get fucked at all.' De Sade was always tricky in the Anglo-Saxon market, but his *Justine* appeared 'complete and unexpurgated' as a 6s. Corgi paperback in 1965. (It was to figure sensationally after the Moors trial.)

As striking as the paperback catch-up was the faster throughput from hard to soft cover. *Lolita* was published by Olympia in Paris in 1955. Weidenfeld brought it out (courageously) as a British hardback in 1959 and reprinted four times in the year. In 1961, the Corgi edition was out (it went through seven editions in a year). *Lolita* thus progressed from banned new book, to mass-market paperback in half a dozen years. Unlike its predecessors, James Baldwin's *Another Country* took only two years to get into soft covers (1963-5). It was strong stuff but the most sensational paperback of the early 1960s was Harold Robbins's *The Carpetbaggers* (Blond hardback, 1963, Four Square paperback, 1964). This sex'n violence *roman-à-clef*, based loosely on the life of Howard Hughes, inaugurated a new mode of hard-boiled bestsellers, exploiting to the uttermost post-*Chatterley* freedoms. As one reviewer estimated, there is sex and/or sadism every seventeen pages of *The Carpetbaggers*. The following scene, in which the hero's father and Indian mother are tortured to divulge the whereabouts of gold they haven't got, is typical:

> The man pressed the burning coal against Sam's neck and shoulder. Sam screamed in pain. 'They ain't got no gold!' His head fell sideways. The man withdrew the burning coal and the blood welled up beneath the scorched flesh and ran down his chest and arm.
>
> The man picked up a bottle of whisky from the table and took a swig from it. 'Th'ow some water on him,' he said. 'If'n he won't talk for hisself, mebbe he'll talk for his squaw.'
>
> The youngest man picked up a pail and threw water over Sam. Sam shook his head and opened his eyes. He stared at them.
>
> The oldest man put the bottle down and walked over to Kaneha. He took a hunting knife from his belt. The other men's eyes followed him. He cut the rope that bound her to the chair. 'On yer feet,' he said harshly.
>
> Silently Kaneha rose. The man's knife moved quickly behind her and her shift fell to the floor. She stood there naked before them. The youngest man licked his lips. He reached for the whisky and took a drink, his eyes never leaving her.
>
> Holding Kaneha by the hair, his knife to her back, the oldest man pushed her toward Sam. They stopped in front of him.
>
> 'It's been fifteen years since I skinned an Injun, squaw man,' he said. 'But I ain't fergot how.' He moved swiftly around in front of her, his knife moving lightly up and down her skin.
>
> A faint thin line of blood appeared where the knife had traced from under her chin down her throat through the valley between her breasts across her stomach and coming to a stop in the foliage of her pubis.

To have had anything to do with books like *The Carpetbaggers* before 1960 would have meant certain prison. Now ten-year olds could buy them.

Like other revolutions, the paperback revolution was warily regarded by the authorities. The official view was put by Hailsham, in the Lords *Chatterley* debate. He would far rather, he said, that the book had appeared in 'boards at 12s.6d. than in paperback at 3s.6d.' It was this custodial fear of 'cheap literature' (a fear, incidentally, which was very active in the nineteenth century and can be traced back aboriginally, to obstructions on vulgate Bibles) that motivated the subsequent Mayflower–*Fanny Hill* case. The logical target – if the authorities wanted another test trial – was Henry Miller, for whose works, long-written but newly published in America, Grove was currently involved in some 50 prosecutions. As his Paris publisher put it, 'Henry Miller . . . is the first American author to have used sex to provoke the mental revolution now being accomplished.' But in Britain, Miller's *Tropics* were published at a minatory 25s. (twice Hailsham's preferred cost) by John Calder, and prudently withheld from cheap, mass-market paperback. They escaped prosecution, as did the similarly over-price, prophylactically hardbacked *Naked Lunch*. The next major literary-obscenity trial was to be over the comparatively innocent *Fanny Hill* – a book which urged no mental revolution, but had the gall to be a 3s.6d. paperback.

Postscript: Henry Miller

Between 1963 and 1969, a cascade of Henry Miller works came into print in the UK. With the *Tropics of Capricorn* and *Cancer*, *Plexus*, *Nexus* and *Sexus*, Miller must have earned more in royalties than almost any other novelist of the period. There was a certain piquancy in his late best-sellerdom. As Anaïs Nin relates, some of the works which now sold in millions (*Sexus*, for instance) were originally written as custom-built erotica for an individual rich collector. Miller could thus claim to have had the largest and smallest readerships of any writer in history.

The apogee of Miller's 'legitimate' status came with the British Book Club Associates' special offer of two *Tropics* and *Black Spring* in 1981. (BCA is half owned by W.H. Smith – W.H. Smut as *Private Eye* call them, with sarcastic reference to their unwillingness to handle 'doubtful' literature.) With a picture of a naked, spread-legged cutie on a sofa and a topical 'Indecent Display' sticker (WARNING: SEXUALLY EXPLICIT) a flier describes Miller as 'BANNED, but undefeated by the censor's stamp . . . BRAZEN but undaunted by charges of obscenity . . . BRILLIANT but now recognised as classics of modern literature'. 'Even today', the member was assured, 'in this so called "permissive" society, his blunt language has lost none of its power to shock.' It had.

November 1963:

Fanny Hill

History's Most Prosecuted Novel

Cashing in on the prohibited paperback boom of the early 1960s, Mayflower scheduled a softcover unexpurgated *Fanny Hill: Memoirs of a Woman of Pleasure*, to be published at 3*s*.6*d*. on 8 November 1963. It would be the first legitimate publication in full of Cleland's novel (ostensibly the confessions of an eighteenth-century courtesan) since its clandestine appearance in 1749. Mayflower were encouraged in this daring act by the book's having been cleared in the New York courts in August 1963. Mayflower, as emerged in the subsequent trial, were a respectable and 'responsible' publishing firm. But they did not have Penguin's institutional standing. Nor did they retail, like Penguin, exclusively through bona fide book stores and outlets.

Police awareness of *Fanny Hill* was excited by the book's being advertised (some three days before publication date) in the window of G. Gold and Sons' 'Magic Shop' in Tottenham Court Road. A scrawled window display announced: 'JUST OUT: FANNY HILL. BANNED IN AMERICA.' It wasn't just out (at least officially) and it wasn't banned in America. An inspector called. He had a few words with the manager who declared the book to be 'on a par with Lady Chatterley' and averred that he would never ever sell such a thing to anyone under eighteen. In fact, the shop's wares were about half magic tricks and party novelties, half pulp reading matter – naturally children would be somewhere around buying their stink bombs and naughty fidos. (Interestingly, the Golds were to go on to become a major force in the British skin mag industry; at this period, the glossy soft porn market was entirely dominated by American imports.)

The police took a copy of *Fanny Hill* to the Bow Street magistrate, Sir Robert Blundell, who was later to try the case. He read the work, bristled and issued a search warrant. In a swoop on the Magic Shop 171 copies were seized, and Ralph

Gold summonsed on 18 December under Section 3 of the Obscenity Act. This meant that the retailer was to be tried, summarily, before a magistrate. The publisher was necessarily *hors de combat*, and the verdict of the magistrate would only have authority within the court's area. By December, Mayflower had distributed some 82,000 copies, and could have made a killing had they chosen to exploit the prurient interest whipped up by the forthcoming trial. The novel had been warmly reviewed by, among others, V.S. Pritchett and Brigid Brophy.

Mayflower, understandably, wished the *book* to be charged rather than these shady entrepreneurs; and like Sir Allen Lane, they wished to go to the dock and protect Fanny as self-sacrificingly as he had Connie Chatterley. For the same reason, they wanted trial by 'the public' – i.e., jury – rather than Sir Robert Blundell who had already decided that the book warranted police attention. They were put out and alarmed to discover, however, that although they could 'intervene' they could not be defendants. G. Gold and Sons were to have that front-line duty thrust on them (they, doubtless, wouldn't have minded stepping aside, in the interest of literary freedom). The publishers' solicitors complained bitterly at this: 'Our clients [Mayflower] may be faced with a multiplicity of appearances in other petty sessional areas whatever the outcome at Bow Street.' Penguin had fought one heroic battle; for Mayflower, it might mean an impossibly long guerrilla campaign, defending *Fanny Hill* up and down the country from Auchtermuchty to Barnstaple, wherever local police decided to move against it. The (Conservative) DPP was sympathetic, noting that the firm had acted with a 'proper sense of responsibility' by withholding the book in the period between the summons and the trial in February 1964. But he nonetheless decided that acting against a single bookseller was not oppressive, given the fact that Mayflower could 'assist' the defendant (i.e., pay for the Golds' legal costs.)

With Mayflower footing the defence bills, a re-run of *Chatterley* in the lower courts was set up. As at the Old Bailey in 1960, the prosecution was conducted by Mervyn Griffith-Jones ('that indefatigable scourge of the impure' as Roy Jenkins called him, after the trial), and the defence by Jeremy Hutchinson. Sir Robert Blundell (who by now claimed to have read the novel twice) presided. The defence had two planks. First was that *Fanny Hill* was an historical source book in which scholars of the eighteenth century

could find a rich supply of primary evidence. Actually, this
defence has never gone down well in British courts. Lawyers
are always suspicious of academics as double-talking charla-
tans, and astutely note that they rarely have trouble getting
the dirty books they want for professional purposes. The
second plank was that *Fanny Hill* comes over as a joyous
celebration of straight, unkinky sex. It is 'bawdy' (a Chester-
tonian plus word) not obscene, or pornographic. Toeing this
line, Peter Quennell (who wrote the preface for both American and British paperback editions) asserted that 'Fanny is an
advocate of the pleasures of straightforward sex.' Marghanita
Laski described it as 'a gay little book . . . a jolly book . . .
It made me feel cheerful.'

In fact, Cleland's novel is extremely defensible for its
joyous, sprightly manner and its stylistic delicacy. (There is
no four-letter word in the whole text; erotic references are
handled by skilful periphrasis so that the most frequent
conjunction in the book is between the heroine's 'tender and
critical parts' and the 'mighty machines' of her customers and
lovers.)

This line of defence was, however, methodically obstructed. The prosecution had been caught out over *Chatterley*. They could read *Encounter* as well as the next lawyer,
and they now knew that Lawrence's book was not all 'tenderness' and 'holiness of sex' as had been protested at the Old
Bailey. Again and again at the trial, Griffith-Jones was to
hammer away at one particular (and entirely untypical)
scene in *Fanny Hill* – that of the 'flagellation'. The episode
opens with Fanny being introduced to a new client by Mrs
Cole. He is 'exceedingly fair and smooth complexion'd' and,
apparently uneasy. Fanny discovers why – he has a 'peculiar
taste'. She, although unpractised in these specialist arts,
prepares a bench and cushion for him. With some wonder-
ment, she observes that he is in a state of less than priapic
excitement, his 'humoursome master movement' being
'almost shrunk into his body, scarce showing its tip above
the sprout of hairy curls that clothed these parts, as you may
have seen a wren peep its head out of the grass'. Fanny lashes
into his 'chubby, smooth-cheek'd and passing white
posteriors', wearing out no less than three sets of rods. He
masturbates unclimactically (his master movement now has
'something of the air of a round fillett of the whitest veal'.)
Now it is Fanny's turn to be beaten. He begins gently and
with caresses, concludes with sadistic ferocity:

At last, he twigg'd me so smartly as to fetch blood in more
than one lash: at sight of which he flung down the rod,
flew to me, kissed away the starting drops, and, sucking
my wounds, eased a good deal of my pain. But now raising
me on my knees, and making me kneel with them straddl-
ing wide, that tender part of me, naturally the province of
pleasure, not of pain, came in for its share of suffering: for
now, eyeing it wistfully, he directed the rod so that the
sharp ends of the twigs lighted there, so sensibly, that I
could not help wincing, and writhing my limbs with pain;
so that my contortions of body must necessarily throw it
into infinite variety of postures and points of view, fit to
feast the luxury of the eye. But still I bore everything
without crying out: when presently, giving me another
pause, he rush'd, as it were, on that part whose lips, and
round-about, had felt this cruelty, and by way of repara-
tion, glues his own to them; then he opened, shut, squeez'd
them, pluck'd softly the overgrowing moss, and all this in
a style of wild passion–pleasure; till, betaking himself to
the rod again, encourag'd by my passiveness and infuriated
with this strange taste of delight, he made my poor posteriors pay for the ungovernableness of it; for now showing
them no quarter, the traitor cut me so that I wanted but
little of fainting away, when he gave over. And yet I did
not utter one groan, or make any angry expostulation; but
in heart I resolv'd never to expose myself again to the like
severities.

Later that evening, Barville and Fanny are aroused by their
mutual beatings to make love – the weals on their buttocks
forcing them into weirdly acrobatic postures. It is an oddly
unsavoury episode in a generally jolly and goodnatured
narrative, and it offered a chink into which the prosecution
could insert forensic levers, intimating that the general tenor
of the book was perverted.

   The adroitness with which Griffith-Jones impaled defence
witnesses intent on arguing the 'straightforward sex' and
'historical interest' angles, is evident in *The Times* account of
Quennell's cross-examination.

Mr Griffith-Jones referred to Barville, the man who delighted in flagellation and the passages in the book which
told of how Fanny was dressed – in the finest linen, white
uniform gown, petticoat, stockings and satin slippers, with
her hair in dropped curls – before 'being led like a lamb to

the slaughter to some horrible brute who could not have sexual intercourse unless he was whipped first'.

Mr Quennell said that the description of the dropped curls was interesting from the point of view of the ladies' hair styles of the period.

The defence had distinguished witnesses (H. Montgomery Hyde, author and former MP; Karl Miller, literary editor; Ian Watt, author of the definitive study of eighteenth-century fiction *The Rise of the Novel*). As with *Chatterley*, the prosecution offered none. But the taint of the seedy Magic Shop was very strongly in their favour. Nor was the defence case helped when, in the adjournment just before judgment was given on 10 February, the firm of G. Gold and Sons was the subject of an injunction granted John Calder by the Court of Chancery. This injunction was to stop the Golds from selling bootlegged copies of *Tropic of Capricorn* (in which Calder had the English rights). Mayflower were also unlucky in that the climate of moral opinion at the time was generally hysterical. The Profumo scandal was currently raging and the British public in one of its periodic fits of punitive moralism about 'vice'. It was not, as seasons go, a good time for liberal causes. Anything which might be alleged, however farfetchedly, to rot British moral fibre was suspect. Fanny Hill would be scourged for the fornications of Christine Keeler and Mandy Rice-Davies. It is instructive to compare proceedings in the Stephen Ward (i.e., the Profumo scandal) case, in the last week of July 1963. Griffith-Jones had again been prosecuting, and he gave Vicki Barrett – one of Ward's callgirls – a gruelling time in the witness box:

> Ward also asked her, she said, to provide a service for his friends who had strange tastes; they were middle-aged or elderly men who required not normal sexual intercourse but beating with either a cane or a horsewhip. Mr Griffith-Jones asked: 'For the whipping, what is the market price?' '£1 a stroke', said Miss Barrett.

If vengeful British justice could punish filthy, flagellant Ward on his suicidal deathbed (he was sentenced while in terminal coma) for this immorality, it would have no compunction in coming down hard on filthy, flagellant *Fanny Hill*.

Sir Robert found *Fanny Hill* guilty (after giving the matter 'two minutes reflection', it was later alleged in Parliament). The 171 seized copies were ordered to be forfeit. The consequent uproar was immense and confused. 'The legal authorities of this country can be relied upon to mishandle any issue touching the censorship of books', observed Roy Jenkins, adding bitingly, 'unfortunately this record of ineptitude does not make them fight shy of this subject.' The Publishers' Association declared itself 'disturbed'. In a leading article, the *Guardian* declared that justice had been thwarted. *The Times* began its leader by observing – correctly – that it was the cheap, paperback format of *Fanny Hill* which was its main offence, pointing to 'the present immunity of an expensive [42s.] edition of the book'. But then the leader-writer went on to argue that *Fanny Hill* was a dirty book anyway, and no great loss: 'There is no health in the current cant of pretending that such books as *Fanny Hill* will become bestsellers for any but the obvious reasons', the paper concluded. According to the *Daily Express*, 'there is universal relief at the ruling of the Chief Magistrate.' In its Sunday sister paper, John Gordon (who had single-handedly made *Lolita* a British bestseller by calling it a filthy book) was very cheered, and went on to demand a general Augean cleansing. In the *Spectator*, Leo Abse plausibly thought the verdict and the prosecution behind it were a panic reaction to Profumo. Peter Jenkins (*Guardian*) and Norman St John-Stevas (*Sunday Times*) made impassioned liberal protests. In the *Sunday Telegraph*, Peregrine Worsthorne worried about the unexpurgated *Fanny Hill* as a threat to Christian marriage: 'it would surely be odd for a society pledged to monogamous marriage to allow any citizen with a few shillings in his pocket to buy *Fanny Hill*.' It was presumably safe to allow the citizen with a couple of guineas to buy it. Here again, it was the mass-market paperback form rather than its contents which was most worrying to society's guardians.

The same controversy was played out in the formal rhetoric and manoeuvring of Parliament. An all-party motion was put down, deploring the verdict. The Attorney-General, Sir John Hobson, stood his ground, and refused the compromise proposal that he might exonerate from prosecution under the 1959 Act all books published 'more than a hundred years ago'. Sir John informed Leo Abse that the prosecution of *Fanny Hill* had cost the authorities £296 3s. Mr Gresham Cooke (Conservative, Twickenham) intervened to say 'there are hundreds of thousands of parents of teenage children who think the £296 was very well spent.' Dingle Foot related to an amused House a personal anecdote illustrative of the pickle censorship regulations had now arrived at.

'I purchased a copy of *The Perfumed Garden* at London airport in December (laughter) – and when I returned to London airport, the book was seized.'

The score now stood at one each. The liberals had won with *Chatterley*, the reactionaries with *Fanny Hill*. Both sides mustered afterwards for what promised to be a lively period of skirmishing. In the Commons, Jenkins made strenuous efforts to plug the hole now evident in 'his' 1959 Act. When in 1964 the Conservative administration introduced certain amendments (to do with the status of film negatives, what was entailed by 'publication' and the 'moral asbestos' conceived to surround the police purchasing obscenity) he urged that a *right* to jury trial should be allowed. Henry Brooke – the most illiberal of postwar Home Secretaries – was 'firmly' against allowing this. Where bulk confiscations were involved it would impede the police and make the juries' task impossibly onerous. A concession was made by the Solicitor-General, however. In future, if a defendant indicated his intention to continue publishing, even if the magistrate ordered forfeiture, then the DPP would normally refer the case to trial by jury. Jenkins could be said to have won his point, though it was not enshrined in law; it was merely an 'assurance'.

The reactionaries were doing rather better. The period after the *Fanny Hill* trial is marked by savage crackdown, especially in Northern England. In February and March 1964, the Manchester police raided city bookshops and seized both the expensive and Mayflower editions of *Fanny Hill* – together with an assortment of other juicy items (*A Cold Wind in August, Tropic of Capricorn, The Kama Sutra*). The unlucky Manchester printers, C. Nicholls and Co., had 4,000 copies of Cleland's novel in their warehouse. This stock was impounded and the firm summonsed. In April, the Manchester magistrates found *Fanny Hill* obscene, and the 4,000 copies were ordered to be forfeit and destroyed. Birmingham, Brighton and Sheffield police similarly moved against *Fanny Hill* in their territories (although the book was now no longer on supply from the publisher).

It is uncanny how inevitably *Fanny Hill* crops up at critical moments in the history of censorship. It was the first obscene book to be prosecuted as such in America, in 1821. It was at

a subsequent American trial of the book that the 'redeeming
social value' consideration was enunciated, paving the way
for the 'public good' plea of the 1959 British Act. Three
trials of *Fanny Hill* in America in the 1960s cleared the air
for what Charles Rembar called 'the end of obscenity'.
(Prematurely; in the flush of 1968, Rembar did not foresee
the moral majority's victory in 1973 and the return of
censorship authority to 'local community standards'.) It was
a decision in 1964 by the Danish Supreme Court, refusing
to condemn a Danish-language edition of *Fanny Hill* (although the original English text had earlier been banned),
that led to the most radical emancipation of pornography
ever. The Danish publisher was, however, cannier than Mayflower; he 'published' the work by sending 60 copies to the
Public Prosecutor and to a selection of critics and public
figures, asking if they saw any reason why *Fanny Hill* should
be banned.

In other circumstances, the *Fanny Hill* trial in the UK
should have consolidated the beachhead made by *Chatterley*.
For a variety of reasons (Profumo hysteria, the Golds' association with Soho smut, the greater strength of British
backlash) this was not to be. What the verdict produced in
the UK was that favourite Anglo-Saxon commodity, fog.
Mayflower decided not to appeal – it would be too expensive
and simply spark off a series of other local prosecutions in
all parts of the country. Instead they brought out a bowdlerised edition. (Not bowdlerised enough for some provincial
tastes, however. In straightlaced Edinburgh even this
neutered thing was found indecent in October 1964.) It
resulted in a nonsense over the next few years. In 1968, for
instance, the foul-mouthed and ultra-violent *Last Exit* was
legitimately on sale – but not the softer *Fanny Hill*. Eventually an unexpurgated Mayflower text crept back into print
in 1970, the year when decensorship was at its height. It was
not prosecuted – though presumably still technically a
banned book.

The hangover from *Fanny Hill* contributed to a general
caution among British publishers (verging on timidity with
paperback publishers) over the next few years, and widened
the gap between when a contentious work might appear in
France, in America, and over here.

Thus *The Story of O* (an updated, French *Fanny Hill* –
with a lot more flagellation) was published in France in 1954,
in America in 1966, in the UK in 1970. The same pattern is
evident with Terry Southern's *Candy* (a modernised, female

Candide, she runs through amazing sexual adventures and ends up making it with her deified father). This work was first commissioned by Girodias and published in his Traveller's Library in the late 1950s. It was brought out, in full, and in paperback, in New York in 1964. In September 1968, there was an English edition by Bernard Geis, marred by heavy and clumsy cutting. This was reissued by New English Library as a paperback in 1969 - still cut but with no indication to the reader of the fact. Meanwhile at some shops in London, and intermittently (depending on the nerve or greed of the shopkeeper) the uncut American Lancer paperback could be found. Finally, an unexpurgated British edition was brought out in 1970 - encouraged by the unpersecuted reappearance of *Fanny Hill* in print.

April 1964:

Cain's Book

Junkies, Revolution and Obscenity

Exile is the theme of Alexander Trocchi's writing and of his life. His first major *départ* was from postwar Glasgow (where he had taken a philosophy degree). In the early 1950s he drifted into the coterie of bohemians, avant-gardistes and pornographers centred in Paris around the magazine *Merlin* and Girodias's Olympia Press. He edited *Merlin* from 1952-55, presiding, as Girodias recalls, as 'the erratic pope of that pagan church'. Pagan it might have been, nevertheless, *Merlin* stands in literary history as a journal of distinction with contributions from then little-known authors like Samuel Beckett, Christopher Logue and Robert Creeley. As a producer of books Girodias considered Trocchi 'the first of Olympia's all-out literary stallions'. Olympia brought out Trocchi's autobiographical *Young Adam* in 1955 (toned down, it appeared in the UK in 1961). Under the pseudonym Frances Lengel, he also produced at the same period a number of hot, semi-parodic pornographic novels such as *Helen and Desire*, *School for Sin*, *White Thighs*. A sample of Trocchi/Lengel's out and out pornography (which has never been printed above ground in his home country though it still circulates profitably under counters and in back rooms) may be given for comparison with his later 'serious' fiction. (The heroine in *Helen and Desire*, in the hands of Arab white-slavers, reminisces about an early rape in her career):

Duke leaned over me, gripping my upper arms in his powerful hands and forcing my shoulders back into the straw. Rippling under the sweat, all the wounded muscles of my soft underside were thus exposed to the man's eyes which at once fixed themselves on the nervous clot of hair between the lip of my belly and the podgy bowl of my tightly closed thighs. He released his grip to unbutton his trousers, leaving red splotches where his fingers had pressed into my upper arms. Then he bared his lower front to me, a powerful flower, stuck close with wiry black hairs under which his skin gleamed moistly like a mushroom in moonshine. At the sight of his desire, my fear left me, my belly and thighs took on the consistency of spawn, the latter opening as my legs arrowed at the knees, anticipating the bandit shock that would scrape the bottom of me like a ship's keel.

Trocchi will have an entry in the history of narrative pornography for such exuberant writing. He will probably have a somewhat larger place for the 'Fifth Volume of Frank Harris's *My Life and Loves* which he wrote (again for Girodias) in 1958. The mass-market paperbacks of Harris's massive confessions – which sold well in Britain and America in the late 1960s – incorporate Trocchi's pastiche addendum without comment. So good is it, that a reader would be hard put to say whether the following is Harris-original or Trocchi ersatz. Frank's Indian pandar, Mrs Redfern, brings her master what would elsewhere be called a French Tickler:

A few days later she drew out a 'hedgehog' and showed it to me: it was a silver ring with a number of very tiny fine feathers brought in all round it. The ring was not closed and Mrs Redfern slipped it over my thumb and said, 'There; if you use that, you will make all the girls crazy for you.'
'Really,' I exclaimed, 'you mean if I put it on, it will give them more pleasure?'
'You try,' she exclaimed. 'Don't tell them; but try and you will soon see that I've made you a wonder-worker.'
'All right.'
. . .
That evening Winnie was coming to spend a couple of hours with me. At first she seemed less passionate than usual, but after half an hour or so of love's dalliance, when I thought she had reached the height of feeling, I slipped on the ring and began the final essay.
In a moment I knew that Mrs Redfern was justified. Almost at once Winnie spread herself feverishly and soon for the first time began to move her body uncontrollably and utter strange sounds, now whimpering, now gasping, 'Oh! I can't stand it; oh! stop, please, or I shall go mad! Oh! Oh! Oh!'

In the late 1950s, Trocchi followed the action to New York. He became involved with new movements in pop art, the Beat generation and, pre-eminently, the drug culture. Out of this experience came the work on which his international literary reputation and his status as an obscene author in the UK rests – *Cain's Book*. Sections of it were pre-published in the *Evergreen Review* and the whole was brought out by Grove in the US in 1960.

Cain's Book is a random performance – 'my little voyage in the art of digression' Trocchi archly but all too accurately calls it. It is presented as the journal of someone like the author (though a preface reassures his immediate family that resemblances are accidental) living a hand to arm exist-ence on a scow, somewhere on the Hudson River. 'Half an hour ago I gave myself a fix' opens the first chapter. His mind and his prose style apparently permanently unjointed by hard drugs, the narrator muses, sometimes reminscently, sometimes philosophically. The philosophy that protrudes through the egotising is anarchic. Two sets of laws in parti-cular are defied: that enforcing censorship ('I say it is imper-tinent, insolent and presumptuous of any person or group of persons to impose their unexamined moral prohibitions on me') and that prohibiting psychotropic drugs ('To think that a man should be allowed a gun and not a drug'). 'I demand that these laws be changed' the narrator tells us, the Ameri-can authorities, the world at large, or possibly God.

For all its cosmopolitanism, its knowingness about Paris and New York, the sharpest vignette in the book takes us back to black-out Edinburgh. (As a very young man, Trocchi had served in the war-time Royal Navy):

> I made love for the first time with a prostitute. Princes Street, Edinburgh. Ten shillings for a short time in an air-raid shelter. I had never seen such ugly thighs nor ever imagined it like that, exposed for me in matchlight, the flaccid buttocks like pale meat on the stone stairs, the baggy skirt raised as far as her navel and with spread knees making a cave of her crotch, the match flickering and this first sex shadowy and hanging colourless like a clot of spiderweb from the blunt butt of her mound. She rubbed spittle on it brusquely, as my mother with a handkerchief rubbed spittle against my cheek when we were visiting She rubbed spittle on it and it was like someone scratching his head. It bristled then, and bared its pretty pink fangs. She told me to hurry up. The stone steps were cold. Above

in the street there was a fine rain and I could hear the swish of tyres on the wet macadam. At my naked thighs I felt the night wind. The match was out. In the almost total obscurity of the shelter I lay on top of her and felt her belly sink cool and soft and clammy under my own.

I was a seaman in the Royal Navy at the time. I remember walking alone back to the Y.M.C.A. where I was staying. I went over it again in my mind, and by the time I reached the Y.M. little feeling of guilt remained. I was even in a vague way proud, callow possibly, but I experienced an authentic feeling of relief. I savoured it with a cup of milky coffee in the tearoom of the Y.M.

The atypical pace and concreteness of this passage – unsavoury though it is – makes one wish that Trocchi had after all stayed with his own folk and realistic modes of writing.

Trocchi attracted great publicity in the UK (where virtually none of his fiction had been as yet published) in 1962, at the Edinburgh Festival Writers' Conference. He had a blazing row with Hugh MacDiarmid in which he argued for internationalism against the older poet's Scottish chauvinism. The controversy was widely reported, and identified Trocchi as a literary figure who centralised the divergent streams of French, American and British culture. John Calder (who had organised the 1962 Writers' Conference) had as his programme the foundation of a 'New British School' of writing, nourished by the rich cosmopolitanism of Robbe-Grillet, Beckett, Ginsberg, and Burroughs. He accordingly took up Trocchi enthusiastically, announcing him as 'a leading figure in the "beat movement" also experimenting with drugs and their effect on creative writing'. The wanderer Cain had returned. 'Trocchi', Calder announced, 'has now returned to Britain and is living in London with his wife and child' with the air of a man who might say 'Sam Beckett has opened a bar in Grafton Street.' It was no retirement, however. Trocchi was bringing with him the exciting doctrines he had picked up in his exile. Together with Calder and other forward spirits he became active in the 'sigma' project. This was ' "a revolutionary proposal" to bring art into life, leisure and popular culture, by means of "spontaneous universities" and cultural centres, and by making art available everywhere, from hoardings to matchboxes'. This proselytising phase of Trocchi's life culminated in June 1965, when he was master of ceremonies at the Albert Hall mass poetry reading which featured, *inter alia*, the patriarchs of beat, Ginsberg and Ferlinghetti.

By now, Trocchi was a read author in his own country. In early 1963 *Cain's Book* came out under Calder's imprint. It was received deferentially – the author even receiving the ultimate accolade of a publication-week interview with Huw Wheldon on 'Monitor'. This monumentally straight figure (later to head the BBC) solemnly enquired about Trocchi's 'controlled' use of junk to stimulate his muse and alluded darkly but approvingly to the post-*Chatterley* 'frankness' of the language.

'Outsiders' were very voguish in the early 1960s and *Cain's Book* evidently sold well – even at Calder's pricey 25s. When a new edition was called for in June 1963, any censorship threat would seem to have passed. But with the post-*Fanny Hill* backlash, especially in the provinces, Trocchi's book was again at risk. Generally, Calder took the wise precaution of supplying only bona fide 'carriage trade' bookshops. These were safer from police raids than 'novelty shops' with a sideline in French letters and dirty books, or seedy newspaper shops with high shelves and back rooms. In Sheffield, however, a number of copies of *Cain's Book* had seeped through to the sewer channels of the book trade. In February 1964 it was scooped up together with 48 other novels and 906 different magazines in what seems to have been a massive, if decidedly indiscriminate, operation. (One Sheffield bookseller complained 'the police took away the August issue of two romances which contained a knitting pattern . . . but left *Tropic of Cancer*'.) Calder gave notice that he intended to defend *Cain's Book* for its literary merit when eventually the trial came round (the magistrates were given six weeks to read the mass of material scooped up). The police justified their seizure of *Cain's Book* at the preliminary hearing on the grounds that it 'seems to advocate the use of drugs in schools so that children should have a clearer conception of art. That in our submission is corrupting.' (This, incidentally, must stand as one of the most extraordinary official synopses of a work of literature ever, rivalled only by *The Times*'s repeated description of *Last Exit to Brooklyn* as 'the story of a man's struggle against homosexuality'.)

When *Cain's Book* at last came before the Sheffield courts on 15 April, Calder told the jury that it was 'one of the most important books written by a British author that has an affinity with the beat movement which is a revolt against conventional values'. Rather more an upholder of conventional values, the Sheffield City Librarian informed the court that there were twenty copies of *Cain's Book* in his library 'kept in a reserve category available only for adults'. Sheffield was not willing to tolerate even this limited access. After a mere three-quarters of an hour retirement, *Cain's Book* was determined obscene and all copies in the Sheffield area ordered confiscated. The verdict did not, apparently, chasten the book's producers. At the Edinburgh Festival in September 1964 Calder and Trocchi went on to work together on an 'underground poetry conference'. A *je m'en foutiste* gesture was devised against the authority that was currently persecuting them. After a meeting at the Traverse Theatre the novelist and sympathisers adjourned to the Grassmarket for a public burning of *Cain's Book* 'in the form of a large incendiary containing fireworks, muzzle to the sky'.

Less anarchically, Calder lodged an appeal. It was dismissed with costs going against the defendant in December 1964. Justifying the negative decision the Lord Chief Justice made an interesting extension of the idea of obscenity, as it had hitherto been conceived:

> This book – the less said about it the better – concerns the life or imaginary life of a junkie in New York and the suggestion of the prosecution was that the book, highlighting as it were, the favourable effects of drug taking, so far from condemning it, advocates it and that there is a real danger that those into whose hands the book comes might be tempted, at any rate, to experiment with drugs and get the favourable sensations highlighted by the book.

In his Lordship's judgment 'there was no reason whatever to confine depravity and obscenity to sex . . .'

Suppression in Sheffield was not disastrous for publisher or author – indeed, it might even be helpful to sales elsewhere on the 'banned in Boston' principle. Nevertheless Lord Chief Justice Parker's decision was highly significant. It marked a new phase of obscenity-hunting in which the primary target would not be the work's text (for instance its incidence of four-letter words) but the *lifestyle* it advocated, or that was associated with its author or even its readership. If it was risking 'obscenity' to be a junkie and a beat, it was also soon going to be similarly risky to be a hippy.

After the furore of *Cain's Book* and the excitement of the Albert Hall poetry event, Trocchi faded from view. His later work is largely translation. This writer on whom Calder hoped to found his 'new school of British writers' remained in the public mind only vaguely as one of that company of Americans (Burroughs, Ginsberg, Bruce were others) who had come over and 'talked dirty' in the early 1960s, ruffled a few feathers, but made no lasting impact.

October 1964:

The Naked Lunch

Trial by TLS

William Burroughs's *The Naked Lunch* deals explicitly with pederasty, cannibalism and drug addiction. It is therefore not surprising that its publishing history in the early 1960s was vexed; more surprising, perhaps, that it escaped formal prosecution in the UK. It was, however, given the most thorough going-over of any novel of the period in Britain's main opinion-forming literary journal, the *Times Literary Supplement*. It would also appear that the paper used its immense authority to try to stop *The Naked Lunch* ever being published, taking on itself the role of pre-censor.

In 1957, Burroughs offered his, apparently rat-gnawed, manuscript to the Paris publisher Girodias, who sent it back for tidying up. In 1958, a chapter was printed in the *Chicago Review* and stirred up some controversy. Girodias's Olympia Press edition of the complete text came out in 1959. In 1962, emboldened by their success in the courts and the marketplace with Miller's *Tropics*, Grove brought out an American edition. This sold more than 14,000 copies by March 1963. Inevitably, it was also banned in Boston. But after a well-publicised trial, the legality of *The Naked Lunch* in the US was clinched and by 1965 the book was generally available there. (For the detailed career of the novel in America, see M.B. Goodman, *The Case History of William Burroughs's The Naked Lunch*, New Jersey, 1981.)

Things went contrarily in France. In 1965, after the puritanical De Gaulle came to power, Girodias and his fellow libertine publishers were persecuted mercilessly. Girodias himself was fairly driven out of the country where he, and his father before him, had been publishing some of the most important books in the English language for thirty years. Taking fright, Gallimard (the most eminent of houses) did not dare list the translated *Naked Lunch* in their general catalogue in 1965. In Britain, the book was published by

John Calder in October 1964. Various tactics were adopted
to forestall prosecution. It was priced at 35s. - about twice
what the standard hardback novel of the period cost. More
provocatively, Calder took out large advertisements in the
literary papers in August and September 1964, describing
The Naked Lunch as 'one of the most significant literary
works of our era . . . a book that is lectured on in British
University courses . . . British publication is a matter of
historical necessity'. This rousing description of the novel
was accompanied by a cut-out coupon, to be returned to
Calder. It ran:

> I/We the undersigned wish to support you in your decision
> to publish *The Naked Lunch* in October. A sufficient
> number of eminent members of the literary world have
> read and praised the book for there not to be any doubt
> that it is a work of serious intent and literary value and I
> think it desirable that it should be made available to the
> British public as it is already available in America and most
> continental countries.

Finally, Calder took particular care over the way in which
The Naked Lunch was released to the trade, and thence to
the public:

> By refusing the book to wholesalers, and in supplying only
> the most respectable booksellers, we made it extremely
> difficult for the police to seize the book and bring it in
> front of local magistrates . . . in fact it becomes impossible,
> providing we print small editions and scatter them thinly
> around the country, to prevent publication of the book
> except by taking it to the Old Bailey and this the DPP is
> not willing to do as there is obviously no official confi-
> dence in a jury. (*Censorship*, summer, 1965.)

In fact, a copy was bought at Zwemmers in London on 31
December 1964, and sent to the DPP who obviously decided
not to take action. Calder's ruses apart, he may have felt that
the recent successful agitation to reform the 1959 Act had
created an unfavourable climate for prosecution. But for
whatever combination of motives, expedients and historical
factors, *The Naked Lunch* (on the face of it a far more
dangerous book than *Fanny Hill*) got through unscathed.

In his advertisements, Calder pigeon-holes Burroughs very confidently. He is: 'the most important writer so far thrown up by the "beat" movement . . . the principal American post-Joycean . . . a writer who at his best can be compared to Kafka, Beckett and Eliot.' In fact, Burroughs is a notoriously hard writer for British readers to grasp or place, and for that reason has never made the headway in this country that his publisher originally hoped for.

Burroughs's first attempt at explaining his work to the British public cannot have helped much. He visited the country in early 1964 (under grudging sufferance from the immigration authorities) and made a broadcast for the Third Programme with his principal British explicator, Eric Mottram. *The Naked Lunch* was imminent, and Burroughs expatiated on his 'cut up' techniques, his view of society as a 'terminal sewer', the importance of 'addiction structure' in his fiction. (Thus, for instance, the author–reader and active-passive homosexual relationships are conceptualised on the pusher–addict model of human behaviour.) It was baffling stuff, and would have been outraging if, for instance, the BBC retained one of Burroughs's asides to Mottram: 'Did I ever tell you about the man who taught his asshole to talk? His whole abdomen would move up and down and, you dig? farting out the words. It was quite unlike anything I ever heard.' And quite unlike what listeners to the Third were used to hearing.

The Naked Lunch has at least three main elements. It is (1) an essay on drug withdrawal; (2) a 'scholarly' study of addiction; (3) a paranoid-sexual fantasia. In themselves, these themes could be handled in 1964 without offending the British establishment. But Burroughs's novel (if indeed it was a novel) introduced a jolting quality of vividly described necrophilia and cannibalism:

> Mary: 'No, let me.' She locks her hands behind Johnny's buttocks, puts her forehead against him, smiling into his eyes she moves back, pulling him off the platform into space . . . His face swells with blood . . . Mark reaches up with one lithe movement and snaps Johnny's neck . . . sound like a stick broken in wet towels. A shudder runs down Johnny's body . . . one foot flutters like a trapped bird . . . Mark has draped himself over a swing and mimics Johnny's twitches, closes his eyes and sticks his tongue out . . . Johnny's cock springs up and Mary guides it up her cunt, writhing against him in a fluid belly dance, groaning

and shrieking with delight . . . sweat pours down her body, hair hangs over her face in wet strands. 'Cut him down, Mark,' she screams. Mark reaches over with a snap knife and cuts the rope, catching Johnny as he falls, easing him onto his back with Mary still impaled and writhing . . . She bites away Johnny's lips and nose and sucks out his eyes with a pop . . . She tears off great hunks of cheek . . . Now she lunches on his prick . . . Mark walks over to her and she looks up from Johnny's half-eaten genitals, her face covered with blood, eyes phosphorescent . . . Mark puts his foot on her shoulder and kicks her over on her back. . . . He leaps on her, fucking her insanely . . . they roll from one end of the room to the other, pinwheel end-over-end and leap high in the air like great hooked fish.

According to Jeff Nuttall, '*The Naked Lunch* actually caused at least one unprepared square to vomit on the carpet.' And it was with a gagging 'ugh' that the archetypally square *TLS* was to receive Burroughs's book.

It is useful at this point to go back to *Chatterley*. As the most authoritative literary journal in Britain (indeed, the English speaking world, since the *New York Review of Books* had not yet started), the *TLS* had been Olympian but somewhat ambivalent over the events of November 1960. While not as hostile as *Encounter* to the trial's 'humbug', it had nevertheless taken exception to the view, expressed so clamorously, that the Old Bailey verdict represented the victory of one class and generation over an older and higher class with whom the *TLS* naturally identified itself.

Over the next year, the *TLS* rumbled intermittently about commercial exploitation of the new publishing freedom and the 'big fish', the 'professional pornographers' (15 December 1961) waiting to pounce. Three-and-a-half million copies of *Lady Chatterley* had been sold – where, the *TLS* asked on 6 July 1962, was it all going?

> After *Lady Chatterley's Lover*, what? It must surely be a matter of months [indeed it was] before *Tropic of Cancer* is freely published in the country. And after *Tropic of Cancer*, what then? An edition of de Sade in translation? [Right again – though the harder de Sade titles never made it.] The liberation of Olympia Press publications from Soho bookshops specializing in pornography so they are given the freedom of Charing Cross Road? [Wrong. You still have to get them in Soho.]

'It might even have been a good thing', the editorial concluded, 'if *Lady Chatterley's Lover* had been published at five guineas rather than between orange paper covers.'

This was the period when Henry Miller was flooding the British market. Weidenfeld and Nicolson brought out *Plexus* and *Nexus*, leaving the harder *Sexus* and the *Tropics* for the intrepid Calder. For the *TLS*, Miller was 'nauseating'. The *Tropic of Cancer* it found 'verbal cancer' (12 April 1963). Miller was a bad writer and (a word used to full biting effect) 'dull'. When *Plexus* was reviewed (1 November 1963) the paper took a loftily amused view of 'this comedy of a reputation based on ignorance'. Now that Miller was at last open to inspection, the bubble of his literary reputation was pricked.

On 14 November 1963, the *TLS* continued in this vein by hatcheting a group of William Burroughs's novels: *The Ticket that Exploded*, *The Soft Machine*, *Dead Fingers Talk*, *The Naked Lunch*. The main venom was reserved for the last title. Two damning points were made. First that Burroughs, like Miller, was a negligible, overblown writer once the glamorous aura of Prohibited Writer was removed. As the anonymous reviewer put it in a reply of 21 November: 'The case against William Burroughs is that he is a second rate writer who would have attracted little critical attention if it were not for his shock effects.' The second criticism of Burroughs was pungently expressed in the title of the review, 'Ugh'. For the *TLS*, Burroughs was simply disgusting: 'glug, glug. It tastes disgusting . . . pure verbal masturbation . . . vomit . . . unspeakable homosexual fantasies.'

What was surprising about this review was not just the violent antipathy it gave vent to, but that *The Naked Lunch* had not been published in Britain, and was not imminently to be published. This was, in fact, a preview. More purposefully, it was a pre-emptive strike against anyone intending to publish *The Naked Lunch* in the UK. For the *TLS* to rage in this way about a book to which its readers, let alone the larger reading public of the country, had no access was extraordinary. One assumes that the purpose of the exercise was to warn off the 'responsible' British publisher from dabbling with Burroughs. And since this was exactly the period of the *Fanny Hill* affair, it is quite likely that many in the book trade were in a state of nerves about dodgy books.

Moreover, the *TLS* was evidently prepared to flout, or sail close to, the law in order to crack down on *The Naked Lunch*. Earlier in the year, it had published a letter from a London student, who received a copy of *The Naked Lunch*

from abroad, through the post. He was visited by two policemen:

> They asked me if I had requested the book to be sent, and
> I said 'No'. 'It's lucky you said that, my friend,' said one
> of them, 'because otherwise you'd be liable for prosecu-
> tion as it is an offence to send, or cause to be sent, obscene
> publications through the mails.' I asked them in what way
> the book could be considered obscene and whether there
> had been a case about it. They said there had, and that it
> had been banned along with about twelve other books.
> (5 April 1963.)

Did the same two policemen visit the *TLS* reviewer, whoever
he was? How did he get his copy?

The *TLS* received an immediate vote of thanks from
various pillars of the establishment. Two letters, from Edith
Sitwell and Victor Gollancz, are worth quoting in full for
their astonishing pharisaism (they were published together
on 28 November):

> Sir,   I was delighted to see, in your issue of the 14th
> instant, the very right-minded review of a novel by a Mr
> Burroughs (whoever he may be) published by a Mr John
> Calder (whoever he may be).
>
> The public canonization of that insignificant, dirty
> little book *Lady Chatterley's Lover* was a signal to persons
> who wish to unload the filth in their minds on the British
> public.
>
> As the author of *Gold Coast Customs* I can scarcely be
> accused of shirking reality, but I do not wish to spend the
> rest of my life with my nose nailed to other people's
> lavatories.
>
> I prefer Chanel Number 5.
>
> Edith Sitwell, C.L.

> Sir,   Allow me to thank you cordially for 'Ugh'. The
> question is not one of pornography, the better sort of
> which, in a poor, second-hand sort of way, is to some
> degree life-enhancing: like the aroma that might faintly
> come through to a tramp at the half-open door of an
> expensive restaurant. I am told, for instance, that *Fanny
> Hill* can give a mild kind of pleasure to anyone except a
> puritan.
>
> But the bogus-highbrow filth you attack – and its

publication has proliferated horribly – is life-denying; spiritually as well as physically disgusting, and tasteless to an almost incredible degree, it offends against value of any kind (including intellectual value) every bit as much as against public decency. And you are right in suggesting that the current orgy may imperil the freedom of literature by provoking the kind of 'authority' that prosecuted *Lady Chatterley's Lover*. This would be a disaster: better an infinity of open drains than a pinpoint of censorship.

Victor Gollancz

Correspondence on the subject continued unbroken for thirteen weeks, and the 'Ugh' controversy bubbled on, intermittently, for a year. Among the correspondents drawn in was Burroughs himself. In January 1964, he was visiting Calder in London (presumably laying plans for the publication of *the* novel). On catching up with the fevered letters about himself in the *TLS*, he was led to ask 'who is Mr Gollancz?' (As much a lese-majesty as to say 'What is the *TLS*'?). He also ventured the reasonable objection that 'Ugh' was hardly a respectable critical judgment: 'the job of evaluation was not done by your reviewer, whoever he may be' (23 January 1964). The reviewer, whoever he was, wasn't interested in evaluation but in exclusion.

The *TLS* summed up the state of play with an editorial entitled 'Whither Ugh?' on 30 January, which stoutly supported its reviewer. It made dark allusions to Burroughs and Arab boys, and concluded: 'If Mr Calder chooses to compare *The Naked Lunch* to *Coriolanus* and *King Lear* [as he had ventured in letters to the journal] there is little that can politely be said about it.' And if nothing polite could be said it was, apparently, *causa finita*. The *TLS* had spoken.

It was not finished for Calder, however. As we have seen, he set about publishing *The Naked Lunch* in Britain in October 1964, taking a number of precautions. The *TLS* was still unforgivingly severe after the event. In an editorial on general censorship matters entitled 'Not for the Children', it noted that Calder had defied the canons of good taste (as enunciated by itself, the *TLS*) and brought out *The Naked Lunch* 'with a number of additionally disgusting amendments'. The earlier opprobrium was repeated:

the book is a mess, where mess itself, the cult of the shapeless and haphazard, has become a conscious technique. Unless it is to be taken as merely clinical – which it is not

- its horrors can only be acceptable to those who become insensitive to them or see some value in indiscriminate hatred of the human race.

The editorial concluded with the promise, that as a 'maker of taste' the *TLS* would continue in its resolute stand against this tide of nihilism. It didn't, of course. Like some giant tanker it slowly but majestically came round to the easy-going attitudes which were *de rigueur* in the late 1960s. (It is instructive to compare the stern 'Ugh' editorials with the almost flippant good humour with which the *TLS* received the news that *Oh! Calcutta!* was not to be prosecuted: or, as the paper archly put it, that Tynan's '*sexe*' was not going to be '*caché*'.)

Naked Lunch II: The Publishers

Burroughs's novel was published in France by Girodias, in America by Grove and in the UK by Calder. These three spearhead publishers share many of the other controversial titles of the period such as the *Tropics* and *Cain's Book*. Comparing their styles - especially those of Girodias and Calder - gives a useful indication of the strategy by which risky books were introduced into the British market.

Girodias

Maurice Girodias (b. 1919) was a second generation 'book-legger'. His father was Jack Kahane, who between the wars published in Paris such prohibited authors as Henry Miller, Lawrence Durrell, James Joyce, Frank Harris. Kahane died in September 1939, and to avoid the Gestapo, Maurice took his mother's maiden name, Girodias. During the Second World War he took up publishing. Thereafter, his career thrived in the margins and gaps between what was permissible by the discrepant standards of French, British and American censorship. Particularly useful to him was the fact that the French authorities would normally tolerate anything so long as it wasn't in French: relying, safely enough, on the monoglot prejudice of the Gallic race, which regards it a loss of national honour to know another language.

After the war, Girodias revived his father's Obelisk press. He still had Henry Miller copyrights and texts like *Fanny*

Hill and de Sade's were there for the taking. In this post-war period, Paris was crawling with GIs and tommies. Many barrack rooms and billets must have found the Obelisk volumes a welcome change from the worthy American Service Editions and Penguin paperbacks sent from the home front.

In the 1950s – a period which he regards as lapsarian – Girodias began to feel the chilling blast of 'bourgeois ex-tremism'. He was increasingly harried; by 1960 he had had 41 titles banned and had been indicted no less than 25 times for publishing obscene books. But it was not so much censor's hostility as financial mismanagement and too old-fashioned and literary a list which brought the venerable Obelisk Press to bankruptcy and Girodias to 'bumhood' in the 1950s. *In extremis*, he started a new line, 'Olympia Books', with an aggressive modern flavour. From the first, it was an outlaw operation. These were books for Americans and British (now coming back as tourists), 'Not to be sold in the USA or Britain' as they proclaimed. Hence, the famous, super-pornographic 'Travellers Library'; and many must have travelled to Paris just for its volumes.

Perhaps because of his mixed parentage and bilingualism, Girodias seems always to have been able to devise new cosmopolitan literary mixtures. Under the Olympia imprint, he gave first publication to *Lolita*, by a Russian professor of English at Cornell (who had also in his youth been an emigré writer in Paris). *Lolita* was, of course, unpublishable in either Nabokov's country of birth or adoption. It went on to become Girodias's biggest hit (before the Anglo-Saxons finally let it in), selling 15,000 in the two-volume and 40,000 in the cheap edition. Olympia also published *The Ginger Man* – a comic study of Dublin life by an American living in London and unpublishable in Ireland, Britain or America. Although he fell out with some of his most famous authors – with Nabokov over business, with Donleavy over cuts to his text – Girodias uniquely combined the skills of the literary ringmaster with those of the 'booklegger'. He made personal contact with and drew heavily on Trocchi's early 1950s *Merlin* group. Through them, he encountered the 'beats', which led him to Burroughs (then resident in Tangiers). It would have been enough for most publishers to have tapped such an extensive literary reservoir. But Girodias took his Paris-based, Merlin-centred writers and turned their energies to hilariously obscene ends. His intention was to 'beat censor-ship out of existence'. Thus Trocchi was transvested into the 'literary lady of little virtue by the name of Frances Lengel' who wrote *Helen and Desire*. (When the novel came under suspicion of being 'contre bonne moeurs', Girodias successfully disguised it in his list as *Desire and Helen* – he was nothing if not skittish.) Christopher Logue was another of the group. He wrote *Lust* for Girodias, who bestowed on him the majestic pseudonym 'Count Palmiro Vicarion'. As 'Marcus Van Heller', John Stevenson did such pornwork as *Roman Orgy*. Not mincing his words, Girodias proudly called these his 'Dirty Books', DBs for short.

In this way, Girodias's Olympia list had DBs and 'Literature' cheek by jowl. Samuel Beckett (another Girodias discovery) would find himself alongside *Whips Incorporated*. Olympia DBs carried outrageously provocative titles (*White Thighs*, *With Open Mouth*) and overpitched blurbs. 'It was great fun', Girodias recalls. 'The Anglo-Saxon world was being attacked, invaded, infiltrated, outflanked and conquered by this erotic armada.' Girodias was also making money. For his DBs, he paid a flat fee and did a standard 5,000 run. He usually cleared an edition very fast. Only occasionally did he miscalculate, as with Terry Southern's sly *Candy*, which was too clever for its own (pornographic) good: 'the book was much too hip to enjoy a normal sale as a DB and it took much more than the customary six to nine months to dispose of the 5,000 copies we had printed.'

Girodias displayed an odd mixture of the desire to scandalise and to evangelise. For him, 'eroticism is a constructive force' and offensiveness a useful weapon: 'Enough has been said about the influence of the printed word. But never enough about the liberating effect of the printed four-letter word . . . no reader was ever reported killed by a four-letter word.' But, he felt, their minds might thereby be purged; according to Girodias, his DBs were essentially hygienic: 'Those literary orgies, those torrents of systematic bad taste were quite certainly instrumental in clearing the air and cleaning out a few mental cobwebs.'

Girodias conceived of himself, his literary authors and his DBs making a 'common fight against the square world'. But the squares had history on their side. Always precarious, Girodias's fortunes turned decisively in May 1958 when the Fourth Republic fell and the puritanical De Gaulle took power. Girodias, in what he called a 'grandiose judicial farce' was haled up on charges of 'outrage aux bonnes moeurs par la voie du livre'. ('Dirty book' does not, apparently, translate into French.) He was penalised with ludicrous severity:

80-years ban on all publishing activities, four to six years unsuspended prison sentence, £29,000 fines. (All later reduced or commuted – but they remain an indication of extreme bourgeois indignation.)

Suffering persecution in France, Girodias was induced to move his flamboyant publishing activities to newly liberated Britain and America. But his attempts to transplant himself were not fortunate. He could no longer recruit exciting new authors. In America Grove were adapting literary pornography to the new 'industrial' style of American publishing. Girodias was an older-fashioned kind of publisher and set in his Parisian ways. Britain, for its part, was culturally uncongenial. Girodias made some attempt to launch an 'Olympia Magazine' and some of his Travellers' Library via the paperback firms Four Square and New English Library. But, despite the fact that (as Kenneth Allsop put it) 'Miss Keeler has replaced Mrs Grundy as our Britannia figurehead', the juicier DBs could not safely be published in the UK. And Girodias's gay, anti-bourgeois style was unacceptable. The British do not want dirty books to be innocent 'DBs' – they must be either ponderously 'literary' or 'criminal'. By 1965, Girodias claimed to be virtually inactive. (This account of Girodias is taken from a number of sources, but particularly his self-portrait in *Censorship*, summer 1965.)

John Calder

Girodias's 'I am a pornographer' was one approach to the new literary publishing freedom. Another approach was that of Barney Rosset's Grove Press in the US. He would probably have said, 'I am a tycoon'. Grove made the new 'liberated' material big business: their style was bestsellers, diversification into film, going always for the mass market and the big, fast buck. A third approach was John Calder's. 'Canny' is the best word to describe his practice as a publisher; 'intellectual' the best word to describe the preferences by which he (with Marion Boyars from the mid 1960s) put his list together.

Calder is a Scot and in the 1960s would have been described as 'anti-establishment'. He was also a gifted organiser. He was a prime mover behind the Defence of Literature and the Arts Society in 1968 (after *Last Exit*). And in the early 1960s it was his aim, no less, to promote a 'new British school of writing'. He had little time for the old school.

As he put it, in one of his polemic advertisements of 1964:

> British writing during the last thirty years has consisted
> principally of social chronicles that stylistically have taken
> little note of the revolutions of Proust, Joyce and Kafka.
> Now the younger writers are moving to a new kind of
> novel, rivalling the achievements that have already been
> made by younger writers in the theatre.

The 'New British School' (Ann Quin, R.C. Kennedy,
Aidan Higgins, Alan Burns) was one component of Calder's
list. Others were 'The American Scene' (Henry Miller, William
Burroughs, Robert Creeley – the 'Beats' generally); 'The
Nouveau Roman' (Robbe-Grillet, Sarraute, Pinget, Duras:
'What these writers have in common is a total rejection of the
old concept of the novel. What they have put in its place is
still undervalued in England'); 'The Avant-Garde Theatre'
(Ionesco, Weiss, Arrabal, Mercer); and one overwhelming
single figure, Samuel Beckett:

> Beckett is the father of both the modern theatre and the
> modern novel. All his six novels are published by us and
> together they undoubtedly constitute the most important
> literary achievement since Joyce.

Calder's colours were: modernist, anti-censorship, international. With historical hindsight, we can see that his hopes for
the 'New British School' (which he must have patronised at
considerable publishing cost) were over-pitched. But as an
invigorator of 1960s consciousness, and as a non-profiteering
exploiter of the 1959 Act, his record is unparalleled. In the
late 1960s, he involved himself rather more with the 'underground' scene. In the middle and late 1970s (after he separated
from Marion Boyars) his style became less avant-garde and
(his own term) more 'solid'.

Calder contrived more successfully than Rosset or Girodias
to escape prosecution. This was not because his choice of
books was tame, nor because the British climate was more
favourable to 'obscenity'. His immunity was the result of
strategy and what in court would be called 'excellent charac-
ter'. Strategically, he priced his books high: 25s. for the
Tropics, and *Cain's Book*, more for *The Naked Lunch* and
Last Exit when they first came out. In every case, the price
was notably higher than the standard for hardback fiction.
Nor did Calder put his books quickly into paperback. Most

importantly, Calder had nothing to do with Girodias-type DBs or the filth-blockbusters with which Rosset was making a killing in the US. Calder would never have admitted *White Thighs* (Olympia) or *Juliette* (Grove) on to his list. He was not offensively anti-bourgeois, nor commercially vulgar. Just right, in fact, for the British market.

December 1965:

Poetmeat/Golden Convulvulus

Blackburn was a long way from the literary hub of things (unless one took seriously Allen Ginsberg's claim that Liverpool was the centre of the universe) and the *Poetmeat/Golden Convulvulus* trial centred on an entirely ephemeral publication. But it may be taken as a significant straw in the 1960s wind. It was the first of the 'political' obscenity trials; that is to say, where a magazine and its editor (and by implication its readers and especially those who used classified ads) were at risk primarily because of the lifestyle they avowed, rather than for any actual offensiveness to the general public of what was printed. From this obscure prosecution in Lancashire runs a trail which climaxes in the Old Bailey and the *IT*, *LRSB*, *OZ* and *Nasty Tales* trials of 1970-73, and which peters out with the *Libertine* acquittal in 1977.

Selling at 3s. (with an optimistic '75c' added), *Poetmeat* described itself as a 'bimonthly platform for the local avant garde'. Local was Blackburn, Lancs. The magazine was founded in 1963. A home-made product, it had the appearance of an office memorandum; it was mistyped, cyclostyled and stapled. But it did carry good reviews of books, and evidently served as an outpost of the 'scene' that was developing so excitingly in London. In keeping with the time, *Poetmeat* was radical and anti-authoritarian, whether in the politics, aesthetics or the lifestyle it represented. (Issue 11, for instance, carries a long gardening feature on how to cultivate hemp.) Its editorial statements and manifestoes were uttered with fashionably bellicose (but 'loving') anarchist rhetoric. The editor was Dave Cunliffe, a 'guerrilla poet', the author of such works as 'Thunderbolts of Peace and Liberation'. Cunliffe declared his hand with engaging frankness: 'I advocate complete sexual freedom for everyone and the constructive use of mind illuminating chemicals.'

The trouble with the police ('the State Authority Machine', as Cunliffe called it) centred on an anthology, reproduced in *Poetmeat* house-style (i.e., very amateurishly) entitled *The Golden Convulvulus*. Unlike the contents (a typical poem runs: 'Flesh! Thighs! Breast! Crotch! Sky!'), the title has some subtlety. It is a Kama Sutraish reference to the 'yoni', and also alludes to Morning Glory, a vine discovered at the period to have interesting psychotropic qualities. The anthology's editor was Arthur Moyse, who favoured (like *OZ* after him) the collage method. The contents juxtapose graffiti, street songs, newspaper items, erotic poems. The whole was designed to be, as Moyse put it, 'a literary and sociological therapy insight into sexual attitudes'.

Cunliffe, the director of the press (Screeches Publications) which put out *The Golden Convulvulus*, described it as 'a limited edition of literary erotica'. Limited was an understatement. It would seem that some 30 copies were sent out 'worldwide'. There were 130 copies in stock for the police to 'seize'. In bulk, this would have gone into a briefcase and still left room for the Inspector's sandwiches.

The anthology's brush with the law began in the Blackburn sorting office. According to the GPO, packets containing *The Golden Convulvulus* had been 'routinely' opened on 13 July 1965 to make sure that they were conforming with printed paper rate regulations. Since by the 1953 Act the Post Office may not carry materials which are indecent, the horror-struck officials felt obliged to pass Moyse's publication on to the police. It was very implausible, and Cunliffe naturally assumed it was a case of police interception. However they came by the magazine, the Authority Machine wanted more. Cunliffe was asked for a list of *Poetmeat* subscribers and mailees. He refused. On 10 August he made a voluntary statement, explaining what *The Golden Convulvulus* was, and what was his connection with it. On 19 August there was a police 'bust'. The 'fuzz' seized, according to Cunliffe, all office material and most of his stock. They also took original manuscripts, an address book and items from the editor's personal library.

On 1 December, Cunliffe (not the anthologist Moyse) was hauled up before the Blackburn Quarter Sessions on two counts: for offences against the 1953 Post Office Act and for publishing 'an obscene article for gain'. ('Gain' rings somewhat hollow; Cunliffe reckoned that every 2s. copy of *The Golden Convulvulus* cost him 2s.3d. to produce.) Under the Solicitor-General's 1964 'assurance', he could elect for trial by jury, and had done so at an earlier hearing.

The prosecution's case was that *The Golden Convulvulus* constituted a risk to 'unstable, unintelligent and inexperienced people' because of its advocacy of 'promiscuous, wholesale, sexual intercourse'. A psychiatrist was dug up to confirm that 'if read by children or young persons of either sex under the age of sixteen, it would tend to deprave or corrupt them'.

Cunliffe mounted an articulate defence on the obvious libertarian and democratic grounds. The graffiti which Moyse had collected were, he maintained, 'the poetry of the underprivileged'. His view was that 'no literature of any kind can do any considerable harm to any person.' But, damagingly, he was also induced to say that he considered buggery between man and woman, 'normal pre-sex play'. (Pre-sex?) He had considerable moral support, from a whole regiment of liberal heavyweights (John Arden, Michael Foot, etc.). All opposed the prosecution on principle – but none could bring themselves to say that *The Golden Convulvulus* had the slightest literary merit. Christopher Driver of the *Guardian* (then more strongly Manchester based than now) was willing to stand as a defence witness – but was firmly of the view that 'although excessively innocent, its literary value in my judgement is nil'. The National Council for Civil Liberty was 100 per cent behind Cunliffe, but could see 'no literary merit' in *The Golden Convulvulus*. John Calder managed a tepid compliment. He thought it 'somewhat undergraduatish in nature', but 'the book would, if published commercially, attract some favourable critical attention.' It was clear enough, however, that Calder was not the commercial publisher who would take it on. All in all, it was probably fortunate for Cunliffe that 'expert' defence witnesses were not admitted to the December trial by jury. None would have perjured themselves to say that *The Golden Convulvulus* might be obscene, but nevertheless had redeeming literary merit. The wretched thing's best chance was to be judged of no literary merit whatsoever but neither obscene: insignificant.

The jury took several hours to return a verdict, and eventually came up with a muddle. They found Cunliffe guilty of sending a postal packet containing indecent material, but not guilty of publishing an obscene article. The flea of indecency was thus discriminated from the louse of obscenity. Cunliffe was fined £50. Henceforward, as he said: 'I am allowed to sell *The Golden Convulvulus* to schoolchildren,

but I am not allowed to mail it to poets, writers and critics.'
It was a preposterous verdict. Immediately after the trial,
the British Museum wrote to say that they had not had their
free copy 'under copyright regulations'. If he wished to
escape another prosecution by them, Cunliffe would have to
take *The Golden Convulvulus* down by hand. But as far as
I can make out, the BM never got its copy. *Poetmeat* lasted
two more issues, before it subsided into a humble newssheet.

The trial raised questions disproportionate to the magazine. As Ray Gosling asked in *New Society*:

> In this case the DPP took charge and prosecuted. Why?
> Was he worried about the growth of little magazines? Did
> he think the case, miles from London, away from the
> literary limelight would give him a chance to prove a
> point? make a legal precedent?

Historically viewed, the answer would seem to be 'yes' to
everything. The *Poetmeat* trial starts a series of actions
against underground, subversive and radical magazines. It was
a platitude to observe that although the ensuing trials were
ostensibly on the counts of obscenity or conspiracy to
corrupt public morals, they were *really* political. But the
confusion started with the journals themselves. They too,
saturated everything with political tendency. Mrs Whitehouse
was, in the late 1960s, fond of quoting a Blakean dictum of
Richard Neville's: 'the weapons of revolution are obscenity,
blasphemy and drugs.' Holding revolutionary sentiments is
no crime in Britain; but possessing obscene articles for gain,
blaspheming and taking drugs are crimes. It was expecting
too much of an authority (especially one which saw itself
cast in the role of pigs and fascists) not to use the counter-
revolutionary weapons so conveniently put in their hand.
Obscenity busts and drug busts were the state's answer to
demonstrations and sit-ins.

January 1966–July 1968:
Last Exit to Brooklyn

Segments of Hubert Selby Jr's *Last Exit* had emerged in America as early as 1957. 'Tralala', subsequently the most objected-to of the book's six narratives, was prosecuted in New England around the time of the *Chatterley* trials. It tells the story of a mindless, amoral whore who lives a life of utter squalor and dies raped to death by a gang of bar-room scum. The final passage – probably the most horrific of Selby's many snapshots of his New York hell – was to be a main focus in subsequent proceedings:

> soon she passedout and they slapped her a few times and she mumbled and turned her head but they couldn't revive her so they continued to fuck her as she lay unconscious on the seat in the lot and soon they tired of the dead piece and the daisychain brokeup and they went back to Willies the Greeks and the base and the kids who were watching and waiting to take a turn took out their disappointment on Tralala and tore her clothes to small scraps put out a few cigarettes on her nipples pissed on her jerkedoff on her jammed a broomstick up her snatch then bored they left her lying amongst the broken bottles rusty cans and rubble of the lot and Jack and Fred and Ruthy and Annie stumbled into a cab still laughing and they leaned toward the window as they passed the lot and got a good look at Tralala lying naked covered with blood urine and semen and a small blot forming on the seat between her legs as blood seeped from her crotch and Ruth and Annie happy and completely relaxed now that they were on their way downtown and their deal wasnt loused up and they would have plenty of money and Fred looking through the rear window and Jack pounding his leg and roaring with laughter . . .

Last Exit was published as a book in America in 1964 by Grove Press, to generally good, if somewhat shocked, reviews. (There was a violently hostile notice in *Time*, however, which was to be much quoted in the British trials.) Rights were acquired by Calder and Boyars and the work was published in the UK on 24 January 1966. It was the usual two-year lag between trail-blazing America and follow-my-leader Britain. By now, parts of the printed text were ten years old. Nevertheless, the British publishers took the precaution of getting the prior opinion of Professor Barbara Hardy (who advised for publication) and of the DPP. His reply was cloudy: 'I get no help from the acts' he confided, himself unhelpful.

Last Exit was received by British reviewers with a bruised respect. It was, thought Kenneth Allsop in the *Spectator*, a *ne plus ultra*: 'the end of the pitshaft. There is no lower level to be probed.' (Such pronouncements are foolhardy. When Selby's *The Room* appeared in 1972 the *TLS* observed that its central rape scene was 'so brutish as to make the gang banging in *Last Exit* look like U certificate material'.) Anthony Burgess headed off trouble in his *Listener* review with the paradoxical assertion that 'No book could well be less obscene.' (Burgess's Joycean view, which he has elaborated in a number of places, is that obscenity is 'kinetic' – it moves to lustful action; it can therefore never be 'literary', a quality of writing which produces stasis. *Last Exit*, Burgess maintains, does not excite one to lust; if anything it is emetic.) The *TLS*, the *Observer* and *The Sunday Times* did not notice Selby's book. Whether this was deliberate or merely oversight is not clear.

At 30*s*. the novel was an unusually expensive hardback, but did well. By September 1966 some 11,247 copies had been sold and had made £1,184 profit for the publishers. It had, however, sent out ripples in high places. One of the bookselling Blackwell family sent a copy to Sir Charles Taylor (Conservative, Eastbourne) who shared the concern. On 28 June he brought the Attorney-General's attention to a 'filthy and disgusting book' which he declined to publicise by naming. Sir Elwyn Jones apparently knew what was alluded to, and replied that Sir Charles's worries were late in the day: 'the book had now almost ceased to be sold. Literary Criticism was almost unanimous that it had literary merit. The DPP had concluded that it was far from sure a prosecution would succeed.' A couple of days later, Tom Driberg and some other Labour backbenchers tabled a motion congratulating

the DPP on not prosecuting *Last Exit*, which they provocatively named. Sir Charles Taylor was further taunted by an
advertisement placed a week later by Calder and Boyars in
The Sunday Times. It ran: 'Sir Charles Taylor, MP has
described *Last Exit* as filthy, disgusting, degrading. It is
one of the most important novels to come out of America
since . . .'

It was all very cheeky, and got the rag up of a group of
Tory backbenchers. One of their number, Sir Cyril Black
(Conservative, Wimbledon), 'a highly successful property
dealer, lay preacher and campaigner against liberal causes'
(Calder's prejudiced description) decided to counter-attack.
It was still possible to take out private prosecutions under
Section 3 of the 1959 Act, and Sir Cyril set this expensive
operation in process. On 28 July he moved at Bow Street
to have *Last Exit* banned. The magistrate who heard the
application was Sir Robert Blundell – he who had been so
hard on *Fanny Hill.* Sir Robert took the book away to read,
was duly shocked, and on 4 August issued a search warrant
for copies to be seized from any local bookshop. Calder, on
his part, declared pugnaciously that 'we do not intend to stop
publishing it under any circumstances'.

The case was heard at another Magistrates' Court, Marlborough Street, in mid November 1966. For once, there was
a powerful array of prosecution witnesses. They included H.
Montgomery Hyde (who had earlier appeared *for* the Mayflower *Fanny Hill*), Robert Maxwell, MP and publisher (he
declared *Last Exit* to be 'muck', and made a great stir by
suggesting that publishers should set up a body to censor
themselves, like the Press Council) and David Holloway,
Deputy Literary Editor of the *Telegraph.* Counsel for Black
was Michael Havers – later to be an Attorney-General himself.
Defence witnesses numbered eleven and starred Anthony
Burgess. The magistrate, Leo Gradwell, was, as Richard
Boston later described him in *New Society*: 'benign, genial,
tolerant and humane and repeatedly showed a wide knowledge and appreciation of literature and art and made some
genuinely funny remarks'.

But he found the book obscene, and passed sentence with
severe comments:

> I must tell you this book in its descriptions goes beyond
> any book of a merely pornographic kind that we have seen
> in this court. One passage I am thinking of is more likely to
> deprave and corrupt than any of those cyclostyled horrors.

(He was, apparently, comparing the death of Tralala with what are technically called 'Soho typescripts'.) The symbolic three copies which had been seized were ordered destroyed. In itself, this was a minimal loss; but it meant that no bookseller in the country could confidently stock the book, if it had been condemned by what was - normally - Britain's most liberal court. Nor was it just *Last Exit*'s publishers who were aggrieved. A joint letter from 18 publishers was sent to *The Times*, dissociating themselves from Maxwell's pious proposals and stating that as a profession they were happier with the decisions of juries than with those of magistrates. In the House, Driberg and his crew tabled a motion deploring the prosecution. In the press, it was widely held that, as Martin Seymour Smith put it, 'Britain had made herself the laughing stock of the civilised world.'

Calder and Boyars decided on a course of considerable hazard. They declined to appeal, on the grounds that it would place the matter *sub judice* and stifle comment. They indicated that they intended to continue publication, and in January enquired of the DPP what he in his turn intended to do about it. On 6 February, he served notice that he would prosecute. This was, in the legal nature of things, a more protracted business than summary proceedings before a magistrate. The case first came before the Marlborough Street Court (again) in April, when the defendant elected for trial by jury later in the year, at the Central Criminal Court.

Legal expenses for this kind of defence are necessarily high. There was also the chance that the publishers - who had acted aggressively (unlike Mayflower, who withdrew *Fanny Hill* at the first sign of trouble) might land themselves with a vindictive penalty. In the long interval before the trial the book was necessarily out of circulation and earning nothing. They had to take out an injunction to prevent unscrupulous dealers such as Arthur Dobson of Bradford (later to be nailed for *My Secret Life*) from circulating photographic copies of the American edition. All in all, Calder and Boyars must have needed steady nerves in summer 1967 and their vow to risk liquidation of the company to protect the book (which had yielded them a measly £1,000) was, in the circumstances, courageous.

The second trial began at the Old Bailey on 13 November 1967, and was to last nine days. The jury was, by Judge Graham Rogers's direction, all male. This was to spare ladies possible embarrassment (so much for Professor Hardy). It was an odd, if gallant decision and went down badly with

The Times who risked contempt with a critical leader on 14 November. The twelve men were sent off to read the book – an exercise over which there was to be some later bad feeling. A couple got through the 234 pages in an hour (as Calder protested – it took the likes of Professor Kermode and Al Alvarez fives times as long). Another told the judge, when asked if all was well, 'we would need an interpreter to understand some of the language.' These formalities over, the trial began. The prosecution panel of experts (who had the advantage of appearing after the defence was concluded) were further strengthened from the earlier trial. A good impression was apparently made by Professor George Catlin, of Canada (his subject was political science and philosophy) who infuriated defence counsel by dropping the fact that *Last Exit* had sold a quarter of a million copies in North America. (That Calder and Boyars were not in it primarily for the money was one of the defence's main planks.) David Sheppard, another prosecution witness, had everything going for him. He had given up a sporting career as opening batsman for England to take orders. He now worked as a social worker in the East End of London. He was not, he asserted, helped in his vocation by having read the low-life descriptions of *Last Exit*, though he could match them from personal acquaintance. Sheppard went on to make history by admitting that he had indeed been depraved and corrupted ('not unscathed', as he phrased it) by Selby's novel. Sheppard's confession was echoed by Sir Basil Blackwell, who felt the few years remaining to him (he was in his late 70s) had been defiled by having to read *Last Exit*.

For the defence, Calder and Boyars assembled what would have been a distinguished party list at their Brewer Street headquarters: Professor Frank Kermode (professor of English literature), Eric Mottram (lecturer in American literature), A. Alvarez (poet and critic), Professor Barbara Hardy (professor of English literature), John Calder, Professor Dan Miller (professor of sociology), Dr Michael Schofield (sociologist), Professor Ronald Atkinson (professor of philosophy), Quentin Crewe (journalist and critic), Marion Boyars, Jocelyn Baines, Jeffrey Simmonds (publishers), Kenneth Allsop (writer and television commentator), Anthony Storr (psychologist and writer), Martyn Goff (writer and bookseller), Edward Lucie-Smith (poet and critic), Eric Blau (writer), Philip French (critic), Lyman Andrews (lecturer in American literature and poet), Professor Bernard Williams (professor of philosophy), Olwen Wymark (playwright), Dr David

Downes (sociologist), Judith Piepe (social worker), Alan Burns (writer), John Arden (playwright), Dr David Galloway (lecturer in American literature), Professor Gorham Davis (professor of English literature), Stuart Hood (writer, TV producer, former comptroller of BBC TV), Robert Baldick (lecturer in French literature) and the Rev. Kenneth Leach (curate of St Anne's, Soho). There was much eloquence, and unstinted praise for Selby from this eminent band. Kermode alluded to Eliot, Dickens and Galsworthy in his evidence and declared that Selby 'has succeeded in his theme in biting terms'. Calder predicted that in 50 years, *Last Exit* would be studied in schools. For Alvarez, it was 'a masterpiece of quite outstanding merit'.

It would seem, however, that the jury did not welcome instruction, even from a company of the best literary critics in the world. After retiring for five and a half hours, they returned a verdict of guilty. Judge Rogers, who had seemed sympathetic to the defence, agreed that the book had been published in good faith by a highly respectable firm. But he nevertheless felt some (small) financial penalty was in order. The publishers were fined £100 and ordered to pay £500 costs. Calder and Boyars estimated themselves between £10,000 and £15,000 out of pocket – an immense liability for a house their size. As a direct result, the Defence of Literature and the Arts Society was formed, to look after funds raised from the sympathetic public and to keep up momentum generated by the trial. DLAS remained in existence for years after, organising defence in various liberal causes.

Calder and Boyars must have felt themselves frustrated. They could not complain at the conduct of the prosecution, which had been correct and unhysterical. The judge had been if anything leaning towards them. So they turned on the jury. On 2 December they sent to *The Times* what was certainly a misjudged letter of complaint, in which they accused the jury of not understanding 'demotic American', of skimping their reading of the novel and of being incompetent to deal with clever literary books. With supreme arrogance they argued that 'at least "A" levels' should be required as qualification for selection in obscenity cases. In an answering letter, Quintin Hogg poured rich scorn on this proposal: 'It seems they read too quickly, and, though intelligent enough to try the most complicated financial frauds, were not well educated enough to assess "the complex literary concepts" involved in books like *Last Exit*.'

More constructively, the defendants lodged an appeal. This was heard in July 1968 (the delay, of course, entailed even more expense for the publishers, with the volumes locked up in the warehouse, and their tenure of rights ticking away). John Mortimer appeared for Calder and Boyars. Following his submission, the appeal judges found that the judge at the trial had not sufficiently instructed the jury on the complexities of the 1959 Act. They also seemed to suggest that at its core, the act was anyway inexplicable: how could a work be obscene, deprave and corrupt *yet* be for the public good? Judge Rogers had left such things, as he said in his summing up, to the twelve mens' 'commonsense'. According to the Appeal Court this was to 'throw them in at the deep end and leave them to sink or swim in its dark waters'. On this technicality, the sentence was overturned.

It did not mean that the book was cleared, of course, but there was no likelihood of a re-trial, at least with this Attorney-General. So *Last Exit* could at last reappear in proud 1960s colours, a post-trial, complete and unexpurgated edition. The whole affair had been very touch and go. It was evident that the authorities had never in the first place wanted to prosecute *Last Exit*, or any other book with accredited literary pretensions. The current Government's instincts were distinctly liberal in censorship matters (this was the period in which the Theatre Act was passed). If this private prosecution, aided by a peculiarly wrong-headed jury, had succeeded, it would have encouraged the forces of reaction to an orgy of book burning.

As it was, the emergency was averted by the verdict of the Court of Appeal. The loophole by which the 1959 Act could be used to bring private actions was prudently closed. In a larger sense, the prosecution of 'literature' for obscene libel was closed as well. *Last Exit* stands as the last serious novel, poem or play to be prosecuted under Jenkins's Act. Sir Cyril Black had, however, a last laugh. In America Girodias issued a spiteful, obscene burlesque called *Sir Cyril Black*; it resulted in $100,000 damages for the aggrieved puritan MP, plus a public apology. (The account of the trial given here follows that by John Calder in the post-trial edition of *Last Exit*.)

April 1966:
Sadism/Bradyism

In the 1970s, the British reader was well served by a new full-length study of de Sade (Angela Carter, *The Sadeian Woman*, 1979) and a new biography (Ronald Hayman, *De Sade: A Critical Biography*, 1978). What was odd was that neither of these writers was able to refer to English (as opposed to American–English) texts of their subject's manifold works. Since 1966, no British publisher has been prepared to put his name to the Divine Marquis's more notorious books. We may not, in the words of Simone de Beauvoir, have burned de Sade – but we have effectively confined him to the Private Case. Meanwhile, in America, Grove Press have made available all the major texts (some illustrated) in modern translation. In France, de Sade's most scandalous works are openly available in their original form – if with the 30 per cent impost levied on avowed pornography. In 1973, the *Oeuvres complètes: edition définitive* (ed. Gilbert Lély) was brought out by Éditions Tête de Feuilles in 16 volumes.

In Britain, de Sade exists as a potent vacancy. Everyone knows about 'sadism' but few will have read *Juliette* or even the tamer *Justine*. (The Grove editions can be imported, but are rarely found, even in Soho.) To understand this curious British edginess about de Sade, one starts with the RSC *Marat/Sade* in 1964. Directed by Peter Brook, the production won seven theatrical awards in four years. The action of Peter Weiss's play is described in the full, sesquipedalian title: 'The Persecution and Assassination of Marat as Performed by the Inmates of Charenton under the Direction of the Marquis de Sade.' (At the end of his life, de Sade was dramatic director in the asylum where he was prisoner.) The original Berlin production was, by all accounts, a rather wordy affair. Brook drew on the current Artaud cult to stylise it as theatre of cruelty, with multiple 'happenings' on stage. The RSC *Marat/Sade* was a stunning experience. It was also close to

72

the impermissible (in 1964 the Lord Chamberlain was still active). At one point, de Sade is made to say: 'And what's the point of a revolution without general copulation?' Sexual anarchy, political protest, agitational theatre and cruelty were all fused. (Brook developed this last aspect daringly in his subsequent anti-Vietnam play *US* - a butterfly was nightly burned on stage.) *Marat/Sade* was a cocktail for the 1960s. There was some stuffiness and disquiet from those rooted in quieter, more orderly times; the *TLS*, for instance, asked Brook if he had not observed 'that books about concentration camps . . . turn up in shops dealing with near-pornography'. But on the whole, the *Marat/Sade* 'break-through' was approved and the British congratulated themselves on their new worldliness and unshockability.

De Sade for the first time was coming on to the market in cheap translation. By 1966, there was every expectation that like Genet (who was originally a difficult author for Anglo-Saxons) he would be gradually integrated into the new map of permissive Britain. However, 1966 was the year of the Moors murder trial, an event which thrilled and horrified the nation. Between December 1964 and October 1965, Myra Hindley and Ian Brady had murdered two little children and one young person, aged seven, twelve and seventeen. Their crimes were carried out with a truly Sadeian degree of cold cruelty. The couple took photographs and tape-recorded their torture of the screaming ten-year old girl 'fancifully concluding the performance with seasonal music - "Jolly Old Saint Nicholas" and "Little Drummer" '. The mutilated bodies were disposed of on the Lancashire moors.

The sixteen-minute tape was played in court. Also divulged were the contents of Brady's library. It included a Nazi Germany collection (*Mein Kampf* was not yet available in English but Brady, no scholar, had hopefully acquired a 'Teach Yourself German'); some bondage–fetish–flagellation porn (e.g., *Kiss of the Whip, High Heels and Stockings*); and, most significantly, there were books about de Sade. Brady, the court was told, had meditated deeply on the particular Sadeian instruction: 'Is murder a crime in the eyes of Nature? . . . Destruction is Nature's method of progress . . . Murder is often necessary, never criminal and essential to tolerate in a republic.'

The Moors trial was quite vile enough to contradict Orwell's nostalgic view that the English murder had declined; so horrible, indeed, that Ludovic Kennedy suggested - in all seriousness - that such proceedings should be given the equivalent of an X certificate, and reporting accordingly curtailed. Newspapers were, however, in no mood to restrain themselves. There was an orgy of press coverage in April 1966. In it, the name 'de Sade' occurred so frequently as to fix it indelibly in the minds of those unlikely otherwise to encounter the writing of a revolutionary French philosopher. And all this coincided with the arrival of de Sade as a best-selling author in English mass-market paperback. The 'complete and unexpurgated' *Justine*, translated and edited by Alan Hull Walton, had first appeared as a high-price hard-back in 1964. The Corgi paperback came out in 1965, and had gone through four editions by the end of 1966.

Walton's is an extraordinarily over-edited text. A passing comment by de Sade, for instance, to the effect that animals feel no affection is answered at the foot of the page with an indignant 'most untrue . . . I have known many dogs and cats who displayed amazing gratitude for the care given them.' The piffling objection is sustained over some 200 words with reference to Byron, Gide, Henry Miller and various church authorities. This *cordon sanitaire* of editorial stuffed-owlism can have obstructed Brady, and other voracious readers, not in the slightest. The following is one of the innumerable episodes of capture and ritual torture to which the 'unfortunate' heroine is subjected and which the prosecution alleged served as the murderers' blueprint:(An 'honest gentleman', Dalville, who has apparently saved Justine's virtue from assault by highway vagabonds, reveals himself to be a monster. Justine is thrown into a pit, to work at a wheel with other prisoners and to learn the lesson of 'the priority of the strong over the weak'):

Dalville then seized a horse-whip which was always kept near us, and with all the strength of his arm, gave me five or six lashes over every part of my body. 'This is how you will be treated here, you lazy slut,' he said . . . Each blow tore away strips of my skin; and, never having felt such infernal pain, either in the hands of Bressac, or in those of the barbarous monks, I screamed loudly and shrilly as I struggled in my chains. Such writhings and twistings, and such cries of agony, only aroused the mocking laughter of the monsters who were watching me; and I had the cruel satisfaction of learning that, if there are men who, ruled by vengeance or by a vile sense of the voluptuous, are able to enjoy the pain of another, there yet remain individuals so barbarously organised that they relish the same delights without any other motive than the gratification of pride or the most terrifying curiosity. It seems, therefore, that man is naturally wicked.

Justine was evidently a money-spinner for Corgi. Had the trial not intervened, it would have been followed up by the stronger *Juliette* and the ultimate *One Hundred and Twenty Days of Sodom* (compared to which, *Justine* is the proverbial vicar's tea-party). Ian Brady put a stop to that profitable series. In the recriminations after the trial, Maurice Temple Smith, a highly respectable publisher who had two scholarly works in his list dealing with de Sade, wrote to the *TLS* indicating his determination to keep the titles in print 'as important to the evolution of modern literature'. But he insisted some degree of censorship must be exercised, intimating that he would not publish de Sade's scandalous books himself. In the same paper, Girodias, who had the temerity to defend de Sade (his Obelisk Press had, after all, authorised the first English translation of *The Bedroom Philosophers* in the 1940s), was severely put down by George Steiner, the most formidably intellectual of anti-pornographers: 'Total freedom of publication includes Streicher on the need to castrate all Jews . . . If Mr Girodias is in favour of such publications, let him say so.' (*TLS* 26 May 1966.) Ludovic Kennedy, in the *Spectator* (29 April 1966) voiced the general view of the Moors trial and book-trade responsibility when he declared 'No respectable publisher would print a novel containing what is alleged.' De Sade's novels contained just such scenes as Hindley and Brady played out; ergo, no British publisher who valued his respectability should publish de Sade. Thereafter, none did.

The most impassioned discussion of the Moors trial was offered by Pamela Hansford Johnson in *On Iniquity*. As the uncompromising title indicates, for her Sadism was not to be tricked away with intellectuality or ingenious special pleading; it was simply evil. In the case to hand, Brady and Hindley were not sick but wicked, iniquitous. Hansford Johnson noted as highly significant that Brady had acquired his most inflammatory de Sade material in 'fairly recent paperback' form (she did not identify Corgi, perhaps for libel reasons). Publishers, she solemnly observed, 'have a very heavy responsibility towards the society in which they live'. Not that the society of 1966 deserved much respect; it was rotting with permissiveness and pornography. Brady and Hindley were the monstrous offspring of:

> the all permissive, the swinging society under its big top;
> the whole garish circus of the new freedom; freedom to
> revel, through all kinds of mass media, in violence, in
> pornography, in sado-masochism. The walls of the police
> store-room are almost bulging outwards with the pressure
> of tons upon tons of dirty books.

Without any evidence, Hansford Johnson assumed that the
main consumers of these dirty books were 'simple minded
. . . semi-illiterate . . . early school leavers' like the Moors
murderers. In fact, as American research conclusively
showed, the typical 1960s user of porn was 'dressed in a
business suit', middle aged, married and college educated;
exactly the kind of person who read Hansford Johnson and
her husband C.P. Snow's novels. History shows up other
naivety in *On Iniquity*. One chapter is indignantly entitled
'Seventy Five Tons'. This avoirdupois refers to the accumu-
lated confiscations of the London Obscene Publications
Squad. Their haul, in Hansford Johnson's fevered portrayal,
takes on the symbolic significance of a Dickensian dustheap,
and she paints a quite pathetic picture of the labours of these
tireless enforcers of morality:

> At Scotland Yard, the Obscene Publications Squad has
> fourteen men who devote almost all their time to the
> pursuit and seizure of filth. Working all round the clock,
> in twenty-four hours they often make seven or eight raids
> on shops in the Metropolitan area alone. They now have
> a stock of *seventy five tons* of obscene material: it has
> grown so much lately that they have been forced to take
> over more stores in which to accommodate it.

As emerged later, the OPS elegantly solved their storage
problems by recycling 'filth' back on to the market, and were
extorting up to £2,000 per copper per month from it. And
someone seems to have taken advantage of Hansford Johnson's mathematical gullibility. In a written answer of 17 May
1966 (prompted by the Moors trial furore) the Attorney-
General revealed that in 1975 some 35,377 articles were
subject to seizure and forfeiture. To make up the author's
warehouse-bulging seventy-five tons, every article (i.e.,
magazine, book, film) would have had to weigh five pounds.
On Iniquity is a compound of genuine shock and ingrained

pomposity. In *Encounter*, Kenneth Allsop put the tract down as 'hot flush' and 'untruth'. Had Miss Hansford Johnson not looked into the mass of Victorian pornography, he asked? Did she not know that the middle-class motor car slaughtered many more children than de Sade-inflamed proles? But Allsop's was a minority voice. Hansford Johnson articulated a rampant English hysteria, and she was not obliged to be precise about history or any other facts. Even society's drop-outs and rebels were inclined to agree that things might have got a little out of hand. Jeff Nuttall, the underground ideo-logue, made a 'there but for the grace of God' recantation in *Bomb Culture* (1968):

There was the widespread vogue of sado-masochism in the arts [in the mid 1960s]. When Brady and Hindley were carrying out their first murder plans, Otto Muhl and Herman Nitsch had already carried out their first cere-monials with entrails, flesh and smeared food . . . I with other members of the sTigma team did a fake disembowel-ling in Better Books basement. 'I thought you'd murdered her' said Tony Godwin. 'It'll come to that' said John Calder.

There were a number of after-effects of the Moors trial and the panic it provoked. One was that the authorities became acutely nervous about obscenity. On occasion this manifested itself as excessive prudence. There was, for instance, a major Beardsley exhibition at the Victoria and Albert Museum in May 1966. Five of the eight illustrations from *Lysistrata* were, however, only viewable by special application (anyone desperate to see them could more easily find them in various books on Beardsley). The Museum authorities took this absurd decision after consulting Scotland Yard and the Home Office. In other areas, nervousness made the authorities trigger-happy. In the kind of swoop which was eventually to make Scotland Yard worry about its 'Knacker' image, Metro-politan police swooped in September 1966 to seize twenty-one pictures by Jim Dine from the Robert Fraser Gallery, Duke Street Mayfair. Admittedly the pictures were of genitalia, but the artist was world famous, and the gallery eminently respectable, and four of the pictures had already been sold for up to 250 guineas each – rather high for the porn market. Nonetheless, the owner was charged under the 1838 Vagrancy Act and fined £20.

There was at least one constructive outcome of the Moors

murder/pornography debate. Following Hansford Johnson's initiative, a high-brow anti-pornography lobby was mobilised. Previous pressure groups – the Viewers and Listeners Association for instance – tended to be low-brow, Moral Rearmament tinged and crassly populist. After 1966, intellectuals (notably the erudite David Holbrook) had a more effective intervention on the obscenity question. As for the trial itself, it has never been forgotten and probably still resonates, mentioned or unmentioned, in most discussions of censorship in Britain. Lord Longford's tentative advocacy of parole for Myra Hindley in 1977 provoked an extraordinary fury and some quite convincing death threats. As with the Marquis de Sade, society could not trust itself to have her out of prison.

Postscript: Hitler's Mein Kampf

Brady had a copy of *Mein Kampf*, but frustratingly for him it was in German. In the 1960s, the copyright-holder of Hitler's book was Hutchinson, and they judged the work still too offensive to bring out in English. The firm ran into stiff opposition with a translation intended to have been brought out in autumn 1965. Principally outraged were the West German government and British Jewish groups. Publication was postponed. (Had it not been, Brady could have had his copy in a language he understood.) In 1969 an expensive hardcover edition was brought out and, as the publishers claim: 'the selling price was set intentionally high so as to avoid any imputation of catering to a mass audience.' In 1972, a paperback version was at last issued, to great indignation. The publishers claimed that at £1.95 it could not be termed a 'mass market' commodity.

September 1968:
The End of the Lord Chamberlain

Performance arts raise trickier aesthetico-legal problems than obscene libel (i.e., written obscenity). Is a cockfight, a strip-tease show or an audience-participation sex event 'censored' by being ruled illegal? Or is suppression of such things merely a branch of the public order laws controlling prostitution and indecent display? How distinguish 'mimesis' and the 'real thing'? (The 'real thing' blue film achieved an apotheosis with the so-called 'snuff movies' in the 1970s, in which victims were sexually abused and actually killed; but the existence of commercially exhibited snuff movies has not, I think, been conclusively proved.) What if a bona fide play contained within its action what amounted to a striptease? Problems of this kind reached a grotesque pitch of complexity in the *Romans in Britain* trials (1980-82), where the ostensible point at issue was whether a National Theatre director was guilty of inciting two men (nightly during the run) to a 'grossly indecent' act – even though this act of buggery was, all parties agreed, 'simulated' for dramatic purposes.

Perhaps because of the vexatious status of drama, it remained for longer than any other literary form in the grip of simple, authoritarian, one-man censorship. The Lord Chamberlain, whose office was responsible for examining plays before their public performance, was not discharged until 1968 (eventful year). He represents the last vestige of direct, state control over artistic expression in Britain. Primarily a member of the Royal Household, the Lord Chamberlain was first appointed to censor drama with the passing of the theatre-licensing laws in 1737; and his authority was confirmed and clarified by the subsequent Theatres Act a hundred years later. It empowered him to forbid the performance of any play as he felt necessary 'for the preservation of good manners, decorum or of the public peace'. Since he was, aboriginally, a Court lackey, the Lord Chamberlain was also

79

hypersensitive to anything touching the Crown, or the Established Church of whose faith the British monarch is the defender. His power was arbitrary, binding and final: there was no appeal, and once passed by him a play could not thereafter be prosecuted.

After the great liberation for printed literature in 1959 (which, of course, also covered drama in print), the Lord Chamberlain's censorship was the target of growing protest, from playwrights, managers and parliamentarians. In December 1962, Dingle Foot introduced a Bill to phase him out: it was defeated by 134 votes to 77. At this period, Baron Cobbold inherited the post; his qualifications were those of a lifelong banker, City man and top person. The appointment did not, understandably, soothe his critics. It is possible that an enlightened government might have compromised with the libertarians by modifying the Chamberlain's office into the equivalent of the Press Council – in which case he might well have survived to the present day. As it was, the League of Dramatists returned to the attack in 1964, pointing out how absurd, inequitable and anomalous it was that the dramatist should be thus interfered with and not his brother novelist or poet.

Typical of the Lord Chamberlain's interventions in the last ten years of his rule was the disciplining of *Fings aint what they used to be* in February 1961. Two of his agents visited the Garrick, where the play was put on. There followed a high-handed letter, banning in future such ad libs as: 'Don't drink that stuff, it will rot your drawers.' The Lord Chamberlain also ordained that 'the builder's labourer is not to carry the plank of wood in the erotic place.' Technically, any improvisation or departure from the script submitted originally was illegal – an intolerable imposition on a production which wished to keep its night-to-night performance fresh and responsive to audience reaction.

Naturally the Lord Chamberlain was very hot on any lese-majesty or sanscullotism. It was suggested that the punitive raid on *Fings* was motivated primarily by some salty jests about the Duchess of Argyle. No representation of the living Royal Family was allowed, nor of other heads of state, except those of Communist bloc countries. (The Lord Chamberlain was not averse to a little black propaganda.) When Rolf Hochuth's *The Representative* was performed in 1966 (the play deals with the papacy and Jewry in the Second World War), it was licensed only with certain back projected scenes of concentration camps removed and with a view favourable to the Pope's wartime record inserted in the programme. The prejudice of the Lord Chamberlain's office was almost certainly responsible for the inhibition in 1960s Britain of 'docudrama' (e.g., Weiss's *The Examination*) or sharp political burlesque (e.g., the irreverent American *Macbird*). And to this day, representations of British premiers on stage tend to be 'cosy' and blunt edged (e.g., *Mrs Wilson's Diary*, *Anyone for Dennis*). The Lord Chamberlain's iron hand survives as what Orwell would have called the 'gutlessness' of 'good taste'. And where the Royal Family is concerned, his dead body would still seem to have a twitch or two left in it. In 1981, a goodish television thriller series, *Blood Money*, was originally intended to revolve around the kidnapping of Prince Edward. This was changed, mid production, and the son of a fictional 'diplomat' substituted.

Saved, by Edward Bond, was instrumental in finishing off the Lord Chamberlain. The play was commissioned in 1964 for the Royal Court - then the powerhouse of the British dramatic renaissance. When they accepted it, the management were under no illusion about the problems with the central scene, in which a gang of London youths torment a baby in its pram, roll it in its excrement and finally stone it to death. George Devine sent a memo to the play's director: 'As for the baby, I don't think the scatalogical bits will get through under any circumstances. Worse kinds of violence may well be passed, but reference to shit and piss will never pass in my opinion.'

The following is the scene, as it was later published:

FRED *looks for a stone.*

PETE. Get its 'ooter.
BARRY. An' its slasher!
FRED (*picks up a stone, spits on it*). For luck, the sod.

He throws.

BARRY. Yyooowwwww!
MIKE. 'Ear it plonk!

A bell rings.

MIKE. 'Oo's got the matches?

He finds some in his pocket.

BARRY. What yer doin'?
COLIN. Wan'a buck up!
MIKE. Keep a look out.

He starts to throw burning matches in the pram. BARRY
throws a stone. It just misses MIKE.

Look out, yer bleedin' git!
COLIN. Guy Fawkes!
PETE. Bloody nutter! Put that out!
MIKE. No! You 'ad what you want!
PETE. Yer'll 'ave the ol' bloody park 'ere!

A bell rings.

BARRY. Piss on it! Piss on it!
COLIN. Gungy slasher.
MIKE. Call the R.S.P.C.A.

A bell rings.

FRED. They'll shut the gates.
PETE (*going*). There's an 'ole in the railin's.
BARRY. 'Old on.

He looks for a stone.

PETE. Leave it!
BARRY. Juss this one!

He throws a stone as PETE *pushes him over. It goes wide.*

Bastard!
To PETE. Yer put me off!
PETE. I'll throttle yer!
BARRY. I got a get it once more!

*The others have gone up left. He takes a stone from the
pram and throws it at point blank range. Hits.*

Yar!

Even with sensibilities hard-boiled by the last fifteen years
of decensored drama, it is a horrible scene. At the time, it
was sensationally so. In *On Iniquity*, Pamela Hansford Johnson went so far as to link it causally (via the climate of
'anything goes') to the Moors murders. But the brutality is
not gratuitous, and Bond has gone to some pains to justify it.
In 1966, for instance, he took a rather scornful line with
the shock it engendered, implying that those who naively
made a fuss about this stage horror had not taken account of

the historical events of their own lifetimes:

> clearly the stoning to death of a baby in a London park is typical English understatement. Compared to the 'strategic' bombing of German towns it is a negligible atrocity, compared to the cultural and emotional deprivation of most of our children, its consequences are insignificant.

Another, less pungent defence was given eleven years later in an 'Author's Note on Violence', printed in the *Collected Plays*. Bond argues that capitalist Britain tolerates a high degree of general violence in order to protect its privileged elite. Encouragement of aggression is a definite strategy on the part of the ruling class, which thereby contrives to deflect proletarian fury against decoy targets:

> such victims may be innocent, indeed they may be chosen for them by the ruling class, as sometimes happens in racialism. In some respects, the young murderers in *Saved* belong to this group. Some of their cries while they murder the baby are ruling-class slogans. This is the way in which working-class anger and aggression can be used to strengthen the unjust social relations that cause its anger and aggression.

This subtle argument is unlikely to have cut much ice with Baron Cobbold.

The text of *Saved* was submitted to the Lord Chamberlain on 24 June 1965 and kept by him for five weeks. It came back with the instruction that two whole scenes would have to be removed: (1) the murder in the park; (2) the seduction scene between the 24-year-old man and the 53-year-old mother of his girl friend. Certain objectionable words and phrases would also have to go (e.g., 12 'Christs', 3 'sods', 2 'Get stuffed!' etc.).

In an article in *Censorship* (autumn 1966) Bond expressed irritation that novels should be free of this interference and not drama. But, apparently, his first inclination was to kiss the Chamberlain's rod and make changes. William Gaskill reportedly dissuaded him and suggested a remedy. Although it was not specifically laid down as a freedom by the Theatres Act, the Lord Chamberlain's office had traditionally winked at performances by theatre clubs, attended by members only. Thus, when five whole scenes of John Osborne's *A Patriot for Me* were removed in 1965, it was put on for an eight-week run in the Royal Court's 'English Stage Society' (which promptly acquired 3,000 new members). It was proposed that *Saved* should take the same bolt hole from censorship.

The first club performance duly went on in November 1965. But the Lord Chamberlain was no longer inclined to be indulgent. Police officers infiltrated the audience, and on 1 January 1966, various directors of the Royal Court were prosecuted under the 1843 Act for publicly presenting an unlicensed play. There was no status in law for 'club performance'. Despite a court appearance by Laurence Olivier (on 2 March, at the second hearing) the defendants were found guilty on 1 April, and given conditional discharges by a sympathetic magistrate who ordered them to pay 50 guineas costs. The punishment was derisory (compared, say, to the box-office takings on any one night). But the real consequence was that the club-performance loophole was now closed. To persist in it would be to invite genuinely punitive sentences.

The plight of the Royal Court was taken up by the country's legislators. In the Lords, in February, Lord Annan spoke eloquently against the standards of 'Aunt Edna' (he presumably meant his noble friend) being imposed on British theatre. In April, in the Commons, Roy Jenkins as eloquently poured scorn on the historical anachronism of the Lord Chamberlain's censorship. A Private Members' Bill for his abolition, with all-party support, was sponsored by George Strauss. Meanwhile, the Lord Chamberlain seemed determined to supply the nails for his own coffin. In summer 1966, he found 'unsuitable' parts of a modern version of Chaucer's *Miller's Tale*, as performed by a troupe of Keele University students at the Edinburgh Festival fringe.

Gaskill, the Royal Court and Bond continued to goad 'the Queen's Housekeeper' (as the playwright called him). A new play, *Early Morning*, was submitted and returned by the Lord Chamberlain in November 1967, banned in its entirety. The obnoxious text is neatly described by Charles Marowitz:

> a fantasy based on the premise that Queen Victoria was a dyke and had a lesbian affair with Florence Nightingale while the British government, led by a sadistic Gladstone and a Macchiavellian Disraeli, ran the country like a branch of Murder Incorporated.

The official reaction cannot have been sweetened by the fact that a fanciful Lord Chamberlain is also included in the dramatis personae.

Defiantly, club performances of *Early Morning* were scheduled. The Arts Council threatened to withdraw its support from the Royal Court. Methuen, Bond's publishers, were also nervous; as a result the playscript was brought out by John Calder. The performances in April attracted the inevitable police visits, and the expectation of what would have been a very entertaining court case. But, in a neck-and-neck race, the Theatres Bill was pushed through to become law in September 1968. *Saved* and *Early Morning* went into the theatre's public repertory in early 1969 – demonstrating to all that the British drama was at last unfettered; the last link of direct state censorship, beginning with the Star Chamber five hundred years earlier, had been broken. The theatre from 1968, until 1980 (and *The Romans in Britain*), enjoyed an unparalleled period of freedom. Not a single case of any note has been brought (or allowed) by the DPP under the Theatres Act.

Looking back at the English drama 1957–68, firmly under the tyrannic thumb of the Lord Chamberlain, one is struck by a curious paradox. This was, by general agreement, a golden age. It saw the emergence of Osborne, Wesker, Pinter, Whiting, Arden, Bond himself. From the extraordinary vitality of the dramatic form, it would seem logical that censorship – even knuckleheaded censorship of the Lord Chamberlain's kind – might be construed as beneficial for the dramatist. This somewhat perverse line of argument typically bolsters its case by appeal to prestigious writers like Jane Austen or Shakespeare. She (as Harold Hobson argued in 1981, calling for the return of the Chamberlain) could not have had Elizabeth Bennet tell Darcy to 'f—— off'; hence, she devised elegant dialogue. Shakespeare and his contemporaries worked under close supervision by the authorities, and were therefore driven to expedients of highest artistic subtlety when dealing with such touchy questions as, for example, how to get rid of a rotten king.

The alleged benefits of censorship furnish the occasion for Shavian wit, but it is very hard to prove the case either way. It is doubtful, for instance, that Czech playwrights or Polish film-makers would go along with the pro-censors. But in one respect, it is extremely plausible that the Lord Chamberlain had a constructive effect during a critical period. His rule over the 'public' stage in the 1960s drove main streams of creative energy into immune club and fringe activity (also into television which, for a year or two before the abolition, was less restricted than London's West End). This built up an infrastructure of 'alternative' theatre. By 1968, the year in which the Lord Chamberlain was ousted, a valuable and synergistic dualism was firmly established. In the same year, 1968, *Time Out* was set up. A main function of this news-sheet-cum-magazine was to keep open and active the channels of communication, agitation and advertisement by which the fringe theatre lives.

Postscript: Film

Print was liberated in 1959; theatre in 1968. Film, however, remained a few more years outside the terms of 'obscenity law'. As with drama, 'anomaly' was the incentive for a harmonising in reform. In November 1974 a 69-year-old Festival of Light campaigner was given leave to bring a private prosecution against United Artists for displaying (to well over a million Britons, by then) the film *Last Tango in Paris*, in which Marlon Brando is shown, fairly explicitly (less ten seconds cut by the BBFC), sodomising Maria Schneider with the lubricant assistance of some butter. The trial was built up as 'the most important since *Lady Chatterley*'. But it collapsed on a point of law: the exhibition of a film could not be construed as 'publication' under the 1959 Act, nor was the film properly an 'obscene article'.

It is evident that the Attorney-General sanctioned the private prosecution in order to set the ground for a new Cinematographic and Indecent Display Bill. But these were stirring days, politically. There was the miners' strike, the three-day week, the fall and change of government. As regards film, the law remained in a state of anomalous chaos, until mid 1977.

As with the Theatre Act, in 1968, the authorities were clearly reluctant to baptise the 1977 innovation with a *Chatterley*-type trial. There was an opportunity. Pasolini's up-dating of de Sade's *One Hundred and Twenty Days of Sodom, Salo*, was seized just before the amendment which brought films into line was passed in July 1977. When the proprietors of the offending Cinecenta eventually came to trial it was well after the amendment had passed into law. It would have been quite possible to try the film as an 'obscene article', like a book or a play. But the challenge was declined, and the cinema proprietors were charged instead with the obsolete, common-law offence of running a 'disorderly house'. (They were not unhappy – in the circumstances the magistrate felt he could do no more than administer a warning.)

After July 1977, private prosecutions were no longer possible without the consent of the Attorney-General. Effectively, legal action by aggrieved individuals ('one-man DPPs' – as Jeremy Hutchinson called the indefatigable Raymond Blackburn) or by pressure group were now a thing of the past. The Festival of Light took the film reform very badly: 'If the Attorney-General is given the final say . . . things will slide as they have in the London theatre over the last ten years.' In fact, they need not have worried. The policy of the BBFC – especially after the passing of John Trevelyan – has always kept public exhibition in British cinemas at a near-Irish level of decency.

PPS   In September 1980, video cassettes were ruled to be 'articles' under the definition of the 1959 Act.

February 1969:
My Secret Life

'Literary experts' had been pontificating in British and American courts for almost ten years; but Steven Marcus was the first methodically to apply the techniques of literary-critical analysis to pornography. *The Other Victorians* (1966) was a book which brought a cool, scholarly gaze to bear on traditional items of 'erotica': not as they were secreted in the private case (or, perish the thought, pored over in back rooms), but as they had been gathered for just such inspection at the Kinsey Institute. Steven Marcus was, and is, a distinguished academic (Cambridge and Columbia). In 1966 he had made his professional mark with a monograph on Dickens and a collaboration, with Lionel Trilling, on a shortened life of Freud. These qualifications made him particularly fitted to undertake a psycho-historical investigation of the Victorian literary underworld – or as he would have it – otherworld.

The Other Victorians was more successful than most works of literary criticism. (Perhaps for the wrong reasons; it is still to be found in Soho sex shops.) And it had the knock-on effect of a book of an earlier generation which in some ways it resembles: *Eminent Victorians*. The Victorians were, once again, exploded; their dirty little secrets exposed to the surprised, yet insatiably curious, eyes of their descendants. A spectacular follow-up to *The Other Victorians* was John Fowles's *The French Lieutenant's Woman* (1969) – 'A Victorian novel no Victorian would have written', as the blurb puts it. Fowles's portentous sexual-historical bomb-shells (that every sixth London Victorian house was a brothel, for instance) have achieved popularly what Marcus achieved in literary–historical scholarship; the Victorians are no longer regarded as 'Victorian'.

Marcus's study fixes on key figures (e.g., the prurient bibliographer Ashbee, William Acton the sex researcher) and on key texts (e.g., *My Secret Life, The Lustful Turk*). His last chapter on the elusive 'pornotopia' yearned for by every addict, elaborates his general theory of how pornography works. Pornography, Marcus argues, is a transhistorical, transcultural phenomenon, corresponding to certain sexual-biological universals. (Marcus's Freudian pedigree is detectable here.) Hence, the observable fact that *Fanny Hill, The Lustful Turk, The Pearl, The Kama Sutra* are as sought after and aphrodisiac in advanced Western societies of the 1960s as originally in their own times and places: in pornographic matters, all men are brothers.

Most importantly for Marcus, pornography is a historically transient phenomenon. Like others in the 1960s, he firmly believes that 'exposure' will wither pornographic growth. Like dry rot, or Dracula, it cannot stand the light of day. In long retrospect, pornography will eventually come to be nothing more than a kind of adolescent phase in mankind's gradual ascent to sexual adulthood. 'We are coming to the end of an era' he writes:

> in which pornography had a historical meaning and even a historical function. The free publication of all the old pornographic chestnuts does not necessarily indicate to me moral laxness or fatigue, or deterioration on the part of society. It suggests rather that pornography has lost its old danger, its old power.

Marcus's stance is that of the mandarin-wise critic for whom 'literature' is an adult taste, pornography juvenile. (To adapt a current feminist slogan – pornography is to literature as masturbation is to sexual intercourse). Part of *The Other Victorians*'s thesis is a discrimination of literature from pornography – more exactly than it could ever be done in a court of law: 'Literature' he maintains, 'possesses a multitude of functions, but pornography possesses only one.' Pornography, unlike literature, has no shaping principle: 'the ideal pornographic novel . . . would go on forever; it would have no ending, just as in pornotopia there is ideally no such thing as time.' Unlike literature, pornography is 'kinetic', constantly trying to escape the webs of language, to get straight to the action:

> at best [for the pornographic writer] language is a bothersome necessity, for its function in pornography is to set going a set of non-verbal images . . . the prose of a typical

pornographic novel consists almost entirely of clichés, dead and dying phrases, and stereotypical formulas. It is also heavily adjectival.

(Marcus's Cambridge training is evident in this last observation.)

There is, for all its brilliance in analysis, a certain complacency in *The Other Victorians* – too much satisfaction with the competence of literary criticism to pronounce authoritatively on the subject. As Marcus admits in an afterword to the second edition of 1974, this earlier self does not entirely please him, given historical hindsight. For one thing, literary criticism – even under Marcus's own supervision – had changed. After 1968 it was more 'engaged', less contemplative and 'objective'. One of Marcus's former students was Kate Millett. Millett's book, *Sexual Politics*, came out (with an éclat even greater than that of *The Other Victorians*) in 1971. In it, she took head-on a group of 'pornographic' male, twentieth-century writers (Lawrence, Mailer, Miller, Genet). Her thesis is one which has been universally adopted and enlarged by her sisters-in-arms: pornography is *not* transitional (Western society's 'growing pains'); it is an essential and ever more brutal part of the apparatus of oppression by which men maintain their supremacy over women. The issue is not maturity or immaturity, but power. Pornography must not be analysed – it must be combated.

Other aspects of *The Other Victorians* come in for Marcus's self-criticism. Homosexual pornography does not fit his argument (when homosexuals 'outgrow' pornography, do they become heterosexual?). And the whole emphasis on 'books', prose narrative especially, was wrong-footed. As it has developed explosively since 1966, pornography has more and more become focused on pictorial commodities (film, magazine, video, photo-set). The logocentric pornographic 'novel' is as obsolete in 1982 as any McCluhanite could wish.

Marcus's exemplary text is *My Secret Life*, by the pseudonymous 'Walter'. This is a massively detailed (4,200 pages), apparently veracious autobiographical account of an unknown Victorian gentleman's prodigiously active (1,200 women) career in sex. Before the 1960s, copies of this work were so rare that its reputation was as the Kohinoor of English pornography. (The British Museum, for instance, only became possessed of a copy by bequest in 1964.)

Marcus's two chapters of discussion and generous quotation from his source-book were eagerly received by a large, and largely unacademic, public. (*The Other Victorians* quickly went into mass-market paperback, a rare distinction for books with the ·8 Dewey decimal classification.) For Marcus, *My Secret Life* is a text both historically authentic and sexually candid. He treats it as a Freudian analyst would his patient's couch confession. Walter emerges a Victorian everyman: obsessed with sex, but unable to handle it except by the regressive strategy of Don Juanism. Walter, for Marcus, is his age's psychopathology spelled out. And his inability to understand or sublimate his drives explains why his fellow Victorians had such a massive appetite for pornography, and why the industry should have so flourished in the nineteenth century. (Statistics are not to be come by; but it would seem that per-capita of the reading population, there was a higher consumption of porn in Victorian England than in contemporary Hamburg or Copenhagen.) For Marcus, pornography is historically a Victorian phenomenon, just as masturbation (the end to which pornography caters) is typically an adolescent practice. Put bluntly, compared to us the Victorians were only half grown up. And if we still need pornography, it is because we have not entirely outgrown our Victorian past.

Marcus did not have exclusive rights in Walter. At exactly the same period in the 1960s, the American sexologists and collectors (at one time they had a travelling museum of erotica) Drs Eberhard and Phyllis Kronhausen brought out *Walter: 'My Secret Life'*. This was a heavily edited selection, published in Britain as two shabby volumes, 9*s*.6*d*. each, by Polybooks. It was stickered as 'For Sale to Adults Only' and went through three editions in 1967, its first year. For the Kronhausens (disciples of Wilhelm Reich rather than Freud) Walter was not a Victorian everyman; he was unique – an English Casanova. Marcus's Walter they found 'bourgeois', and his analysis imbued with Freud's joyless puritanism on the subject of sex. For the Kronhausens, Walter is a truly liberated man, a 'swinger'. Suspiciously, he is also identified as the first of the 'sexologists'.

The difference in interpretation can be shown by an episode which both commentators address themselves to. At one point Walter becomes obsessed with finding out how much coinage a prostitute's 'quim' can hold. So he gets a bag of silver and tells 'Nellie' that all which goes in shall be hers. Her capacity turns out to be quite remarkable:

Putting the silver into a basin, she washed and dried it,
then washed her vagina, dried it well, and the insertion
began. Shilling after shilling I put up her, until forty were
embedded in the elastic gully. Then she walked up and
down. 'I am quite sure I can hold twenty more', said she,
and I put them up by fives. The last five she squeezed up
herself in some fashion.

'You've put those up your backside', I quoth jokingly.

'Don't make me laugh, that would be unfair', said she,
and, in a business-like way, she now put up shilling after
shilling as I handed them to her, till seventy were in her.
Triumphantly she walked up and down the room, none
falling out of her vagina.

Then I went on slowly, not believing she could hold any
more, adding shilling after shilling, and making her walk
after each addition to the load. At the eightieth, I made
her stand at the bedside and pushed my finger up a little
distance only, until I felt the mass of coin about an inch
up from the entrance. I now laid her on the bed for inside
inspection of the vaginal cavity, pulling open the lips, and
could see the silver. Then, triumphantly, she promenaded
the allotted distance, saying, 'The money's mine!'

After that, shilling by shilling, others were engulfed in
her capacious receptacle, which held them firmly, till the
eighty-fifth tumbled out, and the game was over. She
started to laugh, and more fell on the floor, as her vagina
relaxed its grip. I threw her on the bedside, pulled rudely
open her vagina, and a whole dozen rolled out. She was in
convulsions with laughter now, and with each jerk of her
belly, more silver was being ejected.

Then, squatting over a basin, she relieved her vagina of
the rest of the coins, the last one being got out with the
aid of her fingers. The money was then washed and dried,
and she washed out her vagina with a syringe. We counted
the silver – there they were, all eighty-four shillings, as had
been put up. 'I wish someone would do this every day',
said Nellie, elated.

For Marcus, the episode is distasteful, but candidly exposes
the sexually infantile equation in Walter's mind between
piss, money and genitalia. For the Kronhausens, it is 'a pretty
"far out" experiment', but nonetheless reflects credit on
Walter's ingenuity as an 'amateur sexologist'.

There were, then, two opposite interpretations of *My
Secret Life*. How could the interested reader (and there were

evidently plenty) adjudicate? For the resourceful, there was a copy in the Private Case of the British Museum. More feasibly, Grove had brought out a full text in the US in 1966. In February 1969, the English legality of this book was tested in the prosecution of a Bradford bookseller and publisher called Arthur Dobson. The trial was an important one. Dobson, accordingly, was defended by John Mortimer. And there was an equally top-notch set of witnesses – including Steven Marcus, flown in from New York. All in vain; the case was resoundingly lost.

My Secret Life was an important text. But Leeds was not the ground on which the libertarians would have chosen to fight. Nor was Dobson a publisher whom they would have chosen to fight alongside. The events leading up to the trial were vexing – and highly prejudicial to the defence. In February 1965, police had seized a number of books from Dobson's Bradford shop including nineteen copies of *Bawdy Setup*. He was sentenced to two years imprisonment, and fined £500 for possessing for commercial gain obscene books other than *Bawdy Setup*; perversely, this dirty book, the original target of the raid, was judged not obscene and returned. In July 1966, Dobson was freed by Court of Appeal. In August 1967, books were again seized from Dobson's shop, including *Bawdy Setup*. About the same time, Dobson secured rights to be the UK agent for the Grove, eleven-volume *My Secret Life*. This retailed for $30 in the US, and the British net price was advertised £11 15s. Dobson sold some 250 sets, before the Bradford police made one of their apparently regular calls, informing him that he could expect another prosecution. Grove – perhaps realising the kind of bookseller they had got mixed up with – withdrew their support and revoked their agreement. Inexplicably, Dobson went on to reprint in paperback the first two volumes of *My Secret Life*, piratically (assuming, that is, Grove could claim copyright in a work originally privately printed 70 years before). But before Dobson could sell any of these paperbacks, charges were brought. The omnipresent *Bawdy Setup* was joined in with *My Secret Life*, but Mortimer managed to get it hived off, and the Victorian text considered separately. It was fruitless effort. As it turned out, the court did not make any distinction between the nineteenth and the twentieth-century dirty book.

Leeds was a hard venue for 'Mortimer's circus' to play. Partly, too, the defence strategy seems to have been wrong. The line adopted was that *My Secret Life* was a vital historical document. A group of historians was assembled as distinguished in their specialism as the literary critics at the *Last Exit* trial (e.g., J.H. Plumb, E.P. Thompson, J.A. Banks). By all accounts (the fullest is by Alan Watkins, *New Statesman*, 14 February 1969) the historians ran rings around the prosecution. Nor did they stoop to 'humbug'. When, for instance, Geoffrey Best was asked what value for the historian lay in Walter's account of sodomising a prostitute, he replied, 'none whatsoever' – making it clear that documentary evidence was elsewhere in the work and had to be carefully sifted out. Marcus, like all the witnesses, was asked if Walter's violation of a ten-year old girl in Vauxhall Gardens were not the most evil passage he had ever read. 'Do you mean that literally', he returned. And when reassured on the matter of literalness, referred the apparently unworldly prosecuting counsel to immeasurably nastier reading matter. When the prosecution suggested that the work might be a fabrication by a modern hand (along the lines of Trocchi's 'Fifth Volume of' *My Life and Loves*) David Foxon, Reader in Textual Criticism at Oxford, proved on bibliographical grounds that *My Secret Life* was irrefutably Victorian.

The experts acquitted themselves superbly. But they did not acquit the book or the bookseller. He got two years (later reduced), a £1,000 fine and estimated himself £17,500 out of pocket. It had been evident to the court that the clever historians could make good use of *My Secret Life*. (And as evident that they already had no problem in acquiring it for professional purposes.) But they were not general readers. Nor had they been able to demonstrate that this invaluable 'historical document' should be generally available to the raincoated patrons of Mr Dobson's shop. Such was the severe conclusion of Mr Justice Veale passing sentence on the luckless bookseller: 'You were not printing *My Secret Life* to make it available to professors and students. You were deliberately proposing to make money out of the sale of filth because you thought it had money value.'

The *Last Exit* trial showed that the 'literary merit' line of defence was growing threadbare, and could no longer automatically win over juries. The *My Secret Life* trial was the first in which pornography was wholly defended as 'essential historical evidence'. (The argument had been brought in by the *Fanny Hill* defence, but only in support of the primary contention that Cleland's novel was sexually wholesome – clearly not something that could be said about *Walter*.) Leeds showed that the 'historical' ploy was a non-starter.

What was left now was the 'therapeutic' defence. Boiled down, this went: 'pornography is good for you, insofar as it releases tension.' Pornography as safety-valve was to be pushed *ad nauseam*, until 1977 when the exasperated Law Lords ruled it inadmissible.

It was left to the *TLS* (7 February 1970) to complain that *My Secret Life* was neither available, nor clearly banned in the UK. (The trial, perversely, dealt only with the first two volumes - the obscenity of the other nine was untested): '*My Secret Life* is no doubt a nasty book', the paper observed, 'but it is also a significant one.' No British publisher has subsequently taken it on although the imported Grove paperback edition slipped into officially tolerated availability in the 1970s. The abysmal Kronhausen version remains in print to this day.

July 1970:

Mr Tynan's Nude Review

Oh! Calcutta! was not (as some bemused subcontinental tourists were supposed to have misunderstood) about the problems of India's most overcrowded city. The title punned on the French for 'Oh, what an arse you have' – a representative jest. Nor was July 1970 the sex romp's first staging; it had lucratively scandalised New York where it opened in June 1969. In form *Oh! Calcutta!* most closely resembled the irreverent university review. In presenting it, Kenneth Tynan, as in his palmy days as *Observer* theatre critic, was playing the undergraduate *terrible*. 'Mr Tynan's Nude Review' (*The Times*'s frosty description) gathered together sketches from amazingly different hands mixing the crude, the subtle and the erudite with music and dance items. Judged simply by the talents recruited, it was unique. John Lennon, Joe Orton and Samuel Beckett were among Tynan's best-known contributors. Lennon's piece featured a masturbation ring, each member calling out women's names to stimulate fantasy – suddenly one interjects 'Frank Sinatra!' In another playlet, a similar fantasist group is disrupted by a newcomer who is only turned on by violent gun-play. A capsule history of knickers (drawing in part from *Walter*) made up an interlude. All of which was naughty, but oddly juvenile.

    Oh! Calcutta! opened at the Roundhouse in Camden. Since the theatre was (and is) Arts Council supported, predictably feathers were ruffled by 'state handouts for filth'. Tynan revelled in such controversy, and did his utmost to whip up pre-event publicity by having a series of packed 'previews' in advance of the opening night. Well before the play was officially launched he had succeeded superbly in putting the wind up the 'establishment' – as he would have called it in his British satire days, earlier in the 1960s. The unnamed *Times* 'staff reporter' was typically disapproving in the account of his evening at the 18 July preview:

> It will prove of interest to those excited by the prospect of
> unclothed ladies and gentlemen cavorting in a stuffy
> former engine shed . . . it will bore most adults . . . If it
> was for this that the battle against the censor was fought
> and won, then the struggle was barely worth it.

Tynan, throughout his career, had a genius for making his
critics look stuffed shirts.

A whole range of custodians and busybodies were gal-
vanised to the point of providing an off-stage spectacle as
diverting as anything Tynan had devised. Frank Smith, the
perpetually fulminating GLC councillor, complained to the
police after visiting a preview. Finding no aid there, he had
the wild inspiration of inviting the leaders of the nation's
churches to visit what he called 'the shame of London' and
elsewhere, and with a larger patriotism, 'a disaster for
Britain'. The Archbishop of Canterbury replied through a
frigidly formal secretary that 'it is unlikely that Dr Ramsay
will be going to *Oh! Calcutta!*.' Cardinal Heenan, the Archbishop of Westminster, more diplomatically pleaded 'illness'.

On 24 July it was reported that the DPP was 'considering
a complaint' against *Oh! Calcutta!* under the 1968 Theatres
Act. There were, however, difficulties in training the sights of
this act on something as visual, unscripted, choreographic
and impromptu. (In some ways, it would have been easier to
charge Tynan with running a bawdy house – the offence used
for striptease and live sex shows.) If the DPP did proceed
through the 1968 law, testimony would have to largely
taken from 'police accounts'. And notoriously, a clever
counsel could run rings round a policeman testifying to
obscenity. ('And did the sight of these naked breasts corrupt
you, officer?') It would have been much easier if *Oh! Calcutta!* could have been stopped at the point of national
entry, like a film print (which was how HM Customs kept
Deep Throat out). And if it had been a book, with a fixed
'text', it would have been easier still. (Significantly, on 24
July, a man at Dover was fined £150 for importing, *inter
alia*, seven copies of the American book of the play of *Oh!
Calcutta!*) It would have been easier, too, for its libertarian
well-wishers if *Oh! Calcutta!* had not been so ostentatiously unserious. The DLAS, for instance, observed that
it was merely 'light entertainment . . . we exist basically to
defend rather weightier material'. (Who, that is, would go to

the stake for John Lennon's jokes about wanking?) Unlike Penguin Books or Calder and Boyars, Tynan flaunted the commercial appeal of his product. There was no talk of *Oh! Calcutta!* being 'puritanical' or 'tender' or 'sacramental'; nor was it denied that pockets were going to be handsomely lined. *Oh! Calcutta!* provided – as wittily as was compatible with commercial appeal – what Tynan held to be the main gratification of pornography: erections for men, titillation for women. Shrewdly, he banked that the paying public would go for it, whatever the anxiety-makers said.

After the most publicised series of previews in London theatrical history, the play opened on 27 July. Outside the theatre, touts were selling tickets for up to £50 each. A questionnaire was given to the first-night audience, asking them to declare whether they expected to be depraved by their experience. None did. One replied: 'who gives a damn, anyway?' Amidst all the elegance was Tynan himself, a reincarnation of Oscar, 'in a black shirt and what looked like a tropical drill suit'. After all this, the show itself was something of a comedown. As *The Times* critic, Irving Wardle put it in a telegrammatic headline: 'SOMETIMES FUNNY: NOT A MENACE'. The authorities were not even intermittently amused, but were driven to concur about the harmlessness. On 1 August, the Attorney-General, Sir Peter Rawlinson, announced there would be no prosecution of *Oh! Calcutta!* (The decision hit the touts very hard; street prices dropped as low as £12.) The Solicitor-General confirmed Tynan's impunity by refusing Lady Birdwood leave to bring a private prosecution.

An extraordinary rage was unleashed by *Oh! Calcutta!* – not so much by its impudent contents as by the flagrant and entirely unabashed way in which Tynan got away with it. The apparent impotence of the authorities was, for the moral majority, beyond bearing. Lord Eccles, Minister for the Arts, was given a hot time in the House about the Arts Council's involvement. But even he could not vouchsafe that steps would be taken against the Roundhouse, or any other naughty client. Elsewhere, 'leaders of society' saw *Oh! Calcutta!* as 'the last straw'. David Holbrook in a simile severe even by his standards compared Tynan to 'the storm troopers who made Jewesses dance on the tables at Treblinka' (*Spectator*, 5 February 1972). Archbishop Lord Fisher declared that the public exhibition of anyone's genitalia was an invasion of everyone's privacy. A.P. Herbert wrote his famous piece in *The Times* (only a short time before his death) lamenting that the 1959 law which he and his comrades had fought for so persistently and honourably had ended in the 'right to represent copulation veraciously on the public stage'. There was other voluminous correspondence in *The Times* immediately after the production. On some days, it occupied virtually the whole of the letters page, something which had hardly happened since Suez. Discussion was dominated by angry churchmen expressing what one laughably called 'the still small voice of the church'. Their unanimous clamour is summed up by the Bishop of Peterborough (29 July):

> So there is to be complete freedom of expression . . . What used to be called blasphemy or indecency or savage violence or public insult, overt or veiled, to the living and dead are to be hailed as signs of an enriching liberation.

Tynan's contribution to the debate was sublimely insolent. On 7 August he wrote a brief note to *The Times*:

> Sir, Lord Drogheda joins several of your other correspondents in ascribing to me the phrase 'tasteful pornography'. Whatever his lordship may have read, I have never used this expression to describe *Oh! Calcutta!* or anything else. I have a horror of the word 'tasteful'.
>
> Yours etc. Kenneth Tynan

The inevitable *Times* leader appeared on 6 August. Taking the space normally occupied by two editorial items and entitled 'Law and Morals' it began: 'Moralists of the ancient world were in no doubt that lewd spectacles debauch public morals.' Thus launched, it was straight into the fall of the Roman Empire. *Oh! Calcutta!*, *The Times* determined, had 'passed the bounds of decency'. But finally it was forced to admit that the law was, apparently, helpless to control such indecency. The only remedy was in greater collective self-restraint. Disdainful boycott of Tynan's review was called for. The British public was inclined to show no such forbearance. After packing them out at the Roundhouse, the play moved to the West End on 30 September for a years-long run.

Historically, *Oh! Calcutta!* can be seen as a moment of significant provocation. The moral backlash, which was to

climax in 1972, dates from *Oh! Calcutta!*'s shameless appearance in London, unpunished by the law, on a stage subsidised
by the state. As Longford put it in the Introduction to
his *Report*:

> In the age-long argument about pornography a new water-
> shed was reached in this country when, in the summer of
> 1970, *Oh! Calcutta!* was staged with impunity in London.
> Somewhere about that time large numbers of those hither-
> to unconcerned, or positively favourable to greater free-
> dom of expression, began to share the anxieties expressed
> for many years by other citizens. All sorts of people, not
> only those with a religious standpoint, began to say for the
> first time, 'things have gone too far'.

(Even, Longford revealed, Anne Summers, pioneer of the sex-
shop chain which supplied the nation with the bulk of its
vibrators, dildoes and rubber vaginas, thought *Oh! Calcutta!*
was 'pornography'.)

In the months after *Oh! Calcutta!* the moral backlash
attained a remarkable cohesion and purposefulness; to use
the slogan of a later period and another party, all the frag-
ments came together. In September 1970, the Archbishop of
Canterbury called on Christians to mobilise against obscenity.
The Church of England's Board of Social Responsibility
published a report the month after, denouncing pornography,
and declaring, heretically by the doctrine of 1959, 'literary
merit is not sacrosanct'. Lobbies and pickets were mobilised
outside London cinemas. 'Christians' interrupted dubious
plays, and harassed newsagents with too daring top shelves.
Early in 1971, the Society of Conservative Lawyers bent
their legal skills to the future control of porn, and produced a
report, *The Pollution of the Mind*. In March, the ultra-
liberal John Trevelyan was replaced by the more cautious
Stephen Murphy as Secretary of the BBFC. (Trevelyan,
an advocate of the 'Danish solution' of total decensorship,
went on to figurehead for BAPA, the professional association
of skin mags.) In March 1971, the 'concern of ordinary
people' was organised into what was to grow at phenomenal
rate into the Festival of Light (FOL), a movement with a
Savonarola-like programme of social purification. By an
extraordinary stroke of luck the Festival managed to get an
endorsement from Prince Charles – for once forgetful of
royal neutrality. The crusade climaxed with a mass meeting

on 25 September 1971 in Trafalgar Square, but: 'The Festival was not confined to London . . . During the week preceding the Trafalgar Square meeting, others were held all over the country and Festival beacons attracted large crowds – probably a total of about 215,000 people were altogether involved.' 'Ordinary' people were apparently on the march.

Extraordinary minds were also exercised. In June 1971 a letter to *The Times* announced the formation of the grandiosely named "The Responsible Society' headed by the intellectuals Pamela Hansford Johnson (author of *On Iniquity*) and David Holbrook (author of innumerable books, including *The Case Against Pornography*). The 'Great Debate', as it was called, generated a vast quantity of 'metaporn'. As the *TLS* put it (3 November 1972): 'It is a matter of dispute whether or not we are drowning in a rising tide of filth. It seems almost certain that we shall shortly disappear beneath a rising tide of books on the subject.' The *TLS* promptly pitched in with its own book-length series of articles, entitled 'Abuses of Literacy'.

What was striking in the passionate, and sometimes intellectually distinguished arguments, was the pattern of total polarization. Thus Duncan Williams in *Trousered Apes* (June 1971) asserted, eloquently, that 'the flood of sadistic pornography which is making the western world look so hideous . . . is conducive to a madness of our whole society.' This was countered by Jonathan Miller in October 1971 in his dazzling lecture, 'Censorship and the Limits of Permission'. For Miller the fuss about porn was merely symptomatic of other, more fundamental anxieties – 'a vivid symbol of an order in jeopardy'. In his Eliot lectures, published as *In Bluebeard's Castle*, Professor George Steiner was apocalyptic: pornography was a main component of the cultural 'hell above ground' that post-holocaust Western society had made for itself. He reiterated his view (first expressed in the influential anti-pornography tract, *Night Thoughts*) that a popular taste for, and official tolerance of, pornography is a long step towards the death camps. In his coolly sceptical lectures to the Rationalist Association collected as *Crime, Rape and Gin* (1974) Professor Bernard Crick demurred: '*Nothing* is happening in our society at the moment remotely comparable to the rounding up for eventual death of three or four million Jews in Germany: to use this metaphor is to demean the past and to make farcical melodrama of the present.' Nearer the soapbox level, Lord Longford was one week in January 1972 declaiming in Coventry Cathedral that porn was rotting the nation; the next week John Trevelyan (formerly Britain's best-known censor) was arguing, in *Forum*, that all laws against pornography should be repealed. Such legislation would, however, have to pass over a sizeable heap of parliamentary dead bodies. In a February 1972 debate, Gerald Nabarro mustered at least 80 indignant MPs behind his demand that the Home Secretary (the very un-energetic Reginald Maudling) do something. Rear-Admiral Morgan-Giles (Conservative, Winchester) observed: 'this country is sleepwalking into a cess pit.' Very different from these knee-jerk, bone-head authoritarians, Norman St John-Stevas declared himself dismayed by the mess the liberating 1959 law had produced. On 21 January 1971 he demanded a tightening up:

> in view of the Government's concern for the environment, would it not be appropriate for the Home Office to direct its attention at this particular form of moral pollution, about which the patience of both the public and MPs is just about exhausted. (Cheers)

The question was double-barbed, since St John-Stevas was one of those prominent literati who had laboured to bring about the 1959 Act which he now disowned.

In April 1971, the subject was taken up by the Lords. The debate was stage-managed by Lord Longford who had prepared himself by dropping in at such strip joints as the Soho Stokehole ('neither pleasant, nor unpleasant' was his enigmatic verdict). In the passionate and almost unanimous speech-making, Lord Eccles declared pornography to be 'the ugly child of the permissive society. It flourishes most when society is falling apart.' A confessional Viscount Ingleby revealed that 'pornography dragged him down. It pulled his whole personality down. It sapped his strength.' With a flourish worthy of Joe McCarthy Longford told his peers: 'I hold in my hand a piece of hard porn which a headmaster recently found in the possession of a girl of fourteen. Any peer who believes there should be no restrictions should read this book.'

Always the terrible child, Tynan must have rejoiced to have stirred up so big a commotion as the Festival of Light. But perhaps he had done the moralistic, censoring party more good than he would have liked. Before *Oh! Calcutta!* there seemed a strong possibility that Britain might, in her own time, slip gradually towards a Scandinavian situation of complete tolerance within certain no-nuisance regulations. (A number of British commentators, for instance, were favourably struck with the severe simplicity of the Swedish practice by which sex shops were allowed to stock whatever they wanted, so long as external display was limited to the one ugly word, 'PORNO'.) There had been a reasonably friendly response to the 1969 Arts Council conference and Report on censorship, which urgently advocated abolition of the law whose tenth anniversary it commemorated. A sanguine John Calder predicted that in 'five years' censorship in the UK would be no more, the DLAS could disband itself. In fact, after *Oh! Calcutta!*'s 'veracious copulation' there was to be the fiercest popular backlash and official crackdown that post-*Chatterley* Britain had known. Kenneth Tynan looked set to go into history as a modern Oscar Wilde, a dandy whose outrageousness would put a heavy rod in the hands of the philistines for a generation.

November 1970:

IT – 'Conspiracy to Corrupt Morals'

The prosecution of the underground newspaper *International Times* has on the face of it little connection with 'literature'. But it serves as a prelude to the more significant *OZ* trial; indeed, the *IT* proceedings may be conceived at least partly as a dummy run, to see how the 'conspiracy to corrupt public morals' charge would work, if used against an 'underground' publication.

'Conspiracy to corrupt public morals' can be traced back to the 1959 Street Offences Act. This liberalised the laws on prostitution, but also served to clear business off the streets. As a result, it was that much more difficult to make necessary enquiries about 'specialities' face to face. To facilitate 'contact', an enterprising pornographer called Shaw put together a *Ladies Directory*, in 1961. The ladies were, of course, fully professional whores. The police and DPP decided to act against this publication (which would have caught on like wildfire if unprosecuted). They were not confident that a 'living off immoral earnings' charge would stick. They were also nervous that after *Chatterley*, a successful 'public good' defence for the *Ladies Directory* might be ingeniously devised. They therefore invented, out of the plasma of common law, the charge of 'conspiracy to corrupt public morals'. This effectively denied any recourse to 'redeeming social value' pleas. Shaw was duly convicted on the conspiracy charge, and the sentence upheld on appeal.

Contact magazines have a long history in London. An early famous example in the eighteenth century directly ancestral to Shaw's effort was *Covent Garden Ladies*. They are probably always around, in more or less sophisticated forms of publication. The Shaw judgment kept them out of sight for a year or two, but they made a strong comeback in the mid to late 1960s. Now it was not just whores who were advertised, but 'swingers', desperate 'lonely hearts', would-be 'wife swappers' – all hot to get in on the new 'liberated' sex action. The trendsetter was *Way Out* in 1965, which quickly spawned imitators. These new contact magazines could make a mint of money. They set a high cover price (usually £1) and charged as much as 5s. per letter forwarded or advertisement accepted. By 1968, the timid but lustful could have browsed for companionship through *New Friends, Exit, Swingers '68, Blue Circle, Within, Directory, La Plume, Adult Advertiser, et al.* This heyday did not last long. Apart from internecine war among themselves, the liberation that had brought them into business fairly soon took the bulk of the contact magazine's trade away. 'Respectable' magazines – *Time Out, Private Eye,* even the *New Statesman* began to run 'Personal' classified sections that would have meant prison for the editor some years earlier. The raunchier contact magazines survived, but they remained a poor relation of the glossier skin mags and Forum-style sexual advice magazines. (These, of course, also ran contact columns.) And deep in the heart of criminal sexual activity furtive contact services were offered by illegal organisations like Paedophile Information Exchange (PIE).

IT was one of the pillars of the underground press. Less artistically inclined or fashion conscious than *OZ*, it was very much a paper of report, opinion and review. And, in the period after the Sexual Offences Act which made legal homosexual relationships between consenting adult males, *IT* carried their contact advertisements in its personal ads section. A typical example, quoted at the trial, was: 'Passive masculine good looking graduate 36 seeks sexually demanding active male with own pad in London. Daytime preferred.' The legitimised gay-scene had not developed and such advertisements filled a social need.

In January 1970, three directors of *IT* and the company publishing the paper were committed for trial on two charges, one of conspiring to corrupt public morals, the other of conspiring to corrupt public decency. Or as it was put more stiltedly in the formal language of the court they aimed by inserting certain advertisements to: 'debauch and corrupt the morals as well of youth as of divers other liege subjects of the Lady the Queen'. In November, after a trial of six days, all the defendants were found guilty. The three directors were fined £100 each and given an eighteen-month sentence on the first charge and a twelve-month sentence on the second (both suspended). The company was fined £1,500 on the two charges and made to pay £500 costs. As he thus insured the destruction of their journal, the judge agreed that nevertheless the publishers of *IT* were motivated by high ideals.

The success of this trial was clearly encouraging to those behind the systematic purge of the underground press which was now being mounted. And clearly 'conspiracy', once dusted off, had been again found very useful. It was duly introduced as the primary charge in the *OZ* case, eight months later. The *IT* lawyers and defendants were less happy with it, and urged an appeal on the grounds that 'conspiracy to corrupt morals' was no offence in British law. When it finally came to the Law Lords in May 1972, these final arbiters were divided. They agreed sufficiently, however, to uphold the 'morals' part of the sentence and reject the 'decency' part. A journal with advertisements on the inside page, they logically agreed, could hardly offend decent people unless they were indecently looking for offence. And although they could not bring themselves to explode it, their Lordships ventured to doubt the validity of the 'crime' so usefully invented in 1961. Lord Diplock went so far as to call the Shaw judgment an 'unfortunate mistake'.

In the House of Commons, uncomfortable questions were asked. And using his freehold column in *The Times*, Bernard Levin launched a series of flaying articles in June 1972. He seized particularly on the 'assurance' which the Solicitor-General (Sir Peter Rawlinson) gave in 1964 when the 1959 law was reformed. This pledged that no attempt would be made to deny plaintiffs who wished it the 'public good' defence before jury; he had also pledged (Levin alleged) 'conspiracy to corrupt morals' would not be used to bypass the more complex Obscenity Act. Levin's *j'accuse* was uncompromising: 'the *IT* defendants should have a free pardon . . . justice in this country has not been covered in glory by this business.'

British justice was not going to be supinely covered with Levin's insults. The Attorney-General took the unusual step of writing an answering article in the paper. His counter-attack was that the offending *IT* advertisements were not, technically, a 'publication' and could not therefore have justified themselves as being for the public good on the grounds of 'artistic . . . literary . . . scientific merit'. They were, rather, part of 'an apparatus of liaison' (i.e., procurement service) operated by the journal. *IT* was, in short, a pimp. There had been, Rawlinson insisted, 'no breach of any assurance'. Nevertheless, in reply to questioning in the house, the Home Secretary revealed that the whole 'conspiracy' question had been referred to the Law Commissioners. The charge went into limbo for a few years (so *Nasty Tales*, for instance, was proceeded against for obscenity). The Law Commissioners, it eventually emerged, did not like the charge. But it remained in force to nail the PIE organisers, and their peculiarly nasty contact magazine for pederasts, late in the 1970s.

March 1971:

The Mouth

The 'Whacking Off' section of Philip Roth's *Portnoy's Complaint* (1970) inspired other public revelations of what had previously been sex's 'dirty little secrets'. Not everyone was ready to have these closets opened. Brian Aldiss's *The Hand-Reared Boy* (1970, the title is to be taken in a double sense) was stopped by his indignant publisher who came across it in proof. Under another imprint, it went on to become the author's biggest ever seller.

Paul Ableman's *The Mouth and Oral Sex* (in America *The Sensuous Mouth*) was a 'manual' with instruction, history and various diverting material relating to the hitherto hole-in-corner business of fellatio and cunnilingus. The general tendency of the work was seditious as well as salacious – alternative orifices being taken (as in *Deep Throat*) as proper for citizens of the alternative culture. Ableman was, by pedigree, an *avant-garde* writer. He had been associated with the Merlin group in Paris, published his first literary-but-obscene novel, *I Hear Voices* with Girodias in 1958, and was the holder of the *Transatlantic Review* Erotica Prize. *Vac*, a novel brought out by Gollancz in 1968, had run into trouble with W.H. Smith, who refused to stock it.

Christopher Kypreos's Running Man Press was primarily concerned with magazines of a sexual-radical kind, and he chose to market Ableman's book – which he had commissioned – like a magazine. That is to say, he solicited prior subscription through the post. To this end Kypreos/Running Man sent out four brochures for *The Mouth* in what was reckoned at the subsequent trial to be 100,000-a-time mail shots. Like other advertising, these brochures gave a *promesse de bonheur*, and hinted at outrageous revelations if one bought the book. They were, in fact, only mildly offensive. But they fell into the hands of children (protecting the kids – as with the *LRSB* and *OZ* cases – was the seasonal

108

obsession). No less than 17 recipients complained. Another less shockable 2,000 signed up to buy Ableman's book at £2.50 or 3 guineas according to the terms accepted. The book was not otherwise available in British bookshops (though some copies had got on to the German market.) Had it not been prosecuted, the economics of sending out 100,000 letters for 2,000 sales would have killed the venture much more effectively than the vengeful machinery of British law.

Kypreos (not Ableman) was hauled up at the Central Criminal Court on 3 March 1971. He faced a double-barrel charge: that he possessed an obscene article, *The Mouth*, for publication for gain and that he had sent four indecent articles (the brochures) through the British mails. The jury was composed of ten men and two women. They were told by Jeremy Hutchinson (a main *Chatterley* defence counsel) that he intended to defend the 'merit' of *The Mouth*. 'It is not the sort of book which is just scribbled out by some purveyor of pornography.' The presiding judge was Judge Alan King-Hamilton, later to hear the *Gay News* and *Nasty Tales* trials.

The principal witness to testify to the literary merit of Ableman's book was Margaret Drabble (she too would reappear at the *Gay News* trial). She was closely questioned, cross-examined and lectured to by the judge. Her views were unenthusiastic but polite: 'I found it readable, entertaining and well written but not a very serious medical work.' She admired a certain 'clarity and lightness of touch'. Perhaps she was thinking of passages such as the following:

> Many couples spontaneously invent games in which a strawberry, for example, is placed in the vagina and then eaten out of it. Or liqueur may be poured over the penis and sucked off it. An example of how accessible to the popular imagination such games are was connected with a recent scandal in which a well known actress and model was found naked with the members of a pop group. The story circulated that she had been treating the boys to an edible morsel held in a curious way. What was this feast? A banana, a Mars bar, a pickled herring, a liver sausage – before the tale died away one had begun to suspect that the lady must have been equipped in an unusual place with a well-stocked larder!

It was during Drabble's testimony to the literary merit of the work that the judge wearily intervened: 'why is it important to read about it now . . . we have managed to get on for a couple of thousand years without it.' King-Hamilton was even more annoyed by the medical experts. Dr Anne Evans, a north London (inevitably) medical practitioner claimed that some of her patients could be helped by reading *The Mouth*. Dr Leopold Field, a consultant psychiatrist agreed that the book had 'considerable medical and scientific value'. This assertion sparked off the following exchange:

JUDGE ALAN KING-HAMILTON QC. Have you read the *Decline and Fall of the Roman Empire*?
DR FIELD. No.
THE JUDGE. But you know the view has been held that ancient Rome fell because of many years of decadence and immorality?
DR FIELD. Yes.
THE JUDGE. One has only to look at the increasing number of illegitimate births, abortions, cases of venereal disease and increasing homosexuality.

Despite the judge's historical pessimism, and despite the scorn poured by the prosecution on a social scientist who testified to this versatile work's 'sociological merit', the jury, after six-and-a-half hours, found Kypreos not guilty of publishing an obscene article. On the other hand, the jury found the brochures indecent under the definitions of the 1953 Postal Act. Kypreos was fined £250 with £100 costs (though he reckoned himself £5,000 out of pocket). In fining him, the judge declared that 'there is no telling what harm has been done by distributing a brochure of this kind.' (It might be noted, incidentally, that Max Romeo's 'Wet Dream' was featuring in the hit parade at this period – an indication of the younger generation's blithe worldliness.) Referring to the publisher's obviously alien origins, King-Hamilton further observed that selling books in this way 'is something the majority of people in this country do not like'. Outside the court Ableman was also preoccupied with the country: 'I am absolutely delighted. I am weeping. The verdict justifies everything I ever felt for England. I think we will rush out a paperback edition.' The 40p Sphere paperback duly appeared – to the enrichment of all parties – in 1972.

March 1971:

The Little Red Schoolbook

On 31 March, Scotland Yard officers, allegedly spurred by Mrs Whitehouse's complaints, visited the London offices of Stage One, a small publishing house run by Richard Handyside. Handyside was young – younger than Richard Neville, for instance. But he was cut from a different pattern. The son of a policeman, Handyside had been a King's College Cambridge scholar, was short haired and he dressed smartly in acceptably old-fashioned style. Nevertheless, his list had a radical flavour and featured work by Castro and Guevara. Stage One also published *The Little Red Schoolbook*.

LRSB was originally a Danish publication. In Denmark, according to Mrs Whitehouse, it had done 'incalculable harm' (but what more harm could be done in that Gomorrah, one might ask? When Lord Longford made his much publicised trip in August he claimed to have located a Danish farm where animals were to be hired for sexual purposes). Based on Mao's handbook, *LRSB* outlined for children their 'rights' and gave them basic advice on the world, unbiased by parental prejudice. Handyside's translation cost 30p and ran to 208 pages of which less than a quarter were devoted to advice on drugs and sex. These sections were, however, to obsess the subsequent prosecution. Before attracting the Yard's attention, *LRSB* had been noticed in the *Times Educational Supplement*, the *Listener* and the *Spectator*. They tended to find it rather too chic in its anti-authoritarian 'kids' rights' programme, but they dealt with it as a decently provocative publication.

Others were provoked more violently. Ross MacWhirter, for instance, declared that 'the book is not only obscene but seditious'. Much quoted was *LRSB*'s advice on how to handle pornography: 'It is quite possible that you can get some good ideas from it and may find something interesting that you have not tried before.' Among other things that the child may not have thought of trying, *LRSB* instructed on oral sex. Its line on premarital experiment was very permissive: 'people go to bed with one another for many reasons . . . People who warn you against both strong feelings and sex are generally afraid of both.' Great harm was done to Handyside's case by selective quotation of passages like the above (rather than the section on homework) and by *The Times*, for instance, repeatedly describing it as a 'manual on sex and drugs'.

The *LRSB* had, in fact, done well for Handyside. An edition of 20,000 had been printed and another of 50,000 was in hand. But police action, if supported by the DPP, would freeze stock and could mean death for a small operation like Stage One. Effectively, this gave the police summary powers. Need for a quick decision probably explains why Handyside chose to have the 'obscenity' of *LRSB* tested in the Magistrates' Court at Clerkenwell (where the summons was to be returned) rather than go to a higher court with jury, as was his right.

Things did indeed go swiftly if not well for Handyside. The police served a summons on 14 April charging him with possessing 1,201 copies of an obscene article for publication for gain. As a number of publishers pointed out – this formulation seemed to suggest that commercial publishing was in itself suspicious. Publishers generally in London seemed to have felt a tremor of alarm that someone of Handyside's eminent respectability could be so treated by the authorities. On 8 May it was announced that a group of more than 20 'leading London publishers' had banded together to form a protection group. It was reported that they might even go so far as collectively to reprint *LRSB* with their noble imprints attached. This venture testified to the trade's alarm and benign instincts. But as ever with publishing, caution eventually won the day. Publishers began to stand up to be discounted. Weidenfeld and Nicolson – reported as one of the original group – withdrew; apparently the 'direct action' proposal was not to their taste. Faber and Faber announced that *The Times* was 'misinformed' in thinking that they had any part in the campaign. Those publishers who were left (some of whom did not want their names mentioned) indicated an intention of setting up a vague 'fighting fund'. Eventually, the publishing profession withdrew support altogether and Handyside was left with only the ever-ready NCCL and DLAS to stand by him.

When the *LRSB* case came to Clerkenwell Magistrates'

Court in late June 1971, the prosecution opened by alleging that the book and its publisher might well be liable to the charge of incitement; addressed principally to the under-16s, the text of *LRSB* did not make clear that in the UK it is unlawful for a girl under 16 to have sexual intercourse. Supporting this point, Dame Mary Green, Headmistress of the Kidbrooke Comprehensive School in Greenwich, gave her opinion that the book would encourage youngsters to experiment with their own and their peers' bodies. Words like 'orgasm' and 'masturbation' (which she claimed were not in use among *her* friends) would, moreover, have an 'unpleasant effect' on under-16s. In his defence, Handyside stated that he had gone over the text with three teachers and three sixth-formers. He had also taken legal advice on the section concerned with children's 'rights'. He had not, apparently, cleared the manuscript with any headmistresses.

He had a good case, but Handyside must have suffered from the sensational *OZ* trial, going on simultaneously at the Central Criminal Court. More so, perhaps, as he was defended by John Mortimer, who for a period was popping from one.case to the other. Nor can Handyside have been much helped with the magistrates by the familiar and dependable experts drawn up by Mortimer. Dr James Hemmings, for instance, was asked by Mortimer for his reaction to the accusation that *LRSB* insufficiently condemned pre-marital sex between young people. He replied: 'This is the failure point of all adults. If they adopt taboos and negative attitudes towards sex, they do not have the right to hold themselves as advisers.' Another defence witness, Caspar Brook of the Family Planning Association, said the *LRSB* section on contraception was 'wholly admirable'.

The magistrate, Mr J.D. Purcell, was unimpressed. Handyside was found guilty and a relatively painless £50 fine and £115.50 costs imposed. In passing sentence, Mr Purcell said that he didn't think Handyside published the book because of 'his love for children'. His motives were not 'entirely philanthropic'. (Few publishers' motives are.)

One hippy shouted 'you obscene old man!' at the magistrate. Mrs Whitehouse was jeered as she left the court but declared herself 'greatly relieved – for the sake of the children'. It must have also been a moment of some triumph for her. Like Mortimer, she was moving between the *LRSB* and *OZ* cases; both were going her way. She was supported, as might have been expected, by Ronald Butt in *The Times*. With regard to the appeal announced by the publisher, NCCL and DLAS, he declared: 'If the advocates for the book would band themselves into a Society for the Abolition of Childhood we should know where we are.' The advocates for the book were more concerned with the assault on freedom of speech. Tony Smythe of NCCL thought the guilty verdict 'an absolutely sickening decision . . . one of the gravest steps against free expression we have seen in this country for a long time'. For their part, the Advisory Centre for Education pronounced that the banning of *LRSB* was unnecessary and counterproductive - adding the backhanded explanation: 'In our view few children are likely to read the book or want to read it.' (They may have underestimated British youth. On 9 September it was reported that the police had been called into a Brighton school, where 100 duplicated *LRSB*s were said to be circulating.)

On 21 October, the *LRSB* sentence was heard before the Appeals Committee (since it was not a jury case, it could not go to the court of appeal). There was a replay of the original proceedings. For the DPP, for instance, it was asserted that *LRSB* was insufficiently horrific about the dangers of VD - merely pointing out how to recognise symptoms and get cured of them. With some indignation the prosecution added that the booklet 'treats VD more or less as the common cold' (which is, of course, incurable). Miss Elizabeth Maud Manners, headmistress of Felixstowe College 'said that in her opinion the book would prove an incitement to seek out sexual pleasure' (and for young girls to break the law).

On 30 October, the Appeals Committee upheld the sentence. It cited in support of this decision *LRSB*'s advocacy of smoking pot, and its allegations that pornography might be used as a source of 'good ideas' to pep up one's sex life. It is more than likely that if the magistrate had been as heavy handed as his colleague, Judge Argyle, Handyside might have fared better. But £50 was little more than a token fine, and attracted neither much outrage nor much sympathy.

Handyside declared himself 'very depressed' by the outcome. But he was nothing if not energetic. Over the next five years he was to fight his case through the European Commission of Human Rights without ever getting the satisfaction he sought. (He was particularly indignant at the way in which the police had originally occupied and ransacked his premises.) More immediately, he stickered out the most offending passages, made revisions and brought out an edition of 100,000 'amended' *LRSB*s in mid November - helped immensely by the publicity of the trial. This new edition of *LRSB* was scrutinised by the DPP and let pass. In Edinburgh, however, even the amended *LRSB* fell foul of the Procurator Fiscal, and was prosecuted in December for being 'indecent and obscene'.

There are a number of conclusions to be drawn from the *LRSB* trial. From Handyside's point of view, a main irritation (and one which kept him going all the way to Strasbourg) was the high-handed way the police had acted – invading his office, removing material irrelevant to the offending article, refusing to give receipts. At this period the police often seem to have waged all-out war against what they considered, *a priori*, to be subversive magazines, and to have got results by means that exceeded strict legality. In the *IT* and *OZ* cases, files were removed and confidential material violated. There is evidence, too, that mail was monitored in transit. In December 1971, the Assistant Director of the Arts Council of Wales, Peter Jones, was found guilty and fined £20 for procuring through the post the magazine *Suck*. Police claimed that the package, sent from Holland, fell apart spontaneously in the sorting office. (Jones, incidentally, wanted the magazine for a Council-sponsored exhibition. Of the magazine itself, he protested: 'this is not obscene. It depends on your state of mind. This is nature. Throughout history intercourse has been a popular practice.' Since the mails were involved, it was decency rather than non-obscenity and popularity which was at issue.)

The other main consideration arising from the *LRSB* prosecution has to do with authority and 'the young' of whose welfare it is the ultimate guardian. Given the social rule that children are sexually innocent, 'minors' are invariably central in discussions of pornography. But concern about the young takes different forms in different periods. In the middle to late 1970s the primary concern was 'paedophilia' – the young as victims. In the 1960s (especially after the Grosvenor Square demonstration of 1968) the concern was that young people were running wild – enraged by a heady cocktail of sex, dope, rock music and radical politics. This fear runs through the panic reaction to films like *Clockwork Orange*, the prosecution of *OZ* and other underground (i.e., young peoples') magazines and *LRSB*.

There was, of course, something for the older generation to fear. *The Little Red Schoolbook* did, without doubt, incite the young to resistance if not revolution against their elders and betters, as did Richard Neville's *Play Power* and issue after issue of *IT*. And what can have possessed the BBC in 1970 – to introduce a sex education programme for 8 year olds?

Postscript

On 25 August 1971, Mrs Whitehouse attended a *baciamano* with the Pope, and heard her work praised by the Pontiff. As *The Times* put it: 'Only a very limited number of people may attend this semi-private audience, and Mrs Whitehouse seemed delighted.' She had brought with her a copy of *LRSB* and *OZ* 28 to put into the Papal hands (how did she get them through Customs?); but eventually they were delivered instead to an officer of the Holy See, and now doubtless reside in the Vatican's fabled collection of erotica and prohibited books.

June 1971:

OZ 28 – The Longest Obscenity Trial

Founded in 1963 in Australia, *OZ* moved with its editor, Richard Neville, to Britain where, after 1967, it established itself as the market-leader of underground magazines. The name puns on Neville's home country and the psychedelic, technicolour wonderland created by (square) Walt Disney. In style, *OZ* was polychrome *mélange*. Pages changed colour, print came from all directions in a vertiginous riot of typography and disorderly layout. The magazine contained articles, reviews, advice columns, photographs, cartoons, comic strips, advertisements. But it had no set format. (One issue was entirely pictorial – an 'image bank' with no words attached whatsoever.) The perspective was international, and drew heavily, in a spirit of underground syndication on American material (the gifted cartoonist Robert Crumb and the medical columnist *Hip*pocrates were regular contributors). Ideologically, *OZ* embodied Neville's 'playpower' dictum that so alarmed Mrs Whitehouse: 'the weapons of revolution are obscenity, blasphemy and drugs.' For Neville, sexual provocation was a necessary political act. As he put it in *Ink* (a related and shorter-lived underground newspaper, 2 November 1971): 'Actively opposing Mary Whitehouse and her ideas is more important than debating Trotsky's complicity in the suppression of Kronstadt or denouncing Germaine Greer's lowering of her knickers for the colour sups.' (Greer, another dynamic Australian and longstanding *OZ* contributor, was felt to have let the counter-cultural side down with her best-selling *The Female Eunuch*.) Used with proper political consciousness, pornography was thus a blow struck against the Vietnam war and troops in Ireland. It was, apart from anything else, a very marketable doctrine (and more intellectually coherent than the *Sun*'s page three bums and tits). But it let the magazine in for criticism from the more *engagé* of the underground that it was nothing more than a 'wank mag'

117

with radical frills. And when the defence was recruiting for heavyweight witnesses at least twenty refused (including A.J. Ayer, Anthony Storr and Ralph Steadman) on the grounds that the magazine was trivial, dirty minded or both. Nevertheless, it was (as the mailing list read out in court by John Mortimer testified) read in high places by an impressive assortment of Britain's top people.

OZ organised the chaos of its contents by subordinating issues to general themes. There was, for instance, a 'Cunt-power *OZ*' (in court Neville called it more decorously a 'Women's Liberation *OZ*'), a 'Gay *OZ*', a 'Flying Saucer *OZ*', an 'Acid *OZ*', etc. In issue 26, an advertisement announced that 'some of us at *OZ* are feeling old and boring' and invited any under-18 readers to come and edit an issue, free from interference by regular staff. About two dozen volunteered, all still at school. They collaborated in *OZ* 28, 'A Schoolkids Issue'. Children's 'rights' were very much in the air in 1970 and pervaded the tone of their material. There were the usual 'Down with Skool' complaints that would have been familiar to Stalky and Co. The following was by Vivian Berger, the moving spirit of the juvenile collective:

> We have another clever teacher – Mr Butler, who likes the old way of running schools. He canes people. Once he caned me. I had to bend over and put my hands on a low chair so that the muscles of my arse would be tense and it would hurt more. I gritted my teeth because it did hurt and left red marks and bruises.

This lamentation was accompanied by a cartoon of a kind which could have been found in innumerable rough books and on school lavatory walls (fig. 1). Where the issue was specifically about schools it was predictably against exams, discipline, uniforms (and by implication school dinners). It was also for large freedoms. Guilt-free sex and soft drugs were demanded as the schoolchild's right.

> Freedom of sexual expression in public has many tight restrictions. One may kiss in certain places but only fuck in a few places at certain times. Surely this idea is as pretentious and puritanical as the old forms of censorship? Its purpose is to prevent corruption and protect the individual from disturbing or immoral sights. This is ironical in itself and only made to satisfy the so-called moral conscience of society. ('Anne'.)

Figure 1

Potentially harmful and legal drugs are being used as substitutes for the comparatively harmless hash. Surely this is what the authorities should be fighting against with a lot more determination and force . . . It is time hysteria was overcome and situations viewed in the correct perspective. ('Andrew'.)

The juvenile editorial team were not as good with the pencil as with the pen, and the main supporting cartoons and strips were borrowed. Their tone was more brutal than the rather touching doltishness of the written contributions, with their 'surely' this and 'surely' that. Most contentious of the strips in the trial, was that in which young Vivian Berger collaged Rupert Bear into an American 'Gipsy Granny' comic. Violent rape is apparently being committed – though not between any parties who might conceivably appear in a court or a crisis centre (fig. 2).

OZ 28 carried a number of the routine features of the

Figure 2

RUPERT FINDS
GIPSY GRANNY

1   " *It looks just like a ball to me,*"
   " *Open it and see.*"

journal. Its 'camp-porn lesbian orgy' cover was not provided
by the kids. And its classified ads, at the back of the journal,
were certainly 'adult'. For example:

> Voyeurs . . . Homosexuals . . . Lesbians, Heterosexuals, all
> Erotic Minorities . . . Join Contact Club International.
> Ulrikagaten 2, Stockholm, Sweden. Membership £2 only.
> 100% Confidential. Free fucking, Sucking, Hardcore maga-
> zines of your choice! Excellent for masturbations and
> Fuckstimulation!!

Following his success with *IT*, the DPP decided to prosecute
with the whole works. The principal charge was conspiracy
by means of:

> a magazine containing divers obscene lewd indecent
> and sexually perverted articles cartoons drawings and

illustrations with intent thereby to debauch and corrupt the morals of children and young persons within the realm and to arouse and implant in their minds lustful and perverted desires.

The defendants were also charged under the 1959 Act with publishing and possessing for gain an obscene publication. And blasting his third barrel the DPP charged them under the 1953 Postal Act with sending through the mails an indecent article. The persons charged were a trio of *OZ*'s (adult) editorial and managerial staff, Richard Neville, Jim Anderson and Felix Dennis. Also charged was the Company, OZ Publications Ink Ltd.

There were, naturally enough, counter-conspiratorial charges as to why the authorities had chosen to shape up so massively to *OZ*. The commonest was that the proceedings were not to do with morals, obscenity or misuse of the GPO but 'political'. If *Chatterley* had been a 'struggle' between two generations and two classes (as Penguin claimed) this was all-out war to the death. Another theory circulating widely was that *OZ*, *IT* and *LRSB* were singled out because they had grown too big commercially and were threatening 'legitimate' interests. (An analogous argument held that the marijuana habit was threatening the tobacco companies' profitability, and that it was they who were behind resistance to decriminalisation.) *OZ*, before the trial, had a claimed sales figure of 40,000 an issue, and a readership (given commune habits) of half a million. This made it bigger than the *Spectator*, *New Statesman* or even the *Economist*. *LRSB* was going into editions of 50,000. *Time Out* had been started in 1968, and was wiping the floor with its straight predecessor *What's On*. According to this paranoid line of thought, alternative cultures were tolerable, but not alternative economies. *OZ* must go, because it was a threat to big business. (It did not, incidentally make profits because of grotesquely high printing costs.)

We shall probably have to wait the statutory 30 years until 2001 (the date would have pleased *OZ*) until it is revealed why the authorities mounted the trial. As *The Times* noted (with reference to the similarly vindictive Mick Jagger drugs case), they were in the mood for breaking butterflies on wheels. Perhaps they were worried about the silent majority turning nasty politically, and overthrowing the Government. Perhaps it was a belated reaction to the terrifying 1968 Grosvenor Square rally when it looked as if the revolution had started. Whatever the motives, the decision must have been taken at the highest level; apart from anything else, the No. 2 Court at the Old Bailey was to be taken up for nearly six weeks, at a cost of some £80,000.

The underground and its liberal sympathisers rallied to the defence of *OZ*. John Lennon offered to write a song; Tony Garnett to make a film of the proceedings. *OZ* tee-shirts (31s.6d. - profits to the Defence Fund) became uniform garb among the congenial young. The trial itself opened on 21 June with what *The Times* called a 'carnival atmosphere'. Outside and inside the court was packed with 'friends'. John Mortimer was defending Anderson and Dennis (Neville, a law graduate, defended himself). His line was, from the first, that here was a trial about politics, authority and non-conformity. He portrayed the defendants as inheritors of the mantle of British religious dissent: 'When you hear the word dissenter', he told the jury:

> you may think of those who, in past times, used to thunder their denunciations in dark clothes and rolling phrases from the pulpits of small chapels. Now, the dissenters wear long hair and colourful clothes and dream their dreams of another world in small bed-sitting rooms in Notting Hill Gate. In place of sermons with their lurid phrases about damnation, we have magazines reflecting a totally different society from that in which we live.

It was a daring assimilation on which to base defence strategy. On the face of it there was only a tenuous link between John Wesley's preaching and Neville's advocacy of 'fucking in the streets', legalising pot and blowing up the London stock exchange. Nevertheless, Neville piously followed suit in his opening address. *OZ*, he maintained, was 'a sounding board for people with new things to say and nowhere else to say them'. 'So far from debauching the morals of the young', he told the jury, 'our evidence will show that *OZ* is part of a communication network which intends the very opposite. It sets out to enlighten and elevate public morals.'

The trial did not go well for the defence. During its course, Mortimer - who was playing a two-handed legal game - lost the *LRSB* case. Moreover, the levity and innocently reckless tone of *OZ* wilted in the courtroom atmosphere and under heavily literal prodding by the prosecution counsel Brian Leary. Anderson, for instance, described Berger's bit of fun with Rupert Bear injudiciously as 'youthful genius' and was nagged mercilessly:

> LEARY. The youthful genius set to work by snipping out of the Rupert Annual, the head of the bear, That's right?
> ANDERSON. Yes, I suppose that's what he did.
> LEARY. And then, if we were keen to watch a genius at work, we would see him sticking it on the cartoon?
> ANDERSON. Yes.
> LEARY. Already drawn for him?
> ANDERSON. Yes.
> LEARY. Where lies the genius?
> ANDERSON. I think it's in the juxtaposition of two ideas, the childhood symbol of innocence . . .
> LEARY. Making Rupert Bear fuck?
> ANDERSON. Yes.

Dr Lionel Haward, a psychiatrist who was to feature in many subsequent obscenity trials, was similarly trapped into talking nonsense about this item. 'The message of the Rupert Bear cartoon', he asserted, 'was a criticism of the lack of dissemination in sexual education.' Feliks Topolski, giving evidence as a world-famous artist, was hardly more convincing about Berger's now thoroughly mangled collage: 'This, to me, is a tremendously witty putting together of opposite elements from the "comics" culture, thus creating a riotously profound clash. I think it is a great invention.'

The prosecution contrived to make many of the defence witnesses seem themselves dangerous, anti-social subversives. George Melly, for example, was exasperated into admitting that he would, without any remorse, use words like 'cunt' and 'bollocks' in front of his ten-year-old daughter. As he complained to Leary, 'You are trying to make me out an NW1 monster.' Michael Segal (former probation officer and former head of Rediffusion's children's programmes) was made to seem another monster when he admitted that he allowed his four children, including twin boys of eleven, to read *OZ*.

Disastrous damage was done the defence by the testimony of Marty Feldman, then a cultish TV comedian. He began by saying that the Bible (on which he declined to swear) was more obscene than *OZ*, pertly enquired of the judge if he was keeping him awake and concluded his evidence with an audible 'boring old fart' in his Lordship's direction. This was bad enough, but another defence witness, Ronald Dworkin, an American Professor of Jurisprudence at Oxford, ventured to say that in his professional opinion the trial, not the magazine, was a 'corruption of public morals'. It went down very badly with the judge, Mr Argyle. With highlights of this kind, the evidence of more soberly authoritative witnesses (Hans Eysenck, Richard Wollheim) was thoroughly upstaged.

The jury was out for three-and-three-quarter hours. They found the defendants guilty on all counts, except that of corrupting morals. The judge remanded them in prison for seven days, awaiting reports. While there, to the glee of the tabloid press, they had their shoulder-length hair savagely cut – 'at the request of the prison staff'. This gratuitous assault, like the photographs of Mick Jagger in handcuffs, did more for their case in the country than all the expert witnesses put together.

The sentences, when Judge Argyle delivered them on 5 August, were shockingly harsh. Neville drew fifteen months in prison, with deportation to follow; Anderson twelve months; Dennis (on the cruelly mitigating grounds 'You are much less intelligent') nine months. *OZ*, the company, was fined £1,500 with £1,250 costs. So the longest obscenity trial in British history ended.

Judge Argyle was burned in effigy outside the Old Bailey by a riotous crowd of 400 *OZ* supporters. There were eleven arrests. Bernard Levin declared it a 'national disgrace'. Mrs Whitehouse thought it was 'a very good thing . . . this country suffers a lot from people who come into it.' Wedgwood Benn, and other Labour MPs put down an immediate motion, expressing shock at the severity of the sentences. The NCCL described the sentences as a declaration of war on the younger generation. The Monday Club expressed its gratitude to the judge. A number of lawyers voiced disquiet at the trial. The *New Law Journal*, for instance, criticised the judge for 'prolonging the agony'. The sentences were 'indefensibly severe'. *The Times*, in a leader of 6 August, determined that 'the sentences were justifiable . . . the law has a right to protect children.' In Sidney, Neville's father revealed, with sublime irrelevance, that 'Richard's great grandfather was a survivor of the charge of the Light Brigade.'

In granting bail on 10 August, the Court of Appeal came near to criticising the extraordinary harshness of the sentence. Indeed, it was hard to square with, for instance, the prosecution of *Curious*, a highly prurient 'advice' magazine', which was fined £150 at Marlborough Street the day after, the proprietor declaring, piously, that his obscene magazine was *never* designed to get into the hands of children, 'it was in no way "an OZ situation".' In October while the thumping *OZ* sentences were still coming up to appeal, 51,096 obscene books belonging to Sexa Ltd were ordered to be destroyed, and the firm fined £10. In the nature of the current standards of the porn trade (protected by a thoroughly corrupt Metropolitan Obscene Publications Squad) many of these must have been 'harder' than anything in *OZ*. When in August, *Time Out* planned an issue with six pages attacking the *OZ* verdict, their printers refused to make two illustrations taken from skin mags legally available in Soho. The paper appeared with blank gaps where the pictures should have gone.

The appeal was heard in early November. In arguing it, Mortimer claimed misdirection by the judge. Argyle, he maintained, had overlooked in his summing up the dissuasive effect of *OZ* where drugs was concerned. Neither had he pointed out that obscenity could have also an 'aversive' or 'emetic' effect. (This had been the ground on which the American Judge Woolsey had exonerated *Ulysses* in the 1930s.) The Appeal Judges accepted this submission. The 'obscenity' charges were quashed. This left only the offences against the Post Office Act. The six-months sentence for that was suspended. In making this judgment, Lord Widgery significantly revised the understanding of the 1959 law by laying down that an 'article' was obscene if only part of it were judged so. (Just the opposite had been maintained at the *Chatterley* trial.) He also called into doubt the value of 'expert' witnesses, on their showing in this case.

According to Mrs Whitehouse, the appeal verdict was 'a disaster'. From an opposite point of view, the *New Law Journal* agreed the trial was 'an unmitigated disaster . . . it is said to have cost £80,000–£100,000 and occupied no less than 27 working days of a court with one of the most congested criminal lists in the country. And to whatever purpose?' Certainly not to clear up the obscenity law. As Nigel Nicolson pointed out in a witty letter to *The Times*, the logic of Widgery's 'emetic' argument was to suggest that attractive soft core was less innocent than repulsive hard core: 'The harder the pornography the greater its deterrent effect and therefore the greater its social value'. Despite these Alice in Wonderland contradictions provoked by the trial, despite the massive cost and despite the shambles of its eventual conclusion the Home Secretary, Mr Maudling, announced that he was not prepared to look into the workings of the 1959 Act.

OZ: The Aftermath

16 February 1972   It is reported that the police have returned impounded copies of *OZ* 28. During the trial they fetched £5 in Soho. The proprietors now offer the exonerated issue at 50p to 'freaks and the ideologically sound'. The charge for 'academics, librarians and wholesale dealers in pornography' is £1. *OZ* circulation rises to 80,000.

14 March 1972   An OZ 'Police Ball' is held to raise defence funds. The police, uninvited, raid it. Lack of music and refreshment licences result in £5 fines.

16 April 1972   The wife of the clerk of the court at the *OZ* trial is herself tried for having wasted 1,200 hours of police time around mid August 1971. She is accused of fabricating threatening notes to herself. These were taken seriously Argyle was heavily guarded against assassination. She is found guilty and fined £700.

June 1973   *OZ* goes into liquidation with £20,000 debts outstanding.

September 1972:

The Longford Report

Private Eye called him 'Lord Porn', a caricature monster of prurient, geriatric exhibitionism. According to John Calder: 'It is the limelight that draws him to take an interest in pornography.' Whether or not it was an appetite for publicity which motivated him, Lord Longford certainly stage-managed the promotion and publicity of his report with flair. He fuelled pre-publication excitement with a trip to Copenhagen that was a jamboree for the regiment of Fleet Street hacks following him around (viz. the *News of the World* headline: 'Porn Probe Girl Sue to Tell What Happens in Sin City'). To the delight of the British tabloid press and millions of readers Longford actually went to (and was photographed in) a 'live sex show'. In the club 'Longford declined to flagellate a semi-naked girl and had to disengage her whip from his neck.' He emerged shaken but with the comment, quick-witted enough in the circumstances: 'I have seen enough for science and more than enough for entertainment.'

Pornography: The Longford Report was published by Coronet (a firm in which Lord Longford, otherwise a publisher, had an interest) on 20 September 1972. At 500 pages, it represented sixteen-months work by a committee of 53 (of whom only 47 stayed the course; one of the younger members, Gyles Brandreth, left with the sour observation: 'I would not be surprised if they felt *Chick's Own* was pornographic'). Longford's manipulation of the British media for the week of the launch was typically adroit. As a lively parliamentarian, and a good speaker, he contrived to wake up his torpid peers in the upper chamber to the imminent fall of Western civilisation. He took over an 'It's your line' on BBC. The inclusion of Cliff Richard and Jimmy Saville on the Committee assured wide and respectful coverage by the popular and musical papers. There were innumerable features, profiles, editorials, interviews. The paperback became a bestseller. All of which massively went to bolster up Mrs Whitehouse's proud assertion that 'four-fifths' of the English people agreed with the report's outright denunciation of 'the poison of pornography'.

The *Longford Report* is a number of things: affirmation, protest, survey, pressure-group lobbying. Most immediately it urged legal reform – a draft Bill for which it conveniently (if over-optimistically) appended. This reform would abolish the 'public good' test, and define obscenity not as that which depraves and corrupts, but as material 'whose effect, taken as a whole, is to outrage contemporary standards of decency or humanity accepted by the public at large'. The appeal to 'local community standards' (as the criterion was to be formulated by a conservative US Supreme Court, a year later) went against the 'right of the private individual' standard, which had been recommended by, for instance, the 1970 *Report of the American Presidential Commission into Pornography*. This ultra-liberal report (as distasteful to Longford as to President Nixon who took delivery of it) firmly stated that nobody had the superior right to interfere with the citizen's right to his preferred reading matter. The *Longford Report* was all for interference. And not just in reading. Given its subterranean (but tactically played down) links with VALA, a main stress was on control of broadcasting. The BBC, for example, should be 'de-chartered', and its programmes subject to obscenity legislation. (Malcolm Muggeridge's section in the report is polemically the strongest and most entertaining, if the least neutral.)

'The Public at Large' ('Moral Majority' in Nixonian terms) is what Longford felt gave his project muscle. The British people were with him. It was, he claimed, the receipt of a thousand supportive letters after his April 1971 Lords' debate on pornography that first inspired him. The opening section of the report is accordingly entitled 'The Growth of Public Concern'. 'Concern', it implies, is by 1972 well nigh universal. But emphasis on populist consensus gets the report into its most intractable tangle. On one hand, it insists that pornography is 'epidemic' as never before: on the other that the vast majority of Britons are unequivocally against 'filth' therefore any legislation will pass by sheer, unanimous acclamation. It sets up the bewildering spectacle of a British population happily wallowing in pornography which, mysteriously, they want ruthlessly stamped out. This doublethink pervades the report. Take a comment of David Holbrook's attesting to the sadistic tendency of a critically applauded

BBC television drama: 'in the series *Casanova*, a man approached a girl in the bath with an implement saying "open your legs girl!" 12,000,000 viewers watched that scene.' Holbrook intends to incite rage against the BBC; instead, he prompts the reflection that 12 million happy viewers can't be wrong. (If they had felt as indignant as Holbrook, they would have complained or not have watched next week and the ratings-neurotic BBC would have made the appropriate cuts.) If the British wanted both to be thrilled by porn yet have it crusaded against, then they were the moral hypocrites the French and other sarcastic foreigners had always taken them for. Alternatively, the general consensus which the report claimed to have backing its radical proposals was merely propaganda.

In the short term, the report's historical view was apocalyptic. Since 1960 (and ominous *Chatterley*) there had been an unparalleled assault on family life and common decency, producing not the 'permissive' or the 'civilised' but the 'sick society'. It had all peaked in 1970 (*Oh! Calcutta!* was a 'watershed'). Now, at last, there was a fightback. 'Civilisation', the Committee held, 'is a thin crust'. Reforming legislation – perhaps well-meaning but fatally wrongheaded – had eroded this crust dangerously, loosing the dark amoralities which lurk in every human being, and which have always to be checked. The sick society was not, however, just the product of 'mistakes'. The Committee was strongly of the opinion (also popular with Mrs Whitehouse) that in the 1960s there was a conscious and conspiratorial use of pornography for *political* ends, to subvert and debauch the nation, with the final intention of overthrowing our democratic way of life. *LRSB*, *OZ* 28, and Martin Cole's sex education film *Growing Up* (which showed a child masturbating, and recommended reduction of the age of consent to eleven) were clear evidence of this sinister campaign. Had not the Nazis softened up Poland with pornography – more effective than any artillery barrage – before they invaded? The psychologist Hans Eysenck's 'wise' comment was approvingly quoted:

If I were asked by some Martian invader how one could best destroy the human race without overt show of arms, I would have to say that the destruction of the moral and ethical standards which alone maintain a society would be the best method.

The large historical model on which the *Longford Report* rests is as simple. Christianity had served in the Dark Ages to stem the tide of pagan (more particularly Roman) obscenity and had managed to exercise a sanitary control until quite recently (1960, to be precise). Now, Christianity needed to rise again, to put down a second wave of more than Roman amorality. As the Williams Committee was to observe in its condescending dismissal of Lord Longford's effort, the report was fundamentally concerned with much larger fish than the place of pornography in English life. The soul's welfare, the fall of civilisation, the coming of the Lord were what ultimately exercised it.

Suddenly whipped-up collaboration threw strange bedfellows together in the report. There were novelists like Kingsley Amis and Elizabeth Jane Howard (finally, they found the populist crudity too much to take, and dissented); sages like Peregrine Worsthorne and Muggeridge; the Director of the Confederation of British Industry (pornography – among all its other horrors – was the enemy of efficient production); and, of course, Jimmy and Cliff. It would have compromised the report's 'objectivity' to have consorted with overt crusaders like VALA and FOL, so these friends were held at arm's length But there was a nucleus on the Committee from the grandly self-termed Responsible Society. And there was, of course, an ecumenical sprinkling of clergymen (e.g., 'Pornography: A Jewish View'). There were no (declared) gays.

Given the *ad hoc* way in which material was gathered and processed, some of the report's subject panels are better than others. There is, for instance, a good contribution on the soft-porn magazine trade; almost certainly it was the best thing published to date in Britain. The panel report on sex education was, by comparison, appalling. The seven 'Personal Contributions' encouraged some crackpot, hobby-horsical offerings. Peregrine Worsthorne, for example, put forward the Arnoldian view that sex had now replaced religion as the focus of society's yearning for the holy: pornography was, ergo, blasphemous.

The approved reaction to the *Longford Report* was one of knowing, if somewhat weary amusement. George Gale, in the *Spectator*, affected to find it 'funny'. Bernard Levin thought the mountain had laboured to bring forth not even a mouse. Even *The Times* first leader (usually friendly to the anti-porn cause) put it down as merely 'good campaigning stuff'. It was no basis for legal reform; best leave the Obscenity Law as it was *The Times* thought. And like other commentators, it pronounced the ostentatious rigour and scientific objectivity of the report 'only skin deep'. A few readers nevertheless managed to alarm themselves. Leo Abse, MP, termed Longford and his Committee 'cultural fascists', and was convinced they intended to overthrow his, and his parliamentary friends', 'civilized legislation' on divorce, abortion and homosexual acts. John Calder was not an MP, but at this period wanted to be one. He tried to get an emergency debate on the Longford report at the Liberal Party annual conference that he was attending.

What, now that the emergency is over, was the achievement of the report? There were positive aspects. Valuably, it exploded certain glamorous, liberal misconceptions about the 'Danish solution'. Longford's trip to Copenhagen may have been a pantomime; but the report established that it was exactly in the area of live shows (i.e., the pornography/ brothel fringe) that control was tricky, and decontrol most likely to foster crime; even the permissive Danes were tightening up legislation on this matter. The *Longford Report* also made clear what the investigative press had largely chosen not to notice, that the police in Soho were not exactly cracking down on pornography.

The Longford consensual, 'things have gone too far', rhetoric is a pain. But even the semi-literate letters from 'worried' citizens which the report reproduces are less offensive than, say, the mandarin pomposity of the Arts Council 1969 Conference Report on Censorship. It advocated the Danish solution of complete abolition ('May we one day rival that happy state' declared the André Deutsch blurb). The following *oratio obliqua* catches the self-satisfied and imperative tone of those proceedings, compared to which the worthy grubbing of Longford's Committee glows:

Appendix D.1
Report on Discussion with the Lord Annan, OBE, D.Litt., DU., Provost of University College London.
Lord Annan was firmly against the idea of constraining the arts to a level fit for the maladjusted fifteen year old . . .

January 1973:

Nasty Tales

Started in 1972, *Nasty Tales* was a comic magazine for adults, based on American originals, 'with a hippy lifestyle' (prosecution term). It was widely displayed in the retail outlets where *OZ* and *IT* (whose distributors it shared) were found. The first number came to the attention of the authorities and was duly charged under the 1959 Obscenity Act. The case came before Judge King-Hamilton at the Central Criminal Court on 15 January 1973. Accused were three of the editorial staff, including Mike Farren, later to become a well-known figure when the underground press broke up and dispersed in the legitimate branch of the profession. He defended himself. Also prosecuted were the paper's distributors.

In 1972 the property qualification for jury service had been abolished – a fact which was to favour counter-cultural defendants like *Nasty Tales* and later (in 1975) *Time Out*. Defence lawyers might now use their veto powers to sift out a young, male, radical dozen. They did. The *Nasty Tales* trial started farcically. There were not enough reservists in the building and the end of the day found the court with only ten jury candidates (all male). These surviving ten were dismissed the next morning and the selection started over again from scratch. By the time another all-male jury had been agreed on, the defence had rejected no less than 43 eligible jurors. Not only was the jury packed for the defence, but the courtroom as well. Over the next few days the judge was obliged to be frequently severe with insolent 'sniggering', illegal tape-recording and contemptuous shouted interruptions.

The twelve retired to read the comic, reminded by the prosecution that action had been initiated by a mother who found her eight-year-old boy exposed to such illustrations as the full-page 'Grand opening of the great international

132

fuck-in and orgy riot.' Reminded, doubtless, of his own
innocent youth, the judge interposed: 'I cannot resist asking
a question . . . Are *Rainbow* and *Comic Cuts* still published?'
(No).

There followed the usual comedy of cross purposes. The
defendants pointed out to an apparently incredulous prosecution that yes, many people did take drugs; no *Nasty Tales* did
not think it necessarily evil. The prosecution solemnly
pointed to such injunctions as: 'Hi, kids. Don't forget your
Nasty Tales out today. Packed to the brim with drugs, sex
and violence comix. Only 20p.' Was this not incitement of
minors to crime, sin and self-abuse? Farren: no – it was a
parody of consumerist advertising techniques. He went
further and argued that *Nasty Tales* was definitely in the
'public good'. Three experts were scraped up to support
this claim. They were a 'journalist' (the assistant editor of
The Sunday Times colour magazine) a 'humanist' (the judge's
term – he meant a non-Christian) and Germaine Greer. Ms
Greer was labelled 'lecturer in English at the University of
Warwick'. This was certainly true – but she was better known
for her associations with the late 1960s and with feminist
protest. *The Female Eunuch* had been published in 1971.
A 'split beaver' photograph of her, taken at the Amsterdam
Wet Dream Festival in 1970, had been printed both in *Screw*
and *OZ*. At this date many more people had looked at her
reproduced pudenda than examined her PhD on Shakespeare.
It was, however, as the more demure G. Greer, PhD that she
described *Nasty Tales* as 'in the tradition of satire'. ('Rabelai-
sian satire of a very high order' was how one of her fellow
experts justified 'Dirty Dog.') In summary the prosecution,
with some justification, accused Greer of not even pretending
to give 'objective' evidence. Why should she? the defence
asked. Its line was that Greer and the defendants were what
they were: 'Do not convict out of hand because you do not
like hippies . . . You are not trying a generation.'

In his summing up, Judge King-Hamilton bore down very
hard on the journal, its producers and hippies. 'Many people',
he said, thought that 'the pendulum of permissiveness had
swung too far.' Could *Nasty Tales* have the 'artistic merit'
necessary under the terms of the 1959 Act? Similar drawings
might be found on lavatory walls. He confessed himself surprised that any experts had been found to applaud designs
such as that of the international fuck-in. 'But this world is
full of surprises.'

Unsurprisingly, the defendants were acquitted of all

charges to jubilation from the long-haired audience. Outside, one of the jurors said they had thought the trial and the court's 'Edwardian morals' ridiculous from the beginning. The nine-day proceedings had cost an estimated £15,000. King-Hamilton denied costs to the defendants: 'if a company or anyone else publishes for gain material of this kind, which quite apart from sex and violence, according to its three directors freely encourages drug-taking, it can hardly be surprised.'

There was the familiar after-trial declaration of decisive victory for the forces of enlightenment. In fact, viewed historically, the party was over. The acquitted *Nasty Tales* lasted only until 1974. *OZ* also went into voluntary liquidation in June 1973, with debts of £20,000. It was the end of an era - caftans, flowers in the hair, turning on and dropping out, had had their day. One main reason that *Nasty Tales* was cleared was that its kind of protest was, by 1973, out of date and irrelevant. But the battle between authority and the permissible was still being fought as savagely as ever on other fields. In the same week that *Nasty Tales* was cleared, the moral majority scored some notable successes. Ross Mac-Whirter prevailed on the Court of Appeal to grant an injunction (given by Lord Denning) to stop the Independent Broadcasting Authority from showing David Bailey's 'Warhol' programme on Thames TV. Media people were indignant and virtually took over *The Times* letter page for a week. (There was, by contrast, hardly a cheep at the *Nasty Tales* acquittal.) Meanwhile too, the GLC had been terrorised into refusing a licence for the film version of *Oh! Calcutta!* - the stage version of which was still serenely showing as one of the longest runs in West End history. The piquant Lambton affair (in which a junior minister was revealed to consort with whores) fired off a 'vice in high places' panic. The depraved and radical young - so much a worry to the nation in the 1960s - were largely forgotten, a thing of the past. They could have their comics.

January 1976:

Inside Linda Lovelace

The End of Obscene Libel

The *Inside Linda Lovelace* trial preoccupied Fleet Street in the last weeks of January 1976, attracting as much attention as anything since *OZ*. Historically, the acquittal marked the end of an era. As Judge Rigg put it in his summing up: 'If this book is not obscene within the definition of the [1959] Act it might well be difficult to imagine anything that would fall into that category.' The difficulty was prophetic. After *Lovelace*, successive DPPs have accepted that no trial to establish the obscenity of a purely written text (with no taint of libel or racial offensiveness) had the necessary 60 per cent chance of success. There was, hereafter, *de facto* decensorship of the word. This state of affairs was eventually certified by the *Williams Report* with its implicit contention that 'obscene literature' is as muddled a concept as 'obscene music' or 'obscene architecture'.

A number of commentators were curious as to why any case was brought against this 'scruffy little book' in the first place. There had been a *pro forma* complaint from a disgusted 76-year-old ex-barrister of Brighton against Lovelace's *scientia sexualis*. But such stimuli did not normally galvanise socialist Attorney-Generals. Moreover the 'pornographer's friend' (as the relentless Ronald Butt liked to term Jenkins) was at the Home Office. Unless there were some invisible motive, the decision to prosecute (which must have been taken at the highest level) was either odd or stupid. *Inside Linda Lovelace* was soft by current Soho standards. Even in its own professional–confessional genre, it was tame compared to Xaviera Hollander's 'Happy Hooker' series which advocated hedonistic prostitution with more verve than Linda advocated hedonistic fornication. Nor was *Inside Linda Lovelace* the latest thing (pornography, of course, grows old very fast which is why skin mags customarily carry no date of issue). It had first been published as a paperback

135

original in the US in 1973 by Pinnacle Books, and had made the year's bestseller lists, riding the 'porno-chic' wave.

Lovelace herself had appeared at the American Booksellers' Association in spring – a fact less significant for sales promotion than as evidence that she was respectable enough to be shown in public. Cynics might see her as 'a nice girl who sucks cocks for a living', but for the American book trade she was established as a legitimate hot property. Not, of course, that Linda (who claimed that hers and Henry Kissinger's names were now the best known in the world) was principally famous as an author. It was as the star of *Deep Throat* that she had come to public attention. This is the film which together with *The Devil in Miss Jones* confirmed porno movies as big business in America. Masterminded by Gerald Damiano and Lovelace's Svengali, Chuck Traynor, *Deep Throat* was made in 12 days at a total cost of $25,000 and eventually grossed $50 million. Linda (for $100 a day) played the lead role of a nymphomaniac who discovers that her clitoris is in her throat, and takes it from there. A masterpiece of sorts, the film got a maximum 100 rating on *Screw*'s 'petermeter'. (Al Goldstein's New York magazine, before the scandals of its criminal connections were revealed was itself chic in 1973.) In their history of American 'sinema', Turan and Zito concur, finding *Deep Throat* 'a truly fine pornographic film' and place it with *The Devil in Miss Jones* as one of the 'two best erotic motion pictures ever made'. Writing in 1976, they also make the point that the 1973 Supreme Court decision, which returned power to 'local community standards' destroyed the economic base of the porno-film industry which – like its Hollywood partner – needs secure national circuits for prosperity and ambitious productions. Following the Supreme Court decision, *Deep Throat*, the best of the art porn flicks, was likely to be the last. As Turan and Zito foresaw it, after 1973, 'the cheap stuff, made in someone's garage for a total cash outlay of $27.50 would still be around, as always, but the era of class theatrical pornography was, to all appearances, over.'

Why then prosecute Lovelace's tatty paperback in 1976? The answer is probably to be found in the British authorities' extraordinary sensitivity where blue films are concerned. In most censorship matters, the UK has always been willing to play follow-my-leader with the US – bringing out its *Chatterley* a year later, its *Tropics* two years later, its *Oh! Calcutta!* 18 months later and so on. But it was not prepared to go along with American tolerance of 'real thing' sex films.

(The piquancy of *Deep Throat*, of course, was that Linda was actually sucking - there was no way it could be faked.) British law and law enforcement was ruthless on any home production of such sexploitation material. In the Collingbourne trial in June 1974, for instance, a moderately-sized film unit based in Watford was extinguished with the utmost severity. (It was turning out $27.50 features like 'Schoolgirl Fun', 'Kinky Capers', 'Sexy Sisters'.) The manager of this operation prudently decamped to Amsterdam, and was sentenced to five years in his absence. He was described as 'depravity and corruption incarnate' by the judge, who concluded his sentencing with the alliterative observation that 'the shrill petulant protest of licentious libertines has been resoundingly rejected'.

Up to 1975, the British licentious libertine had to go to New York if he wanted to see what was smart and porno. But in August 1975, the French government had virtually abolished control on the importation or showing of hardcore movies. *The Story of O, Deep Throat* and *Salo* were openly available in Paris - the only provision being that exhibitors pay a 30 per cent state tax for being 'pornographic'. There was considerable British interest in this rational Gallic solution, and at least one parliamentary question was directed to the Government as to whether the experiment might not be introduced here. The prospect of licensed filth apparently appalled the Home Office. And if they wanted to buttress Albion's floodgates against it, a successful process against *Lovelace* would be ideal. The film, of course, had never been legally shown in this country (the English dirty mac brigade had to make do with the pallid imitation *Deep Thoughts*). But Lovelace had visited London in 1974-5 with impresario Jimmy Vaughan who held the world rights to *Deep Throat* (and dearly wanted to get a British release). If the book *Inside Linda Lovelace* could be nailed, it would ensure that the more obnoxious film would never get past HM Customs.

The English edition of *Inside Linda Lovelace* was 'published' (that is to say imported from America and distributed) in 1974 by Johannes Heinrich Hanau (66), of Old Compton Street, Soho. It was later stated in evidence, that of a first batch of 50,000 only 38,000 had been sold by 1976. If true, the figure was strikingly little for a work which had enjoyed runaway success in America, and which was connected with a film so criminally hot. But part of the lukewarmness towards *Lovelace* is explained by national indifference to her specialism. Oral sex has never been popular as a British pornographic theme – just as 'spanking' has never appealed to a mass of American punters. (It was British resistance to the charm of fellatio which, I suspect, led to the flop of Paul Raymond's sex romp *Snatch 69* in April 1975. Its predecessor at the Whitehall theatre, *Pyjama Tops*, had run for six years.)

At the Central Criminal Court trial, Hanau was defended by the distinguished legal pair, John Mortimer, and Geoffrey Robertson. At first sight, the book whose innocence they argued hardly seemed to merit the best obscenity case lawyers in the country. *Inside Linda Lovelace* is a strange mixture: part sex manual, part polemic for sexual liberation (at one point the author claims, outrageously, 'I feel like a kind of pioneer who explored a strange and forbidden territory'). It describes, with gusto, those anal and oral expertises associated with the Lovelace of film and publicity legend. Everyone in America seems to have apprehended that the book was, in fact, ghostwritten (by Douglas Warren it transpired – a hired hand provided by editor Marina de Rey). But at the English trial, defence strategy hinged on the assertion that what was being pilloried was the candid confession of a highly experienced, articulate child of the 1970s. In fact, Lovelace's confessions were no more hers than were Maria Monk's or Fanny Hill's.

In its tenor, Mortimer's defence was jaunty and good-natured: 'You will have to ask yourselves', he told the 3 women and 9 men of the jury, 'whether our society is such, having survived two major wars, that it will actually totter to an end because Miss Lovelace cheerfully indulges in all sorts of shenanigans.' If books like this actually depraved their readers, he asked, why wasn't the hum of vibrators audible from the corridors outside?

A visitor from Mars would find us a very wonderful race, at this crisis in our economic existence, that we can spend thousands of pounds of public money and hear many thousands of words, all because a 22 year-old has written a book [she hadn't] which suggests that sex is a bit of fun!

Did we want Big Brother breaking down bedroom doors to order citizens to resume the missionary position?

In the course of what was, by all accounts, a brilliant performance Mortimer made the unblushing claim that *Inside Linda Lovelace* expressed 'joy and pleasure in sex' and explained interesting techniques 'with care, concern and perhaps ingenuity'. Perhaps in this last he was thinking of Chuck Traynor's encomium on Linda's vaginal muscles, which she was supposed to train for hours every day with a wet tubular vibrator: 'I can put my fist in Linda's cunt but if she wants to she can hold on to my little finger so hard that I have trouble getting it out.' Famously, Traynor had passed on to his *protegée* the secret of the 'sword swallower's fellatio' technique which he had had, in the first instance, from the Japanese. Linda passes it on to the reader in her book.

Mortimer was followed by a string of defence experts, testifying unanimously to the usefulness and candour of *Inside Linda Lovelace*. Marion Boyars (publisher) claimed that Lovelace's philosophy allowed women the active participation in sexual pleasure previously monopolised by men. Dr Brian Richards (a GP specialising in sexual difficulties) claimed that the book would be 'helpful to couples' (or trios, he could have added). He did admit under cross-examination that enthusiastic experimenters might kill themselves emulating Linda's tricks. Nevertheless, there was nothing wrong with oral and anal sex and Lovelace's book was the better for being 'in ordinary language'. Anna Coote (28, journalist) firmly asserted that this was an 'honest' and womanly book: 'I think it puts forward a positive attitude to sex and it is written by a woman [it wasn't] and for too long women have felt they must have a passive and negative attitude.' Mervyn Jones (socialist, journalist, novelist) declared himself against all censorship. Johnny Speight ('Till Death Do Us Part') compared *Inside Linda Lovelace* favourably with *Mein Kampf* (he presumably *wasn't* against all censorship). Jeremy Sandford ('Cathy Come Home') saw Linda as fellatio's Anne Frank: 'It is an absorbing book . . . it is almost like a young girl's diary.' Dr Lionel Haward (Governor of the International Academy of Forensic Psychology and Consultant Psychologist to the Chichester Group of hospitals) reminded a thoroughly belittled court that the World Health Organisation 'has been very concerned about the mental and physical effects of impaired sexuality'. Free circulation of *Inside Linda Lovelace* would help this lamentable situation.

The jury took five hours to return a not guilty verdict. The publisher, Hanau, indicated his immediate intention to reprint; well he might, given the huge publicity his book had received. 'There is in the world today a growing sense of freedom', he declared; adding, 'I am referring to countries with democratic forms of government.' Costs were paid out of public funds. There was some inflated speculation as to how much they were, but the Attorney-General estimated a modest £13,000. Sales of the book soared to a reported 600,000.

Linda Lovelace did not subside into the obscurity which might have been expected. It is true that after 1976 her career as a superstar flopped. There was a messy divorce from Traynor; an abortive stage career (*Pajama Tops*); drugs charges. Then, like some other showbiz personalities, she was born again – not as a star, but as a Christian. The result was another confessional book, *Ordeal* (ghostwriter, credited this time, Mike McGrady). In this 'nightmarish portrayal of sexual perversion and enslavement' a very different Linda Lovelace is projected:

> The personal prisoner of a sadistic monster, Linda was regularly beaten, hypnotised and raped. She was threatened with disfigurement and even death. With a knife held to her throat, she was forced to commit unspeakable perversions, sold to the highest bidders and passed from one celebrity to another. She was made to perform regularly for private parties and before movie cameras. She made *Deep Throat* under unimaginable duress and she still bears the scars of the many beatings she suffered.

The difference between *Ordeal*'s gothic terrors and *Inside Linda Lovelace* 'cheerfulness' is evident from the description of her initiation into anal sex in the later book, juxtaposed with the expert 'advice' on the subject given in the earlier:

> 'Let's make a sandwich,' one of the men [at the orgy] said. My first thought was that we were going to stop and get something to eat. By this time I had lost all appetite. But that's not what they had in mind. The man who had called out for the sandwich lay on his back and the others put me on top of him. Then I felt another man climbing on my backside. I understood then that they were talking about a human sandwich. I had never experienced anal sex before and it really ripped me up. I began to whimper.

'Oh, lookie here,' one of the men said. 'We must have a new baby here.' (*Ordeal.*)

When I think back on how hung-up I was on this score, it amazes me to realise what I've learned to do since. Not only did I readily learn to take the fattest vibrator I could find, but this entry point has become as pleasurable as all the other more familiar ones. I can take any man's organ in my rear, and can have repeated and bombastic orgasms by this fucking method alone. I mean I need no clitoral stimulation whatever. It turns me on as though the back entrance had a clit of its own. (*Inside Linda Lovelace.*)

Particularly relevant to the 1976 trial is Linda Boreman/Lovelace's account of how she wrote *Inside Linda Lovelace*:

And so I became a best-selling author. The way you become a best-selling author is this: Every night for two weeks you get a list of questions to answer; Chuck Traynor tells you how to answer these questions and you give those answers to a tape recorder; then a professional writer types it, arranges it, spells it right, and calls it *Inside Linda Lovelace*. The publisher adds a centerfold and a bunch of other near-naked pictures and then you have a best-selling book.

Where did this leave the Old Bailey experts, and their lofty sentiments about 'positive attitudes to sex', 'honesty' and the World Health Organisation? They could of course (together with most of the porn industry) beg to be sceptical about *Ordeal*. Why trust a book ghostwritten by ('in collaboration with') Mike McGrady any more than one ghostwritten by Douglas Warren and Chuck Traynor? But the witnesses in January 1976 had staked their expertise on the book's manifest veracity. In the event they were evidently inexpertly stupid, or cunningly perjurious.

It was not an episode from which the orthodoxy of enlightenment came out at all well. Reflecting on the trial, after Boreman/Lovelace's promotional tour for *Ordeal* in 1981, Mervyn Jones admitted that his appearance in the witness stand 'is not among my proudest memories'. 'In the pub over the road', it would appear, he and some other defence witnesses agreed that the book was atrociously written and probably ghosted, but we declared in court that it had qualities of 'integrity' and 'candour' . . . The real falsity of the situation, in the light of what we read in *Ordeal*, was that both prosecution and defence assumed the voracious enthusiasm claimed by Linda Lovelace to be genuine.

Beaten, raped, multiply entered, sodomised by a dog (and once, almost, by a donkey), forced to insert the candy 'Red Hots' into her vagina, traded like a credit card to buy her husband's clothes: the Lovelace of the first book would indeed have had to be voracious.

February–April 1976: Lovelace II – Exit the Expert

The *Lovelace* acquittal must stand as a black day in the Festival of Light calendar. According to Mrs Whitehouse, since 1976 'the obscenity laws have been in ruins.' She alleges that at this period, the DPP sent out new guidelines, exempting from prosecution all but 'pornography involving actual physical harm, such as flagellation, bondage, what is euphemistically described as "Scandinavian butcher shop sex",' bestiality and certain perversions connected with bodily excreta. Dispiriting as it was for her party, for the authorities it was certainly a relief to let pornography lie. Moreover, defeat with *Inside Linda Lovelace* did not, as was feared, open the way for the lady's film. On 16 July 1976, James Ferman could write with some complacency to the *New Statesman*, contradicting a false report by its film critic:

> The BBFC has never been asked to consider the film *Deep Throat*, since it has never been officially admitted to this country by the British Customs. If it were, we are advised that it would almost certainly fall foul of the British common law charge of gross indecency.

Such has remained the case ever since.

This was small comfort, however, in view of the violent backlash which the *Lovelace* acquittal provoked. The Home Secretary could no longer rely on his own kind to support his contention that the permissive society was a civilised society. Not even the students were with him. In 1969, Mrs Whitehouse had been howled down at Leicester University, defending her position in a debate on pornography.

In October 1976, in a similar debate at Cambridge, she won her motion easily.

Using its privilege of telling the government off, *The Times* voiced indignation at the conduct and outcome of the case in a furious first leader entitled 'The Pornography of Hatred' published the day after the verdict. Not mincing its words, and presumably verging on contempt of court, the paper insisted that *Inside Linda Lovelace* was 'indeed pornographic in that it is an erotic book about a vicious girl written in vulgar language'. Moreover, its sexual instruction was 'physically dangerous'. It was entirely wrong that some wretched back street publisher should have his costs as well as all the sales-boosting publicity. Main chastisement was reserved for Dr Richards, the most persuasive of the medical witnesses. The leader-writer cited a cross-questioning of Richards from an earlier trial where he had been shown a number of pictures and asked for expert comments; as, for instance;

3. *Woman inserting an instrument into back passage of a man.* Dr Richards: Yes, this has therapeutic value . . .
5. *Girl with distress in her face, arms manacled and has cuts. She is tied up. A man with a bayonet is inflicting cuts.* Dr Richards: I have known patients who could benefit by masturbating on this.

The Times alleged jury packing by a defence using their veto to select 'young men of radical appearance'. (Immediately following the trial Mrs Whitehouse had herself complained to the Sex Discrimination Board, arguing for six of either sex in such cases. Nine years earlier, in his disappointment over *Last Exit*, John Calder had argued that obscenity juries should have 'A' levels.)

The 1959 legislation, *The Times* concluded, had failed and was a mockery. It cited an earlier opinion of Lord Denning's that the weakness of the statute was in its 'public good' defence, as validated by 'experts'. According to Denning: 'experts say that *pornography itself* is for the public good – which is quite contrary to what Parliament intended'. *The Times* sarcastically updated the objection in the light of *Lovelace*: pornography was now vindicated by 'Dr Richards's standard defence that anything which tends to promote masturbation is for the public good.' The Victorian myth was reversed – failing to abuse oneself might now lead to the straitjacket and the padded cell.

'It does deprave' was *The Times* subheading. Many voices

were raised to agree that pornography criminalised, it did not cure criminals. 'While that tortured child's scream echoes in tape or in memory', wrote Sir Laurence Grafftey-Smith (3 February) 'no British jury can convincingly pronounce that sadistic pornography does not deprave.' The ever-reliable Ronald Butt used his column in the paper (5 February) to make his routine allusion to the decline of the Roman Empire. William Sargant – a psychiatric expert as weighty as any produced by the defence for Lovelace – gave his opinion (3 February) that 'it is nonsense to say that reading sadistic pornography never has any deleterious effects on the reader . . . We are running real national risks.' In the House, Michael Alison, a Conservative front-bench spokesman, accused the Crown of being wilfully 'negligent' over obscenity cases. The *Inside Linda Lovelace* trial had been 'farcical'. Why, it was wondered, did not the prosecution produce witnesses of Sargant's calibre? Alison indicted the slovenliness of the DPP by reference to the case of a Plaistow man, Brian Jacobs. In February, this merchant was found guilty of possessing some 600 obscene films and a few thousand obscene magazines, for commercial gain. As usual, he had called medical experts to allege that the material was in the public good (two of them, Dr Christine Pickard and Maurice Yaffe, were fresh from giving evidence for *Lovelace*). But in this case 'private individuals' (i.e., the Festival of Light) had gone to the expense of importing a counter-expert – Dr John Court, a psychologist of Flinders University Australia. Court had done field work on pornography and come to illiberal conclusions. When Court was offered to the DPP the gift was accepted 'belatedly' and, as Alison claimed, grudgingly. (Originally it had been intended to call no prosecution medical witnesses.) Court's assertion that pornography was never usefully 'therapeutic' was decisive. On 5 February, Jacobs was sent to prison for a year with £700 costs – and this within a week of *Lovelace's* acquittal.

Court's theory that pornography caused rather than cut sex crime was congenial to the judiciary. In Leeds, on 11 February, Mr Justice Jupp, handing out stiff sentences for rape, observed that 'this is the third case in succession where pornographic material has set in train offences'. Nor was the cause of enlightenment helped by the revelation on 9 February that in Birmingham hard-core pornography was available on the national health for the sexually inhibited. (Apparently therapists acquired their 'medicinal' supplies from the police store of confiscated material.)

The instincts of law enforcers (police, judges, magistrates)
are traditionally less liberal than those of sex counsellors and
publishers. But at this period, the division was particularly
wide and entrenched. In October 1975, for instance, Judge
King-Hamilton (earlier in charge of the Playland vice-ring
case, later to judge the *Gay News* blasphemy trial) sentenced
a London porn merchant with the comment: 'This stuff is
really dreadful. It . . . has made certain parts of the West End
the sink of iniquity [it] leads to all sorts of sexual offences
and corruptions of young people.' That pornography provoked serious crime was evidently the official conclusion
drawn from the most sensational case of the period, that of
the Cambridge Rapist, earlier in October. Peter Cook's
exploits were both horrific and bizarre (he eventually took to
wearing a hood with 'Rapist' emblazoned on it. As he told
police, this saved time in introductions). One incidental
feature which emerged in the proceedings was that Cook
frequented a Cambridge sex shop – the 'Love Inn' – in Mill
Road. A few days after Cook was put away, the Cambridge
police raided it, seizing material which the Cambridge magistrates duly ordered to be destroyed. (The defendants judged
it best in the lynch-law atmosphere to make no defence.)
In Oxford in the same month two named magazines, *Forum*
and *Viva*, were seized by the police. These were freely available in most town centres, and *Forum* could claim to be the
market-leader in 'sexual advice' magazines. (Its then editor,
Philip Hodson, is a particularly articulate and well-educated
journalist.) *Forum* was defended by a familiar battery of
'experts' – including Yaffe, Pickard and Haward, all of whom
were to appear a few weeks later for *Lovelace*. Haward told
the Oxford magistrates that he routinely used *Forum* and
Viva for treatment purposes in his health service clinic at
Chichester. The magistrates were not apparently impressed.
Haward figured again, a week or so later, in the trial of a
blue film unit which the police had busted in October 1974.
The defendants ingeniously claimed that there was no case to
answer, because although the films were made with consenting adults in this country, they were only sold abroad.
(Allegedly they had enquired of Scotland Yard if they were
covered under the Sexual Offences Act, and were reassured
on the point.) Thus a film like their *Anal Rape* was solely for
the German market. A second line of defence was that these
films were anyway 'therapeutic'. Haward testified that he
used similar materials at his (by now surely much frequented)
Chichester clinic. This brought the astonished query from

Mr Justice Wien: 'Do you recommend lesbianism on the health service?' In certain circumstances it seems Dr Haward did.

After the *Lovelace* setback, it was evident that the judiciary had had enough. They also had means with which to suppress these vexatious 'sexperts'. In February and May 1975, prosecutions of two sex-shop owners had taken place at Northampton and Swansea. Both were found guilty and heavily fined. The trial judges had refused leave for the defence to call expert witnesses to show that the seized hard core was helpful to married people and potential sex offenders (Haward, among others, was waiting in the corridor). In March 1976, the Court of appeal upheld the convictions, denying that hard pornography could have redeeming psychotherapeutic value. The disputed evidence was ruled inadmissible. The appeal went a rung higher to the House of Lords, in November, where it was again rejected. Hereafter, the 'medical' justification of obscenity was dead. Haward, Richards, Yaffe *et al.* could hang up their guns.

In its aggressive mood, the judiciary had more rods with which to beat the discredited 1959 law. For some time there had been confusion in film licensing. The BBFC is a self-regulating body set up by the film trade among themselves. Local authorities reserve, though rarely use, a superior licensing right of their own. A liberal tendency in the GLC (associated principally with Enid Wistrich) had recently used this prerogative to permit the showing in London of films denied a BBFC certificate. In these cases, the GLC committee had applied the 1959 obscenity tests - although films, like television, were specifically excluded from the terms of the Act.

Enraged by this metropolitan decensorship, the indefatigable Raymond Blackburn brought a private action against the GLC, on the grounds that they were in breach of common decency. (He selected as his target the Swedish '*More About the Language of Love*' - an avowedly sexological film.) In the Court of Appeal in April 1976, Lord Denning ruled that the GLC had indeed misused their licensing power. In adapting the 1959 Obscenity Act, they were failing the London public. The proper test, according to Denning, was that of decency not obscenity. 'The Customs authorities and the Post Office', he pointed out, 'apply the simple test "is this *indecent*?" ' They consequently had no problem in protecting decent citizens from shame. Nor - of course - were these officials obstructed in their duty by 'experts' and 'public good' testimony. (That this method could not be used had been established in a test case in March 1972, when the Post Office had prosecuted the gay magazine *Spartacus* under the 1953 Post Office Act.)

As if to bear Denning out, Heinrich Hanau, the publisher of *Inside Linda Lovelace*, had his appeal against the Heathrow Customs turned down on 26 April. In 1975, officers had seized sample copies of an illustrated book in which Hanau had just bought rights at the Frankfurt book fair. The work – Tomi Ungerer's *Fornicon* – was, as it happened, much worthier than Lovelace's tawdry paperback. (Although the Uxbridge Magistrates called it 'a cross between Heath Robinson and de Sade', Ungerer was an artist of international standing; *Fornicon* was based on an exhibition shown in New York in 1969.) Geoffrey Robertson (Hanau's lawyer for *Lovelace*) protested Ungerer's merits in court. Nevertheless, the Customs' contention that the item was 'clearly indecent' was upheld – and this only six weeks after the Central Criminal Court had been unable to find *Inside Linda Lovelace* obscene.

The road from 1959 had led to final confusion. The original aim had been simple – to encourage literary freedom and discourage pornography. As it now stood, the Act's provisions against pornography were everywhere flouted, and its protection of literature abused to enrich the publishers of *Inside Linda Lovelace*. The whole notion of the 'expertise' by which redeeming merit was to be validated had been contemptuously overset by the Law Lords.

All this came at a tricky time for Roy Jenkins – the architect of the 1959 reform. The Government intended to make films 'an article' under the terms of the law, so as to head off private action like Blackburn's. Denning's opinion lay athwart this measure. A Law Commission report (supposedly much favoured by Jenkins) had advised in April that the 'conspiracy to corrupt morals' charge, so opportunely devised in 1961, should be scrapped. Now, however, was hardly the time to abolish a law which, whatever its failings, succeeded in getting convictions. It was now that Jenkins must have turned to that favourite device of politicians at bay – the Royal Commission. But before the *Williams Report* was delivered, there were to be changes of government and public mood, and a sensational blasphemy trial.

June 1976:

'The Well Hung Christ' –

Gay News, Blasphemy and the Funny Bone of Society

With the Sexual Offences Act of 1967, homosexual acts between consenting adults ceased to be criminal. Over the next few years homosexuals changed their identity from oppressed sub-group ('queers') to a legitimate minority ('gays'). In 1970, the Gay Liberation Front was started in the UK. A number of magazines and papers set themselves up to cater for a self-aware community which if small (*Zipper* – the glossiest of the 70s magazines never apparently went above 10,000 circulation) was above average in educational standard, earning power and fashion consciousness. Some acted as contact magazines (it was for this service to gays that *IT* drew the authorities' displeasure in the late 60s); some (like *Playguy* or *Quorum*) simply borrowed the commercial formulae of the heterosexual market place. *Gay News*, an upmarket fortnightly paper, was founded in 1972.

Given the relatively closed circuits of the gay community, there was little general offence from its pornography. (*Spartacus's* first full frontal nude, in the late 1960s preceded by some years' *Playboy's* 'going pubic' in 1972, but no one seemed much concerned.) In mid 1975, however, there were some signs of a purge. The veteran spokesman for liberal causes, David Steel, was concerned that the police seized 16,000 gay magazines in London on 20 August. The eventual aim, thought Steel, was to roll back the advances of the Sexual Offences Act. In fact the imminent assault on gay rights was to come not from the expected obscenity and conspiracy laws, but on the quite unexpected grounds of blasphemy.

As an instrument of persecution, the English laws of blasphemy have traditionally pilloried the crazy. (The first blasphemy offender was John Taylor in 1676. He claimed, *inter alia*, to be the younger brother of the whoremaster Christ.) But blasphemy had also thrown up a series of

148

martyrs (e.g., Paine, Shelley, Holyoake) clearly more noble than the laws used against them. Around such martyrdom, some of the most effective pressure-groups for legal reform were organised. (George Holyoake's prosecution, for instance, led to the formation of the still hyperactive Rationalist Press Association.) Free-thinkers have always loathed theocratic laws, and point to America where persecution on grounds of religious deviance is unconstitutional. Nor, in the twentieth century, have the British authorities been all that proud of their potent blasphemy law. The last (as people thought) prosecution was that of Gott in 1921. He was given nine months for publishing matter 'offensive to anyone in sympathy with the Christian religion'. Particularly offensive was Gott's assertion that Christ entered Jerusalem 'like a circus clown on the backs of two donkeys'. Apparently idiotic, this case was important in leaving a state of play in which 'ridicule of Christianity' and 'bad taste' was the legal essence of blasphemy. Mere denial of the tenets of Christian belief (e.g., Edward Bond's 'God is . . . a device of class rule') was not, prima facie, blasphemous. There have thus been no 'monkey trials' in twentieth-century England. But portraying Christ as a monkey might conceivably have its dangers.

It was the reformed Obscenity and Theatre Acts of 1959-68 which turned attention to the lapsed blasphemy weapon. These laws forbid private prosecution. But blasphemy was still available to the indignant individual and to the pressure-group. Perceiving this Lady Birdwood had paid for a blasphemy action against the directors of Oscar Panizza's play, *Council of Love*, in 1970. She failed on a technicality, but cleared the way for future litigation.

Mrs Whitehouse had herself thought of invoking the blasphemy law against a particularly offensive *Till Death Do Us Part* episode in 1972 (Garnet: 'Wot abaht yer virgin birf, then?'). But the 1964 charter of the BBC made it proof against this form of attack as well as against the Obscenity and Theatre Acts. Blasphemy came to mind again in April 1976, when VALA was fearful that a Danish film-maker called Thorsen intended to make 'The Many Faces of Jesus Christ' in England. Thorsen had not had much luck with this project; in November 1973 the Danish Film Institute withdrew a £42,800 loan guarantee for what was then more candidly called 'The Love Affairs of Jesus Christ' when the Vatican complained. Now Thorsen was thinking of England as a location. VALA whipped up a very successful press campaign against this proposal; so much so that the Archbishop of Canterbury, Cardinal Hume and Prime Minister Callaghan declared that they would personally act to keep the blasphemer away.

It was while all this was on the boil, that *Gay News* 3-16 June came Mrs Whitehouse's way. At the subsequent trial it was said that a probation officer (who also happened to be a member of the Responsible Society) referred the offending issue to her. He had unknowingly picked the paper up to read an article on his profession. (Establishing these links of innocence is tactically necessary to VALA and FOL – they cannot snoop around Soho, send or receive obscene materials through the mails, or even, in the case of Mrs Whitehouse and *The Romans in Britain*, go and see a play which is costing £20,000 to prosecute.)

Gay News 96 contained a full-page poem by James Kirkup, entitled 'The Love that Dares to Speak its Name', illustrated by Tony Reeves. The illustration, which runs the length of the right hand margin, shows a conventional Deposition, with the difference that Christ is being lowered by a Roman soldier and the corpse has what Philip Larkin would term 'a tuberous cock and balls'. The poem's title is, of course, an allusion to Lord Alfred Douglas's sonnet about guilt and homoeroticism – a theme taken up by Oscar Wilde under cross-examination (some would say crucifixion): 'The love that dare not speak its name in this century is such a great affection of an elder for a younger man as there was between David and Jonathan . . .'

In the twentieth century, Kirkup's poem suggests, gays can come out and flaunt their preference. The story of the poem has a Roman left alone with Christ's body before burial. He takes the opportunity of entering orifices and wounds and manages to revive the corpse a last time to sodomise himself. The poem ends defiantly with a statement that now homosexuality will always speak its name. Closet homosexuality and crucifixions are presumably, things of the pre-1967 past.

As usual, the literary text suffered a legal tug of war. The adversarial prejudices of the two counsels starkly misrepresented the poem as (a) 'so vile that it would be hard for the most perverted mind to conjure up anything worse' and (b) a poem to be placed alongside Donne's 'Batter my Heart' and St John of the Cross. In fact, Kirkup's is a trivial poem judged by normal critical standards. In form it is a rather soppy dramatic monologue, whose only redeeming feature is an occasional engaging cheekiness. Thus the first stanza is gushily reverent, but ends with the double entendre that Christ was evidently 'well hung' (i.e., 'thoroughly crucified', but in American slang 'well endowed sexually'). And in the middle of the sacramental giving and receiving of sex with the corpse the Centurion (one assumes that he's not an OR) inserts the information that he knows that Christ has previously 'had it off' with Herod, Paul, Judas, *et al.*

Kirkup kept himself studiously away from the combat his poem provoked. But the publishers were not much helped by a statement given to the *Observer* (17 July): 'Of course I knew this would dismay and shock some people – but had I not myself been deeply offended dismayed and shocked by *their* disgusting version of the Crucifixion?' Mrs Whitehouse yielded to no one in the matter of offence. 'The Love that Dares to Speak its Name' she declared to be 'the recrucifixion of Christ with twentieth century weapons . . . the *climax* of anti-religious attacks . . . I felt I had to do something.'

What she did in late November 1976 was to start a private prosecution for blasphemous libel (i.e., written blasphemy) against *Gay News*, its editor Denis Lemon and its distributor (this last target was later dropped). In early December, she was given leave by a judge in chambers to bring charges. The ensuing trial took place at the Central Criminal Court, 4-12 July 1977, with Mr Justice King-Hamilton as judge.

It was all a huge surprise, and caught the liberal establishment somewhat on the hop. Casual blasphemy like lese-majesty had been creeping unopposed into British culture throughout the non-conformist 1960s. People might disapprove on grounds of taste, but no one seriously thought that the Tottenham supporters who dressed in biblical attire after their team won the 1963 cup and paraded the streets chanting 'hallowed be thy name . . . thy kingdom come' could be done for blasphemy in this day and age. The Beatles might say that they were now more important than Jesus, and all that would happen was that the Bible belt of the US would go incandescent with bonfires of their records. One novelist wrote a rather pathetic letter to *The Sunday Times* while the Thorsen affair was at its height. He felt it was unfair that the reading public hadn't been shocked at 'my latest novel, *The Triumph of Vice*, in which Jesus and Mary become lovers'. Such themes apparently no longer had the power to shock any but the lunatic religious fringe.

In fact, Kirkup's poem fitted VALA's desire to resuscitate the offence in all its heinousness better than other blasphemies to hand. Deviant sex and blasphemy was a more combustible mixture than mere obscenity (protected by the 1959 law) mere homosexuality (protected by the 1967 law) or mere blasphemy (protected by the tradition of freethinking dissent against which no British authority had dared take action for 50 years.) Thorsen's film was of course deviantly sexual and blasphemous, but it was also, as *The Sunday Times* called it, a 'phantom target'. 'The Love that Dares to Speak its Name' had already been published, and there was an answerable printer, publisher, poet and illustrator to punish.

One should nevertheless grant Mrs Whitehouse her due of courage. She was inviting an overwhelming volume of personal vilification. Outside the courts during the trial it was reported that there were crowds of gays shouting 'White-house: kill, kill, kill'. At one point she had thought that the DPP would take the burden from her. He didn't. Coggan and Hume, who had been vociferous when the Thorsen visit was imminent, were now silent and offered only moral support. Few senior churchmen, it was maliciously said, dared come out strongly against homosexuality. All in all, Whitehouse confessed to feeling 'dreadfully isolated'. And if things went wrong, as they could in an unprecedented case, she would also look dreadfully foolish.

In bringing her action Mrs Whitehouse was helped by a definite resentment against gays in the mid 1970s, a senti-ment (which often did not dare directly speak its mind) that they were getting rather uppity. Anita Bryant had mobilised similar resentment in the southern US into a crusade. There was moreover rather a lot of coming out in English high places around the time of the trial. Two books of the season were Tom Driberg's *Ruling Passions* and Christopher Isher-wood's *Christopher and His Kind*. Kirkup himself was a younger friend of E.M. Forster and J.R. Ackerley, only recently discovered by the general public to be homosexual mandarins. Altogether it might be thought that there was too much recent deference to Auden's maxim 'there is only one sin: disobedience to the inner law of our own nature.' Mary Whitehouse could think of other sins, and shrewdly felt that the law might help her scourge them.

What Mrs Whitehouse called 'the homosexual/intellectual/ humanist lobby' gathered behind the persecuted journal. Nicolas Walter of the Rationalist Press Association offered to send a return of post copy of the 'blasphemous' poem in exchange for an s.a.e. *Peace News* reprinted it, as at various times did the smaller circulation *Socialist Challenge*,

Freedom, the *Liberator* and *Anarchist Worker*. An *ad hoc* 'Free Speech Movement' was formed with over a hundred signatories (from Larry Adler to Des Wilson) who defiantly co-published the poem after the trial, daring Mrs Whitehouse to come at them.

There was, however, no shortage of tempting targets. VALA's first strategic problem had been who to go for: the poet, the journal, its editor, the proprietors, the printer, the distributors, the wholesalers or even the retailers. First on the list was the poet. Kirkup was indisputably the author and the work had not, apparently, been published without his consent. (How much, if anything, he was paid was never said.) But as an internal memorandum in VALA admitted, 'Kirkup turns out to be rather more substantial than we had supposed.' Not any old queen, that is, but a university professor and Fellow of the Royal Society of Literature with a sizeable entry in *Who's Who*. The printer and distributor would probably have pleaded guilty without a fight. Wholesalers and retailers were simply stooges. Lemon and *Gay News* itself were therefore selected.

The encounter in court was on familiar gladiatorial lines. On the one side John Smyth, VALA's favourite lawyer (later he was to take on *The Romans in Britain*). On the other side, Geoffrey Robertson and John Mortimer, late of the *Lovelace* trial. Since it was blasphemy at issue, there was, however, one point of difference. No expert opinions were allowed. Only Margaret Drabble and Bernard Levin were permitted to give evidence as to the good moral character of the defendants. Both asserted *Gay News* and Lemon to be 'responsible' and stood up to some 'what would you do if you saw a German raping your mother' questioning. Drabble, for instance, was asked as the mother of two teenagers whether she approved of paedophilia.

The prosecution line was that the poem was self-evidently filthy; its blasphemy 'too obvious for words'. The defence line from Robertson was that a poem cannot be read at the level of 'a lavatory limerick'. Mortimer poked fun at the antiquity of the blasphemy charge; it was 'as if we had been whisked on some time machine back to the middle ages'. The jury was out five hours. (Mrs Whitehouse and her supporters helped them with constant group prayer.) Eventually by a majority verdict of 10–2 they found journal and editor guilty of producing a blasphemous libel. According to the Rational Press Association's account, the judge had been hard on the defence in his summing up. He was certainly severe in his sentencing:

> I have no doubt whatever that this poem is quite appalling and is the most scurrilous profanity. It is past my comprehension that a man like James Kirkup can express himself in this way and that the paper should publish it with reckless disregard for the feelings of Christians and non-Christian sympathisers.

It was 'touch and go' as to whether Lemon should go to prison. He was, instead, fined £500 (or six months) with nine months suspended for 18 months. *Gay News* was fined £1,000 and ordered to pay costs (for this purpose the defence fund had collected some £20,000). The prosecution's costs were paid out of public funds, unlike those in Sir Cyril Black's comparably successful action against *Last Exit* ten years earlier.

The appeal was taken to the highest level. But the Law Lords came down with a final five to three vote upholding the sentence.

The two years following her *Gay News* triumph saw Mrs Whitehouse at a zenith of power, capable not just of reviving moribund laws but of actually creating new ones for the protection of British society. Her achievement was the more remarkable in view of the Labour Government's natural reluctance to act in advance of the Williams Commission. Her target in this legislative crusade was not homosexuality (though her 1977 book, *Whatever Happened to Sex?* indicated that she regarded it as 'abnormal') nor blasphemy (the Pythons' *Life of Brian* got through unscathed) but 'the funny bone of society', paedophilia.

Mrs Whitehouse opened her campaign in May 1977 with the announcement that 'unless we are on our guard, there is nothing to stop the impending import of "kiddie porn" from the United States in which children of three are used in sexual poses.' To put the nation on guard, she made her opening thrust not at the new Home Secretary, Merlyn Rees, but at the new leader of the Conservatives, Mrs Thatcher. The two ladies spent 75 minutes together on 3 September and Thatcher emerged 'a deeply concerned woman'. She went on to ask urgent questions of the Government, declaring herself 'appalled that these things are happening here'. Mrs Whitehouse claimed to have seen even British magazines featuring little girls 'six, seven, or eight years of age'. *The Times* offered ponderous support. It was no defence to say that these obscenities originated abroad: 'for the British to be fed by the abuse of children in other countries is no less shameful than if these acts were filmed in this country. One might argue that it is even worse.' Mrs Thatcher and Mrs Whitehouse, the paper opined 'are absolutely right to demand early legislation'.

On 17 November there was a debate on the subject in the House. Rees, who had refused a *tête-à-tête* with Mrs Whitehouse, grudgingly declared himself 'willing to see if the law can be tightened'. But clearly he would have preferred to wait a couple of years for Williams. Whitehouse, however, was not to be reined back. The matter could not wait, she insisted; there must be immediate action. The trusty Ronald Butt lent her support in his *Times* column with an article entitled 'Stamp It Out, This Abominable Evil of Using Children for Pornography.' If the country had to wait for Williams, asked Butt, 'how many lives will be irretrievably damaged?' As usual, he hinted at the 'unspeakable material' which had been shown him – this time by a clergyman hot-foot from Germany. (How did he get it past customs?) 'May we not', asked Butt, 'even see this foul material also defended by a travelling circus of expert witnesses as "therapeutic"?'

A three-front attack by the Festival of Light, the press and blue noses in Parliament whipped up a hysteria about the imminent deluge of child pornography surging across the Atlantic from an already deluged America. In the context of this hysteria, attempts to mount any rational defence of paedophilia simply fueled rage. When, in September 1977, Tom O'Carroll of PIE tried to address a conference at Swansea University on 'Love and Attraction' he was hounded off the campus.

Support for the forthcoming Protection of Children Bill was boosted by the flying in of Dr Judianne Denser-Gerben of the New York 'Odyssey Institute'. This lady was photographed, holding lurid samples of American child porn (presumably imported like herself, and highly illegal), and quoted as saying 'I cannot understand the attitude of your Home Office.' The righteous fever, as is common in Britain, reached comic proportions. The National Association of Head Teachers (21,000 strong) complained in February to the Home Secretary that 'pregnancies among school girls are increasing, and many teachers believe that the increase in pornography can be blamed.' On Valentine's day appropriately enough, it was reported that 'Edward Brincombe, aged 43, of Rattery, Devon, drove a lorry up the steps of the Eros statue in Piccadilly Circus on Saturday night and attempted to attack it with a chain saw as a protest against child pornography.' The Bow Street Magistrates fined him £50 for his quixoticism.

In spring, Cyril Townsend (Conservative, Bexleyheath) had his Protection of Children Bill discussed in Parliament. Despite its manifest emotional appeal and fierce penalties (a fine of up to £10,000, three years in prison or both) it met little opposition. As the Religious Affairs correspondent of *The Times* noted: 'few MPs care to risk seeming soft on such an inflammatory issue.' Debates in the House produced the familiar rhetoric: 'filth . . . profit . . . evil men'. The Home Office was dragged along, although all its instincts must have been to wait till 1979. The Home Secretary, too, would probably have preferred to postpone things until after the general election. But such was popular fury that Government business managers were obliged to wedge open a space for the third reading in a chock-a-block programme. It eventually got through the Commons on 20 April, 'amid cheers from both sides'.

The Bill was received in similar spirit in the Lords in early May. There was, however, one dissenting voice from Lord Houghton who declared it to be 'a buffalo bill, a stampede', observing that pornography had probably corrupted more London policemen than children. But his jaundiced comment was lost in the general jubilation that the tidal wave of paedophiliac porn was now averted from British shores.

The Bill was a triumph for Mrs Whitehouse and for the Festival of Light (though as a charity they were not technically permitted to campaign for changes in law). 'Their first big victory', a *Times* correspondent called it. Less excited than the paper's leader-writers and its resident Comstock, Ronald Butt, he also noted that 'child pornography is being regarded as a useful stick with which to beat the general law on obscene publication.' This general law, together with laws on conspiracy, indecent assault and gross indecency was already quite competent to deal with the abhorrent manufacture and trade in child porn. This was shown by the Hayman affair, when it came to light two years later. PIE, it emerged, was operating quite serenely all through summer 1978 while Parliament and the country was in such a self-congratulatory lather about child porn. What put police on to the activities of the exchange was Sir Peter Hayman's absent-mindedly leaving a packet of 'obscene material' on a London bus. The subsequent prosecutions (in which Tom O'Carroll was jailed for two years) were brought under the old 'conspiracy to corrupt public morals charge', not Mrs Whitehouse's brainchild.

It would seem that the Protection of Children Bill resembled the 'Horror Comic' legislation rushed through in similar circumstances 20 years before. Such measures are not to be taken as useful or practical: they merely mark the extraordinary lengths to which sanctimonious emotion and panic can occasionally drive the British public and its legislature.

Postscript: Brimstone and Treacle

By odd coincidence, there was an unconnected sex-and-blasphemy *brouhaha* at the BBC, exactly simultaneous with the *Gay News* affair. It focused on Dennis Potter's play, *Brimstone and Treacle*. In the mid 1970s, Potter was, by general critical agreement, the country's leading television dramatist. A new work was commissioned from him by the BBC, accepted in script form and paid for in January 1975. It was then produced by Kenneth Trodd (whose Marxism had occasionally been a sore point with the authorities) at a cost of £70,000. *Brimstone and Treacle* was advertised in the *Radio Times* for performance in the 'Play for Today' slot, on 6 April 1976. But at the last minute it was withdrawn, with a maximum of unwelcome publicity for the broadcasting authorities. Taking responsibility, Alasdair Milne, Director of Programmes, told Potter in an explanatory note (whose high-handedness infuriated the dramatist) 'I found the play brilliantly written and made, but nauseating.' The second part of the trilogy of which *Brimstone and Treacle* formed a part was substituted – ironically it contained 'worse' nudity than the piece it replaced. But it was not Kika Markham's bare breasts as much as the contentious religious theme which turned stomachs at Langham Place.

Brimstone and Treacle is a play for four characters. Tom and Mrs Bates are the middle-class parents of Patricia. She has been traumatised into paralytic, grunting dumbness by a hit-and-run car accident. But the dumbness, we are to understand, is less a case of brain damage than moral shock at having surprised Bates in bed with her best friend, just before the accident. The Devil visits the Bates household, in the shape of Martin, a wheedling young cadger. He takes over the nursing care of Patricia, a favour which her unwitting parents gratefully accept. While they are out, he twice rapes the 'vegetable girl'. On the second occasion, he is discovered in the act, and runs away. Patricia speaks for the first time in the play: 'No, Daddy, no!'

The scene of the rape must have been what Milne found particularly nauseating (the secretive, gloating violation of a powerless partner is strikingly similar to 'The Love that Dares to Speak its Name'):

MARTIN. (cont.) (*purr*) Pat-ric-ia! Pat-ric-ia!
PATTIE. Um uk.
MARTIN. Shh! Now let Daddy see dem ickle boo-boos, then. Shall Daddy see boo-boos? Ye-y-es.
He unbuttons the top of her long flannel nightdress. Then he sinks his head down on her exposed body, fondling and kissing. She starts to make louder noises. Her eyes widen.
(Move in B.C.U. Pattie's eyes)

(In a later theatrical production, Potter took advantage of the greater license of the stage to add the direction that Martin removes the incontinent Patricia's plastic pants, before fade-out.)

Medicinally, *Brimstone and Treacle* is the most unpleasant of purges. Thematically, the play argues that true awareness of the appallingness of evil leads to rebirth from primal ignorance – a state symbolised by the vegetable, conflictless but morally null existence of Patricia. She has to experience the worst that can happen to her before she can consciously or articulately respond to her condition. Like the substance of its title the play is, by design, exceedingly unpalatable. Potter himself wrote it, as he later revealed, 'under difficult personal circumstances' and victimised by considerable pain from 'acute psoriatic arthropathy', a pain which apparently strained his Christian conviction. The play, he explained, aimed 'both to parody certain familiar forms of faith and yet at the same time to give them expression'. In 1976, the BBC was in no mood to parody faith to the accompaniment of deviant sexual assaults.

Potter's reputation and career did not suffer. Inevitably, he became an anti-censorship hero. *Brimstone and Treacle* was shown at the Edinburgh Television Festival in 1977, after which the conference members collectively sent a telegram of protest to the BBC. A stage performance was given at

Sheffield the same year, and it went into production as a film (Trodd directing) in 1981.

February 1977:

Libertine

Started in 1974, *Libertine* was one of the myriad semi-underground papers to be found in the larger provincial university towns in the late hippy period. Based in Leicester, *Libertine* described itself, eclectically, as 'a mixture of *OZ*, *Suck* and *Forum*.' It sold at 75p and claimed a circulation high of around 10,000. Early issues specialised in period erotica, sepia Victorian nudes and sub-Fragonard pastoral frisking. But after five issues it was inherited by Dr (psychology) Arabella Melville (who ran the *Forum*-style 'Helping Hand' column) and Colin Johnson. These two declared themselves 'Followers of the Anarchist Prince Kropotkin' and dedicated the journal to 'sexual freedom, past and present'. They also invigorated the radical politics of the paper with horny skin-mag rhetoric. Thus, for instance, *Libertine* 9 advertised its attractions: 'Your lady editor fucks Philip Hodson, *Forum*'s sexiest male editor, we illustrate amazing sex gymnastics and publish erect cocks.'

The couple opened a bookshop in Granby Street, Leicester's town centre. It was under the nose of the police department who, thus prompted, decided to take action against *Libertine* 7, as probably the most offensive of the articles on sale. Johnson certainly thought so: as he blithely told the police officer making the formal purchase 'This one is a collector's item – we will be at the Old Bailey.'

In fact the trial was held in home town Leicester. But despite the provincial setting 'Mortimer's travelling circus' (Mrs Whitehouse's term) rallied to the defence. Francis Bennion, of DLAS, observed the proceedings – to ensure that literature and the arts were properly defended – and gave an account in the *New Statesman* (18 February). One cartoon singled out by the prosecution was peculiarly offensive. It is from a strip entitled 'Home on Leave', and is described by Bennion at some length:

160

The burly RSM, newly arrived from Northern Ireland, greets his decrepit, wizened mum. She offers him oyster pie, and crumpet for afters. 'Tell me son how was it in Ulster?' The bullock-stupid RSM replies: 'It was rough mum . . . there I was surrounded by Micks, after my arse they was, so I cocks me automatic and POW! POW! . . . hee! hee! . . . splattered her brain all over the place. That hee! hee! learned her!' A crude, troops-out cartoon but there is something more. 'Crumpet for afters' means oral sex . . . 'Melvin just loves his mum's hot crumpet' croons the balloon issuing from mum's thin lips as she lies outstretched on the kitchen table.

This is the drawing, which the *New Statesman* prudently did not reproduce:

Since the Lords ruling in November 1976, the 'therapeutic' argument was inadmissible. But Maurice Yaffe (reportedly writing his PhD on pornography) varied his normal terminology expertly by asserting that 'Home on Leave' was 'educational . . . in the sense that it expresses taboo thoughts of incest.' This extraordinary twist of Section 4's 'public good' defence was accepted by the judge. (The other extraordinary feature of Yaffe's evidence was that when he opened his evidence copy of *Libertine* 7, he discovered that a particularly raunchy pin-up of Arabella Melville had been excised. The police were suspected.)

It went down badly with the prosecution that Mortimer should defend in his usual skilfully lighthearted way. (A cartoon of the trial in a later *Libertine* shows the QC with a card reading 'If you lie, we can win' protruding from his gown.) There were also some sneers that expert witnesses were drawn from Hampstead's intellectuals, rather than the Leicester citizenry who provided the jury. But the local team, Melville and Johnson, defended themselves vigorously. She made the 'sex is innocent pleasure' case, he was clever at the expense of official hypocrisy, and finished with a perorating quotation from Harold Wilson's plea for freedom of speech at the Helsinki Conference.

The jury were out for just a quarter of an hour to reach their not guilty verdict, with a speed which suggested the case should never have been brought; the editors were completely exonerated. (They did not of course dedicate the rest of their lives to *Libertine*, but graduated to 'responsible' authorship. Still a team, they brought out *Cured to Death*, an exposé of iatrogenic medicine and pharmacy, in 1982.)

It was one of the many 'ends of an era' that one encounters in a survey like this. As *New Society* put it, the *Libertine* case demonstrated 'that prosecuting publications under the Obscene Publications Acts is scarcely on any more'. So much had been evident since the *Lovelace* trial. But the walkover at Leicester had been significant in that it marked the decisive end of a decade's hostilities whose beginning Jeff Nuttall had announced in *Bomb Culture*: 'between the autumn of '67 and the summer of '68 . . . young people under various pretexts, made war on their elders, and their elders made war on them.' The 'great sexual sermon' (Michel Foucault) preached by the young in the 1960s had been delivered, digested and was now history. A radical style youth journalism persisted in the mid and late 1970s – but it tended to ally itself with rock music and straight agitprop rather than with pornography.

Libertine takes its place at the end of a series of trials that began with *Poetmeat* in 1965, and which peaked in 1971 with the *IT, OZ* and *LRSB* affairs. It was not 'literature' which was at issue in these trials, but attitudes and lifestyles found subversive (rather than merely obnoxious) by the authorities. The charges brought had been various: obscenity, conspiratorial immorality, or the abuse of community services – such as the mails (or occasionally Arts Council patronage). There was to be no more significant persecution of this kind, not because either generation had won but because no one cared to carry on the battle to the next generation.

It was not either the end of persecution or of organised resistance. The *Gay News* trial and the child porn panic showed that. If anything authority (especially in the provinces) was unleashing its thunderbolts with renewed severity. James Anderton, for instance, recently appointed Chief Constable of Greater Manchester, determined to drive pornography far from his city's streets with a Savonarola-like ferocity. In 1977, he launched 286 vice-squad raids collecting 160,000 obscene articles. In every obscenity case he brought to court – some against journals as generally acceptable as *Penthouse* – he gained conviction. In 1976, there had been just five such raids.

March 1977:

The Fall of the Dirty Squad

Investigation of the corruption of the Metropolitan Police Obscene Publications Squad got into gear with the appointment of Robert Mark as Commissioner in the summer of 1972. There was a wave of discreet early retirements and resignations, and the purge culminated in a first trial at the end of 1976. But it was the second trial in March–April 1977 which created the bigger sensation. It revealed, as Mr Justice Mars-Jones put it: 'corruption on a scale which beggars description' (though the popular press did their best). What was shocking was that not just 'men on the beat', but 'upstairs' was revealed to have its fingers in the Soho porn-pie. Ex-Commander Wallace Virgo was (together with Kenneth Drury on a related corruption charge) the most senior Scotland Yard man ever to be brought before the London Courts. He was also the holder of the Queen's police medal. In office, Virgo had overall control of nine squads, including those specialising in drugs and porn. Over the years he contrived to block the many complaints of OPS corruption from ever being followed up. He had done this not out of comradely loyalty, but for payments (as the prosecution alleged) of up to £60,000 in all. What was even more shaming, was that this corruption had coincided with the most ferocious police assault ever against politically subversive 'obscenity' (e.g., *LRSB*, *IT*, *OZ*) and the comparatively innocent use of drugs by the dissident young.

That there was corruption in Soho was apparently an open secret among journalists, lawyers and the Metropolitan Police themselves. (According to one anecdote put around at the time of the trials, the Dirty Squad regularly provided the film entertainment for the police stag parties.) Giving evidence, one defendant (Leslie Alton, former Detective Inspector) made the interesting plea that for thirty years he had seen Soho porn-shops thrive and 'celebrities and politicians' frequent them. 'I formed the idea', he told the court, 'that it was *political* to let them flourish' (*Daily Telegraph*, 1 April 1977). Whether his idea was correct or not, they flourished as never before in the late 1960s and early 1970s. Some measure can be gained from the scale of the payoffs. From mere £50s, sweeteners rose to £2,000 a month, at their height, for the top men. In court, Virgo and ex-Detective Chief Superintendent Bill Moody were accused of creaming off up to £100,000 a year. One single bribe of £14,000 was alleged to have been made to Moody to get a pornographer off a charge.

The Obscene Publications Squad was small: fourteen to eighteen men strong. And although its territory was nominally metropolitan London, activity inevitably concentrated on Soho. Traditionally, CID men worked intimately with the criminal world. This intimacy was thickened by virtue of the fact that the pornography laws were a grey area, leaving total discretion to the officer responsible for initiating charges. The law assisted the bent copper, but gave little help to his straight colleagues. Going by the book, he had to inspect and buy (and be recognised), procure a warrant and authority to search, swoop, itemise the material (possibly tons of it) which he seized, and go to court (if the DPP agreed). If the retailer consented to the forfeiture of his material under Section 3 by signing a 'disclaimer', then the officer would have personally to supervise the destruction of the material. If a prosecution ensued under Section 2, then he would have to sit through a possibly extended trial, and face the likelihood of being made to look a clodhopping Dogberry in the box by clever defence counsel. All this would have been tolerable if porn were *rara avis* in Soho – or if there had been only a handful of dirty bookshops as in the 1950s. But by the end of the 1960s, there were at least 50, diversified into sex aids, film clubs, strip joints, mail order.

Using the letter of the law, a law which ideally required the extermination rather than the supervision of pornography, it is evident that the OPS had an impossible task. Nor were they fool enough to attempt it. They selected a different method of policing their manor – namely the protection racket. For this purpose the vagueness of the law was a positive advantage. In court, a policeman could plausibly appeal to his 'professional judgment' to explain why he had, or hadn't moved against a certain item. In this way he could protect a client or punish a rebel shopkeeper. And Virgo and Moody, whatever their qualities as detectives, were excellent businessmen. They devised, some ten years before the GLC was to come round to the idea, a 'licensing system' for opening new shops. (Top-pornographer James Humphreys recorded in his diary paying Moody and Virgo £16,000 'licence fees' over one sixteen-month period). The most memorable episode retailed in court was how the pornographer Ronald Mason would be given a CID tie by the head of OPS and go with him to the confiscated store of porn at Holborn police station. There he would make a selection for purchase and recycling back on to the Soho streets.

Unlike mere 'gangsters', the dirty squad did not offer protection in name only. Unlicensed interlopers were harassed and driven out. Forthcoming raids on clients that could not be headed off were signalled (by the hilarious code-word, 'W.H. Smith'). Some material would be left on the shelves for the law to fall on; but the most profitable (and legally vulnerable) hard core would be carted away until the heat was off. Sometimes the forewarned pornographer would recruit some luckless stooge at short notice from Piccadilly to stand at the till. He would be arrested and in court would be as 'stumm' as only true ignorance can make a man. Huge payments were made. But the trade could easily bear it in return for the commercial stability which resulted. In court, James Humphreys claimed to have made £216,000 profit (untaxed) in the boom three years 1969-72.

'Blue money' is notoriously difficult to assess. But in a series of articles in the *Observer* Business Review in mid 1971, Raymond Palmer reckoned that there were 100 outlets for pornography across the country, about half clustered in Soho. The overall annual take he estimated at £10 million. The network of distribution was integrated, with Soho acting as the Covent Garden, Billingsgate or Smithfields of filth. The big men of porn, like James Humphreys, were completely insulated from the business end of things by being 'superior landlords', and usually took no smuggling risk. (Thus, in June 1972, a Danish lorry-driver caught near Newcastle with half a ton of porn in his container lorry got six months in prison. Whosoever in London it was destined for got away scot-free.) Porn shops at this period were estimated to have been turning over as much as £2,000 to £10,000 a week. Mark-ups for legitimately produced soft core were high. For hard core they were astronomical.

Judged purely as book-merchandisers, porn shops had great commercial advantages. Their overheads were low. They did not, like W.H. Smith require High Street sites. In fact, the more spectacularly dingy their aspect, the better. Their staff, though doubtless experienced, were untrained; generally all that was needed was one sharp-eyed man at the door. No 'may I help you sir?' but an occasional 'buy up or get out' was all that was required in customer service. There was no net book agreement to worry about. (Sometimes a 'straight' book on, say, the SS or sexology, would be shrink-wrapped and sold at treble the price it cost at Foyle's, a hundred yards away.) Stock did not have to be accurately reflected in its lurid covers – prosecutions under the Trade Descriptions Act were unlikely. Nor need magazines be dated – they could therefore be kept for much longer than their month or year of issue.

Soft core was produced domestically. (A large part of it was distributed through normal magazine supply chains; some even through W.H. Smith and Menzies.) Illegal hard core could be brought in from Europe, where it wasn't hard core. Britain was the EEC member with strictest censorship standards, and porn was therefore sucked into Soho by a siphon effect; especially from Germany, Holland, Belgium and Scandinavia. Mr Heath could have found few better Europeans than the pornographers in 1971. They were also loyal to the Atlantic community. It is recorded that one leading merchant made it his custom in 1972 to jet to New York, fill his briefcase with ultra-hard flagellation/bondage/child porn bought (legally) in Times Square and jet back the next day. His cargo would be on sale in Soho, photo-reproduced, by the end of the week; grainy, perhaps, but thrilling enough for the parochial British punter to pay through the nose for it.

All this profitable jig was up, when Mark was appointed from the provinces in March 1972. He had a number of things going for him. His arrival coincided with the furious moral backlash of the Festival of Light crusade. Investigative journalism had turned a spotlight on porn. Predictably, the criminals could not keep their noses clean, nor, once apprehended, their mouths shut. Humphreys was extradited on a sordid stabbing charge, involving his wife's supposed lover. His revelations (and his indiscreet diary) opened the way for uncorrupted policemen to fall on Soho and its outlying network like a ton of bricks. In early 1973, the new West End Division anti-porn team pulled in more than 40 tons of material and nine of the porn trade's top men. Up to 100 men took part in New Year raids. At the end of 1974, one raid on Soho mustered 200 policemen and pulled no less than 45 pornographers into the net. In May a record was set when a swoop on the Cobham Farm of Gerald Citron, former public-school boy and porn merchant, yielded 100,000 books and magazines. The haul's estimated street value was half a million pounds; 75 per cent of it was classified by detectives as 'hardcore', the remainder merely 'obscene'. As *The Times* reported (22 May) 'Mr Citron pleaded guilty of possessing eighteen tons of obscene publications for gain.'

A whole range of hitherto tolerated soft-core magazines was prosecuted: Goldstar's *New Direction* and *In Depth*; Penthouse's *Forum*; *Viva*; Raymond's *Men Only*; *Park Lane*, *Search*, *Relate*. Soho, stable for years, didn't know if it was coming or going. In their zeal, the police made some injudicious calls. (On a Women's Liberation art exhibition at Swiss Cottage Library, for instance. And arguably the prosecution of *Nasty Tales* was an error.) But there was, unmistakably a new rigour.

In spring 1973, Mark put Divisional Assistant Commissioner Kelland in charge of the biggest ever Metropolitan corruption investigation. It wound up in 1976, with a string of suspensions, early retirements, resignations and dismissals. And on 28 February twelve Scotland Yard officers (some prosperously retired) were arrested. In November a batch of smaller fry were tried. All were convicted and given sentences of from four to ten years. The second trial took place in March 1977. Six officers were brought up on 27 counts of conspiracy and bribery. They all went to prison; Moody (the 'architect') and Virgo (the 'man upstairs') receiving a dozen years apiece.

The impact of the Dirty Squad scandal was enormous. Every sector of the press and media gave it maximum coverage. Until this time, few ordinary people outside the circuit of journalistic, court or prison gossip can have suspected that – rotten apples apart – their police force was systematically corrupt. The notion that officers of the rank of Inspector or Commander were up to their necks in the organised sale of illegal pornography (that most dirty handed of trades) came as a bombshell, undoing years of Dixon of Dock Green indoctrination.

The immediate reaction to the trial was one of relief. The judge declared the proceedings an 'exorcism' and the 'excision of a cancer'. Some stupid things were said in this state

of post-operative euphoria. *The Times* (14 May), for instance,
confidently reported that pornography was virtually extinct,
a thing of the past:

> The newly constituted squad has purged the West End of
> London of the pedlars . . . Trade in pornography has
> dwindled to less than a fifth of what it was in the late
> 1960s and early 1970s and it continues to decline. Maga-
> zines which at one time would cost £5 a copy are worth
> little more than £1 now. A senior Scotland Yard Officer
> said: 'There is just not the money in it any more; certainly
> not enough to contemplate trying to bribe a police
> officer.'

This is probably an inaccurate piece of reporting to rank
alongside the 'unsinkable Titanic' story. In fact, Soho's sex
industry would continue to grow, at least trebling its size
over the next three years. But in the vacuum created by the
uprooting of the OPS 'firm' a new dispensation needed to be
found, and there was a tricky period of adjustment.

The police adjustment was, in the first place, a superb
piece of public relations. It was announced in August 1977
that a woman, Commander Daphne Skillern (48) was to head
the OPS. With her came a new policy of control, rather than
suppression. As she put it in her first interview 'there is no
way that pornography can ever be eliminated, but we can try
to control it at the level where it corrupts least.' A similar
view was expressed by the DPP and by the Attorney-General
in his Upjohn lecture (November 1980). This new 'realism'
in which pornography was accepted as a fact of London life
required new, and less repressive (or unworkable) legislation
than the old 1959 Act. The Indecent Display Bill (which
came into law in October 1981), the 'sex shop' clause
inserted into the Local Government Miscellaneous Provisions
Bill (to come into effect in mid 1982) are, essentially,
measures of control. Pornography was, by the end of the
decade, conceived as a substance equivalent to cigarettes or
alcohol; in widespread use, but potentially dangerous and
therefore supervised by licence. The toleration implicit in
this legislation was bewailed by Mrs Whitehouse (*Sunday
Telegraph* 7 February 1982):

> It was like the slamming of a door at the end of a tunnel.
> 'I can't believe it!' I told the journalist at the other end of
> the phone . . . I never thought I would live to see the day

when a *Tory* government would 'license' pornography . . .
for the Conservatives even to contemplate going down in
history as the party which effectively legitimised pornography – that is incredible to me.

The 'trade' also had to make its adjustments. Police
severity after 1973 hit the soft-core market, particularly, at
a bad time. A new generation of magazine proprietors
(partly inspired by *Playboy*'s going pubic in 1972) had been
rivalling each other in pictorial daring. As a result, the safety
margin between soft and hard had been dangerously
narrowed. The whole above-ground distribution arrangement
(by which the market-leaders' huge 200,000 plus circulations
were achieved) came under threat. The wholesaling trade was,
for instance, intensely upset by the massive police raid on
Johnson's Central News Agency in Bath, April 1974. Ten
thousand copies of 238 different magazines were seized
(including, hilariously, the *TLS* – a slip which provoked
questions in the house). Of these 146 issues were found
obscene by Bath magistrates. They included *Playboy*, *Penthouse* and *Mayfair* – all of which were carried by W.H. Smith.
Given the investment in a single issue of a top skin mag,
confiscation would have been calamitous. When, for instance,
324,000 copies of the Christmas 1972-3 *Men Only* were
seized by the customs (it was printed in Holland and contained fairly explicit female masturbation photo-sets) the
best part of half-a-million pounds was lost to the British
retail trade. Arguably, by 1975 the British newsagent needed
soft porn as much as the magazine proprietors needed the
humble corner shop. There were at this time about a dozen
major publications, six to eight specialist wholesalers and a
supply to some 20,000 outlets. The retailer got a handsome
25 per cent of the 50p–£1 cover price, and since most issues
were undated, sale-or-return was not the problem that it was
with other lines of magazine.

To preserve this valuable business, the British Adult Publications Association was formed in June 1977. It aimed principally to protect members against Section 3 actions (i.e.,
confiscation by 'disclaimer', where to make life easy, the
bookseller agreed in advance to his stock being forfeited).
BAPA sought to deflect the rigours of persecution under
Section 3 partly by group solidarity, but largely by adherence
to 'voluntary' and legitimising thresholds of permissibility.
As its chairman admitted when it was set up, 'we have been
going too far recently'. 'Guidelines' were drawn up by John

Trevelyan (formerly Secretary of the BBFC) and came into force 1 April 1978. Any publishing member who transgressed them (showing, for instance, actual penetration by an erect penis) would find that retailer members of BAPA would not handle his publication. By 1979, BAPA claimed to represent 3,000 members (largely at the selling end of things) and some 80 magazines.

After the 1973-77 hiccup, the porn industry continued its serene boom. In January 1981, the conservationist Soho Society recorded that Soho's 164th 'sexploitation' shop had just opened on the site of the famous delicatessen 'House of Hamburger'. The resident population of Soho was reckoned to have fallen from 6,000 to 2,000 in 20 years, with a corresponding drop in light industry and retail (other than sex-shop) outlets. There were now more 'Swedish' saunas than Italian restaurants. There were also, some 70 'film clubs' in Soho, specialising in porn. The Tottenham Court Road fringe of Soho was suddenly transformed into a video bazaar, about a quarter of whose tapes were 'adult'. Hard video could be had at the inner-Soho sex shops – in which 'books' were now a very minor line of goods compared to 'aids', 'peep shows', and specialist pictorial magazines. According to very credible reports in *Event* and *Private Eye* (indignantly lodged on top of a sex shop in Greek Street) Soho was again thoroughly criminalised, and at risk of Mafia takeover. True or not, pornography was doing bigger business than ever.

July 1977:
Porn and the Treaty of Rome

Legal history was made in July 1977 when defendants, sentenced at Ipswich Crown Court on charges of importing pornography (German and Dutch in origin and legal in its home country) via Felixstowe, were given leave and legal aid to appeal to the higher authority of European law. Article 30 of the Treaty of Rome prohibits any 'discriminatory' restriction on free movement of goods within the community. The British authorities, who took the matter very seriously, based their case for unilateral suppression on Article 36 of the Treaty, which is concerned with the maintenance of public morality. The two defendants at Ipswich were the proprietors of a porn mail-order firm and they had been sentenced, after a 41-day trial, to eighteen months and four-and-a-half years in prison, respectively. If they won their appeal, their penalty would be set aside, their goods returned, a lot of British porn merchants would be instant millionaires, and Soho purchases would cease to smell – as much of it distinctively does – of the Danish bacon that masks its secret entry into this country.

Sir Michael Havers went himself, as Attorney-General, to argue the test case in Luxembourg in September 1979. On 15 December 1979, the European Court determined that it was, after all, a matter for the British courts' sovereign judgment. Where pornography was concerned, the rules governing free trade within the community could be legitimately modified.

So the British porn industry was denied the quick killing of selling a few container-loads of continental product without police interference (or, conceivably, OPS payoffs). But on the whole, the more thoughtful of the 'merchants of filth' cannot have been displeased. For the big business of porn had, by 1977, settled into a prosperous two-tier system by which the soft material was legitimately mass-produced at home and distributed through normal outlets (i.e., corner papershops, bookstalls, W.H. Smith for ultra-soft magazines) at very low standardised price and in circulations of up to 300,000 for the market leaders like *Mayfair* or *Club International*. Meanwhile the hard material was imported ('smuggled') and available by mail order, in Soho or 'private shops' at vast mark-ups to compensate for the salesman's risk. The fact that hard porn was illegal gave it the more savour and justified high prices. In fact, for the connoisseur it would be cheaper and more rational to get the Harwich–Hook of Holland ferry and buy the stuff legally in Amsterdam, gloat over it in a hotel room and come home empty handed but with the imagination fired.

The porn industry, by the end of the 1970s, was indeed massive. Some sense of the scale of the UK operation is given by official statements on confiscations (presumably little is disclosed in income tax returns or official reports in Company House). Commons written answers revealed that 250,000 articles were seized by the police in London in 1975, 375,000 in 1978-79 and 1 million in 1979-80. The increase, Leon Brittan stated, was largely explained by the fact that after 1978, police had been moving against those home-produced magazines which upset the apple cart by going harder – showing erect penises and penetration, for instance. The consequence of this purge was to confirm the two-tier system, ensuring that easily seized soft porn would be genuinely soft in the future.

Other massive hauls testify to the impressive size of the industry. Customs in 1977-78 seized just under 100,000 books, magazines and comics with a street value of £1 million. In another swoop on 2 June 1980, the police and customs seized books, films and tapes (video at this period was the fastest expanding sector of the market) valued at £300,000. In September of the same year, 65 cartons of smuggled books and magazines were found in a lorry-load of vegetables at Harwich; the customs estimated their value at £250,000 – considerably more than the greens they accompanied.

This last discovery highlighted the benign diversification of the pornographer's trade in the UK. The random seizures were pinpricks and could easily be borne as an occasional inconvenience (more so as the courier, not the pornographer was liable in law). Offshore there was a huge supply of high quality, ultra-hard material produced legally and cheaply in its domestic market. Scandinavian porn (the hardest of the hard) had long accommodated to international demand, and offered subpictorial text in three languages (German and English were always prominent). English-speaking America, the main source of UK supply for purely textual porn, was slightly less convenient, the lines being longer and less open. But print was anyway giving way to the international language of photo-imagery. Nowhere than in pornography, incidentally, is McCluhanism more plausible. By the 1970s, the 'dirty book' was virtually obsolete. Different tolerances from country to country, and the fact that the UK was always among the least permissive created an irresistible suction effect. In some ways it could be compared to the North and South-American marijuana traffic; but with the significant difference that pot is not produced *legally* in Mexico or Colombia. Amsterdam, Copenhagen, Antwerp and Hamburg were, by contrast, brimming with materials which needed only to be got across the channel to reconstitute themselves from soft-legit to hard-under-the-counter commodities with all the profit advantages that conversion entailed.

The contrast between the imported and home-grown commodity was spelled out by the woman head of the Obscene Publications Squad, Commander Daphne Skillern, in a press interview (29 May 1978). The 'really nasty stuff', she alleged, came from the continent. This featured torture and the insertions of 'instruments' into women. 'British magazines', Commander Skillern patriotically declared, 'were much straighter.' Item for item, however, these were less valuable than the Continental nasty stuff, which would go for as much as £10–£15 a single magazine – a mark-up of many thousands per cent.

November 1979:

The Williams Report

'The Pornographer's Charter'

Like some other Royal Commissions, the formation of the Williams Committee had its roots in governmental perplexity and desire to prevaricate. At its furthest it can be traced back to February 1974. The Heath Government had unexpectedly fallen, thanks to the miners. This occurred at a period when Robert Carr's Cinematographic and Indecent Display Bill was fairly well advanced. But the new Home Secretary, Roy Jenkins, had no love for the Conservative measure, and it was shelved. In the legislative vacuum which followed considerable confusion developed. The progressive measures dear to Jenkins's heart were blocked (the abolition of the conspiracy to corrupt morals charge, for instance – recommended by a Home Office working party in December 1974). It was not possible to get them past the massive lobby of VALA (who had amassed over one-and-a-quarter million signatures for their 'decent society' campaign), nor was it timely now with the imminent trials of virtually the whole Obscene Publication Squad (about which horror Jenkins was briefed when he took over).

The first specific mention of the Labour Government's intention to 'look into' obscenity was winkled out in Parliament in early 1977. On 1 March of that year, Irving Wardle of *The Times* reviewed the Joint Stock theatre company's *A Thought in Three Parts*; a play by Wallace Shawn, put on at the ICA. Under Max Stafford Clark, and with its workshop technique, this ensemble was in its most creative phase. (Other of its notable productions at the period were Howard Brenton's *Epsom Downs* and Barrie Keefe's *A Mad World My Masters*.) But Wardle disliked Shawn's play intensely, and was scathing about the 'most generous portions of erectile tissue' exposed and vibrated on stage, and the versatile sexual congress simulated. Michael Alison, Conservative front-bench spokesman on home affairs was, as he told the house, too busy a man to go at all often to the theatre. But he read *The Times* and he referred the Wardle review to Sam Silkin, the Attorney-General, with a 'formal' request to consider prosecuting the play, the company, the ICA or whatever. After six weeks, an uncomfortably prodded Silkin indicated that he had consulted the DPP and no prosecution could be expected. But, he revealed, the Government intended to set up a committee to consider generally the question of obscenity. No one was very happy at this news. Alison was 'disturbed and disappointed'. Critics of the Home Office saw it as a time-wasting ruse: from now on, possibly for years, the Government could turn away any uncomfortable questions with a 'wait for the Report'.

On 17 June 1977 more unpleasing details were released. Bernard Williams was to head a Committee with the task of investigating 'Obscenity, indecency and violence in publications entertainments and displays' (excluding, of course, broadcasting). The choice of chairman was immediately protested by the Festival of Light: 'Professor Williams', they complained, 'is a leading humanist' (code word for 'pagan'). Ten years before, he had gone into the witness stand for *Last Exit*! On 23 June, Michael Alison headed an all-party deputation of MPs united in their view that Williams's non-Christianity was prejudicial. Unavailingly; the appointment stood.

Williams had twelve committee colleagues, all distinguished; each was entered in the 1979 *Who's Who*. They had their first meeting on 2 September 1977, and presented their report on 31 October 1979. The Committee's conclusions are as striking for their cool, played-down style as for any positive recommendation. The *Williams Report* seemed primarily concerned to communicate an attitude towards obscenity. This attitude was rational, unexcited, intelligent. Like the *Longford Report*, it accepted the existence of a trend: 'for many years the obscenity laws have been in retreat.' Indeed, after *Lovelace*, a large part of the 1959 law was a dead letter, since it was unlikely that ever again it would be invoked for 'the written word'. But the Williams Committee was not, like Longford, alarmed about this *de facto* development, and felt if anything it ought to be made *de jure*:

the printed word should be neither restricted nor prohibited since its nature makes it neither immediately offensive nor capable of involving the harms we identify, and because of its importance in conveying ideas.

Rationality and individual freedom were the Committee's priorities. Its report repudiated the view expressed in Lord Devlin's famous 1959 lecture 'The Enforcement of Morals' that standards of behaviour need to be imposed from above on a population because 'an established morality is as necessary as good government to the welfare of society'. For the Williams Committee, the welfare of society was the product of its citizens' private 'exercise of reason'. For the rational man, pornography poses no threat because 'most pornography is trash'.

'Trash' should not corrupt the civilised man, but it might irritate him. Hence the report's most positive recommendation was that its power to cause 'nuisance' should be curtailed. The report advocated Swedish-style shops for pornography: 'which announce their nature but do not allow their contents to be seen'. As with Wolfenden and prostitution, twenty years before, the aim was not to suppress (this would be impossible while retaining a necessary measure of freedom for the individual) but to remove what could be offensive – assaultive even – from public view.

The conclusions (unanimous) of the *Williams Report* were generally tolerant, permissive and unalarmed. There must of course be safeguards for children, models, ethnic groups and animals (though perhaps this was the RSPCA's concern). But where no 'harm' was present, only that should be controlled 'which gives unreasonable offence to otherwise reasonable people'. (Unlike Longford, but perhaps as optimistically, Williams assumes a rational rather than a moral majority in the British adult population). The reasonable person, and a society of reasonable people, could dispense with the imprecise, loaded terminology in which the question had hitherto been discussed: 'Terms such as "obscene", "indecent" and "deprave and corrupt" should be abandoned as having outlived their usefulness.' This, therefore, was a commission 'On Obscenity' which advocated the junking of the term under which it was invoked. In place of this vague, moral–legal rhetoric, Williams advocated a calculus of 'harms'. The question to be asked of pornography is not 'does it deprave, is it evil?' but 'what harm does it do' and 'will more harm be done in attempting to abolish it?'

The *Williams Report* was impressively wide in its comparisons with other countries, and deep in its historical reference to Britain's past practice. It dealt with the current porn scene in unprecedented factual detail, and also had a lively section on the aesthetics of the erotic and the pornographic. It contrived to be scientifically exact, philosophically rigorous, and elegantly written. It pleased no one.

VALA were furious, more so as the report had comprehensively trounced 'their' scientific expert, Dr John Court. Selecting the least appropriate adjective in their lexicon, they called Williams 'unbelievably naive' (though they did make the good point that he had overlooked the booming area of video). Mrs Whitehouse demanded that the Government reject the report. At a meeting with the Home Secretary, Willie Whitelaw, she asserted that she had 'evidence which invalidated the Committee's main finding that there was no relation between sex crimes and the availability of pornography'. (She hadn't.) Bryan Cassidy of the GLC declared it 'inconceivable that a Conservative Home Secretary could be thinking in terms of legislation based on Williams'. (He wasn't.) In his *Times* column, Ronald Butt foamed predictably: 'Mr Whitelaw should reflect that the knowledge and instinct of the public in this matter is more important than that of the skill of a handful of committee sitters using their intellectual agility to verbalize a social problem out of existence.' *The Times*, in an editorial (29 November), found the report utterly lacking in gravitas: 'They leave the file as they found it, effectively contested by those who take a more consistently serious view of the matter.' According to Brian McWhinney MP, who had made several attempts to get an Indecent Display Bill into law, the *Williams Report* was 'a pornographer's charter'. The Responsible Society urged rejection of the Report, and the introduction of simple coercive legislation.

Like the American Commission, which in some ways it resembles, Williams was set up by a liberal administration and delivered to a reluctant (in Nixon's case downright hostile) conservative successor. On 30 November Whitelaw informed the House that there would be no 'early action' on the report. Nor was there. And if there were eventual action, it would not come from the Government. After a debate on the subject on 16 January 1980, the Home Secretary saw no way forward to reform except by a Private Member's Bill, which would resuscitate Robert Carr's almost forgotten Indecent Display Bill of 1974.

Backbencher Timothy Sainsbury (Conservative, Hove)

took on this task. His 'modest but necessary' Bill became law
on 27 October 1981. Its penalities were Draconian; up to
£1,000 and a two-year sentence. Not that anyone was ever
likely to suffer this swingeing punishment. The Bill was, by
general agreement, a shambles. For one thing, it rested on the
term 'indecent', one of those value words that the *Williams
Report* in its wisdom, advised abolishing. What was indecent?
As one aggrieved newsagent put it, it was all right if you were
bloody Sainsbury and had nothing more dubious than a
plucked chicken on your shelf. What of pacifists who found
guns 'indecent'? Or animal lovers and fur coats?

Soho sex shops embraced this law, ingenuously intended
to persecute them, eagerly. All over the square mile 'warning
notices' shot up, and hasty screens and curtains were erected.
The punters' imagination could now work overtime, pictur-
ing what criminal excitements lay behind the new barriers.
Soft porn solemnly covered itself with red-banded announce-
ments: 'Warning, sexually explicit, do not buy if you are
easily offended. Newsagents: keep away from children.' It
was wonderful for trade. For a while, even posters for
respectably certificated London films carried such stickers,
following the fashion. (E.g., *The Wolfen*, a horror film,
advertised all in black in November 1981 with a white
sticker: 'This film contains explicit scenes of a most terrifying nature'.)

Even Mrs Whitehouse had second thoughts and was displeased with the Bill. It legitimised pornography, making it a
respectable commodity if sold - like alcohol or tobacco -
under the properly controlled conditions. As one of the
members of the Williams Committee, Polly Toynbee, put it
in an article in the *Guardian* (30 October 1981), it was a
miserable fruit from what had been the most comprehensive
and thoughtful examination of obscenity ever undertaken in
Britain: 'The comprehensive proposals . . . on the workings
of the confused, impractical and intellectually hypocritical
obscenity laws have bitten the dust . . . I can't help feeling
rather bitter.'

October 1980–March 1982:
Buggering Celts –
The Romans in Britain

Howard Brenton has provoked more controversy than any British dramatist since Osborne - and like Osborne, much of the controversy centres on the issue of modern Britishness. Particularly offensive (and legally risky) has been his habit of wedding drama with current political issues and personalities. His *Measure for Measure*, at Exeter, originally had a Macmillan takeoff for the Duke, and Enoch Powell for Angelo. Under threat of libel action, the personations were dropped. *A Fart for Europe* (1973, with David Edgar) made the point its title implies. His 'Churchill' play (1974, RSC 1978-9) returned to the national totem which Hochuth had failed to topple a decade earlier. Its full title *As it will be performed in the winter of 1984 by the internees of Churchill Camp somewhere in England* indicates the play's central heresy. Brenton first attracted nationwide publicity with *A Short Sharp Shock*. (Originally it was entitled 'Ditch the Bitch'; the title was vetoed by Sir Roy Shaw, conscious of what the bitch might do in his next year's Arts Council allocation). Put on in Stratford East in June 1980 and later moved to the Royal Court, this was a lampoon of Thatcherism. A universally deprecated scene was one in which wraiths of the recently assassinated Airey Neave and Earl Mountbatten were made to appear, clutching their *disjecta membra*. Since the Theatre Royal and the Royal Court are both Arts Council clients, calls for punitive grant-removal were made to the Minister. Despite the representation of himself as the limpwristed butterfly of the Cabinet, St John-Stevas turned backwoods wrath aside with soft answers. But among the press (including a majority of drama critics - who loathe him) Brenton was a marked man.

Brenton is one of the younger generation of dramatists to be commissioned by Peter Hall to write for the South Bank National Theatre. His *Weapons of Happiness* went on in 1976, the first new play to be performed there. He apparently relished the challenge of 'establishment' theatre: 'You can go on forever as a playwright earning your living in cultural cul-de-sacs playing to 30 people a night. I now want to be tested on a big scale.' The Olivier, of course, is the biggest theatrical auditorium in the country. The only other big arena for the playwright is television. Brenton has done some work for the BBC – but evidently feels that the freedom allowed by the medium is too little.

His second play for the National Theatre, *The Romans in Britain*, opened in the Olivier on 15 October 1980. The plot is not easily summarised. In the largest sense it is a work about racism and colonialism. It merges, and sometimes deliberately confuses, three planes of action – each analytic of imperialism. Historically earliest is Julius Caesar's second military expedition to Britain in 54 BC and his pogrom of indigenous Celts. The action subsequently switches between 515 (after the Saxon invasion), and 1980 (and the British 'invasion' of Northern Ireland).

Overlooking, for the moment, the critical worth of the play, it is evident that offence was inevitable. There were those who did not like the main stage of their National Theatre profaned by Brenton's 'yob-talk'. The opening in which a prehistoric Mick wanders on stage, looks around and delivers the first line: 'Where the fuck are we?' is a deliberate affront. Even strong and sceptically patriotic stomachs turned at the third scene, in which three Romans come upon three naked Druids. They kill two and, according to the bald stage directions, the third soldier grabs the wounded survivor 'and begins to bugger him'. After some time and much grunting it seems that the Roman's prick has slipped out, or perhaps not succeeded in getting in:

THIRD SOLDIER. Arseful of piles. Like fucking a fistful of marbles. I mean, what do they do in this island, sit with their bums in puddles of mud all year long?

He stands.

Huh.

He looks at himself.

And I'm covered in shit.

(Brenton's supporters call this episode 'attempted rape'. Queen's Regulations for a later army insist that penetration need be neither complete nor sustained for rape to have been committed.)

As disturbing from the National Theatre's point of view was Brenton's provocative version of the contemporary Irish situation. The 1980 dimension of the play moves to a field near the Ulster border where a plainclothes English officer has attempted to pass himself off as an IRA sympathiser. His disguise is seen through, and despite his clear 'liberal' decency, he is executed. A choric speech applauds the ruthless deed:

I don't want to hear of this British soldier's humanity . . . And how he thinks Ireland is a tragedy. Ireland's troubles are not a tragedy. They are the crimes his country has done mine. That he does to me, by standing there.

The passage implies authorial tolerance of a particularly nasty episode in Northern Ireland. On 14 May 1977, Robert Nairac, a Captain in the Grenadier Guards but in civilian clothes and Irish disguise, was captured by the IRA just north of the border. He was interrogated, tortured, gave nothing away and was murdered.

For other reasons, winter 1980 was a tense time in Irish affairs. The Maze hunger strikers had come off their dirty protest and gone on to hunger strike. It was likely that *The Romans in Britain* would be running during the climax of their starvation, and the expected mainland bombing campaign that would follow.

First notices were a universal howl of execration. For *The Sunday Times*, James Fenton described Brenton's play as 'a nauseating load of rubbish from beginning to end . . . banal beyond belief . . . It is advertised as unsuitable for children. It is unsuitable for anyone.' In the *Guardian*, Michael Billington agreed that it was banal and 'a blood-bolter'd agitprop pageant'. Milton Shulman panned it in the *Standard*; in his view *Romans* belonged with the 'sado-masochistic, pornographic literature of Soho'. Its thunder stolen, the *Sunday Telegraph* devoted a leader to the play, labelling it 'artistically worthless . . . and morally offensive'. *The Times* and *The Financial Times* were more temperate, but as negative in their judgments. The consensus view was summed up by the *Spectator*'s Bryan Robertson – 'What a fucking play.'

In the ensuing, post-vilification 'debate', some defence of

Brenton was mounted. Playwrights were drawn in (Hampton, Bond, Pinter, Osborne) and a couple expressed union solidarity with their attacked colleague. While the play was going through the magistrates' courts, Bernard Levin, in *The Times*, delivered a surprisingly favourable verdict (in stark contrast to his stable-mate, Ronald Butt): '*The Romans in Britain*', he asserted, at article length, 'is a very good play indeed.' But Levin's intervention could not overset the now rammed-home conviction that Brenton's play was worthless, seditious and nasty.

The critics' hard words were followed by resolute attempts to break the bones of Brenton, the play's director Michael Bogdanov, and the National Theatre supremo Sir Peter Hall. There were the usual furious questions in the House, which St John-Stevas met with his usual cool: 'Attacks on this play at the National have had one effect – to fill that theatre.' (He was right, the play was promptly booked out for the rest of its run.)

Notably uncool was Sir Horace Cutler, leader of the GLC. He stormed out of a preview and fired off a letter, via an eager press corps, to Peter Hall (currently in New York with the uncontroversial *Amadeus*), drawing his attention to this 'disgrace' to the fair name of London. He also hinted broadly that the GLC annual grant (£630,000 in 1979-80) was in jeopardy. Mrs Whitehouse, uncontaminated by any exposure to the play, but alarmed by reports, complained to the authorities. On 18 October, it was announced that the Obscene Publications Squad would be paying a visit to the theatre the following week.

Hall stood by his protegé. Once or twice a year, he said, 'we take a risk doing new things'. Replying to Cutler, he called *Romans* 'an ambitious and remarkable piece of dramatic writing'. ('Remarkable' was, perhaps, lukewarm for a production on which he had lavished some £100,000 of the state's cash.) Hall insisted that only poor audiences would induce him to shorten the play's run and, given the present publicity, empty seats were the least of his problems. (In late October, touts were marking up tickets 100 per cent.) But the theatre's position was not helped by Brenton's agent who was quoted in *The Times* as saying: 'this is how the Romans behaved . . . in fact it is rather touching.' He added, 'the sad thing about the subsidized theatre is that you have to get your money from such boring sources.' He would evidently have preferred Peter Hall to pull a stocking over his head, like the IRA, and rob a bank or two for the cause's war chest.

The familiar battle lines were drawn. John Mortimer gave his opinion that prosecution was 'unlikely'. VALA's lawyer saw the play ('numbed', as he later claimed) and found a *prima facie* breach of the law. The Festival of Light (like the National Theatre a registered charity) demanded that the Charity Commissioners intervene. The National Front favoured more direct action: a contingent demonstrated outside the theatre, others inside on 7 November pelted the stage with eggs, fireworks and flour bombs.

Britain was once more in a glorious tizzy about 'filth'. And, by a perfect coincidence, the BBC transmitted a twentieth-anniversary dramatisation of the *Chatterley* trial (November 1960), while the furore was at its height. History, however, did not repeat itself. On 24 October Scotland Yard indicated that it would not be making any submission to the DPP. A month later the Attorney-General stated that he would not permit any private prosecution of the play. It was not, he said, unconsciously echoing David Mercer, 'a suitable case'.

Mrs Whitehouse was reported as 'angry'. *Romans* was 'obscene rubbish . . . it had appalling reviews and no critic defended it'. Nor was she to be thwarted. As with the *Gay News* prosecution she looked for other legal instruments, and found one in the Sexual Offences Act of 1956. Using this, and exploiting a loophole in the 1968 Theatres Act, a private summons could be brought against Bogdanov for 'procuring an act of gross indecency between 2 actors in December 1980'. Such acts, of course, would more normally be expected to occur in the theatre's lavatories.

On another front, Cutler's threats were made good. In March, as *Romans* reached the end of its run, the GLC held the 1981-82 grant to the National Theatre at the previous year's level. Since its other main clients had an increase for year-on-year inflation this was effectively a cut. But according to the Council Arts Committee, 'There has to be a line drawn somewhere.'

The ingenious form of the charge against Bogdanov posed problems in that it predicated such a nasty little malefaction. *Romans* could not be defended head on by Hall and Brenton with grand gestures towards 'literary merit' and 'the public good'. Nor, more importantly, could the theatre put its money and its reputation entirely behind their director, should he draw the dirty old man's maximum £1,000 and

6 months.

The committal proceedings took place at the end of June 1981 at Horseferry Road Magistrates Court. Bogdanov pleaded not guilty, and if, in fact, committed he elected for trial by jury (with the consequent risk of maximising his sentence). Giving evidence, Hall revealed that he 'had insisted that the rape scene should take place in full light and down stage'. He made his routine comparison with Gloucester's blinding and defended the brutality of Scene 3 as necessary artistically: 'in my view the scene is a precise and inevitable metaphor about the brutality of colonialism.' In between allusions to Euripides, Ibsen and Shaw, defence counsel pointed out that this was the first time that the 1956 Act had been used for an overtly 'simulated' act of buggery, without sexual gratification to any of the participants. Moreover, if Bogdanov had been a woman, the charge could not have been brought (though presumably Hall might have been had for running a bawdy house). Jeremy Hutchinson (the original *Chatterley* counsel) even discovered some modesty in the offending passage. 'The hand of the soldier', he maintained, 'was over his penis and the penis remained not erect.' (In the later trial it was alleged that this 'penis' was in fact the actor's thumb – how that could have been detumescent is physiologically interesting.)

John Smyth QC (VALA, in his turn a veteran of the *Gay News* trial) ignored any aesthetic sophistication in his submission: if one man thrusts his thing towards another man's rectum in a public place, was that not indecent? The bewildered magistrate (who had not read the play, apparently) decided that it was a 'mundane offence' but 'obviously a case of public importance'. He was sufficiently persuaded to commit Bogdanov on bail for later trial.

British justice grinds notoriously slowly. There was a delay of over eight months between Michael Bogdanov's being committed at Horseferry Road Magistrates' Court on Section 13 of the 1956 Sexual Offences Act, and the case coming to Court No. 1 at the Old Bailey on 15 March 1982. An even longer period of time separated the jury trial from the alleged gross indecency – notionally set as having occurred on 19 December 1980.

In this interval, the opposing propaganda and fund-raising machines were cranked up. Mrs Whitehouse's VALA and the Festival of Light worked through the closed circuits of their membership mailing lists. For Bogdanov (whom the National Theatre could not directly underwrite) a Theatre Defence Fund was set up. Howard Brenton toured the country, giving one-man readings of *Romans*. Equity held meetings and collections. The Oxford Playhouse was organised for readings of the transcript of the day's legal proceedings (tricky, this – since if the performance veered from 'report' to 'dramatisation', there would be a contempt of court). From all sources, the Defence Fund amassed £7,000 by 15 March. They also had solid support from various grandees: the Lords Olivier and Goodman, Trevor Nunn, Harold Hobson, Peter Brook and Janet Suzman were on call to give character witness. Defending counsel was Jeremy (now Lord) Hutchinson; when Bogdanov's age he had successfully defended *Lady Chatterley* in the same court. Reportedly, he had waived part of his fee for this case.

It was, as the press inevitably dubbed it, 'the biggest obscenity trial since *Lady Chatterley*'. Bigger, in a sense: Whitehouse versus the National Theatre promised a clash of Titans. In the event, what the expectant British public got was the biggest fiasco since the second Clay–Liston fight. The trial, originally estimated to go on for two stormy weeks, was all over in three listless and inconclusive days.

The story of the trial is easily summarised. On Monday 15 March the jury of nine men and three women was sworn in, after some mild inquisition as to affiliation with VALA and FOL. (Friends of the National Theatre were not, apparently, objectionable.) Neither Whitehouse nor Brenton were present. Bogdanov was not placed in the dock, but in the well of the court, flanked by supportive Equity officials. The remainder of the first day was taken up with opening addresses, designed to put the jury in a properly grave and open state of mind. On the Tuesday, the prosecution's single witness was questioned and cross-questioned. Mr Graham Ross-Cornes had been Mrs Whitehouse's solicitor for eight years and was a member of VALA. He had observed the play for his client on one night in December 1980, sitting 90 feet away, switching his attention from the stage to a torch-lit text and evidently in a condition of considerable moral pain. He was not, it emerged, an experienced theatre-goer (he admitted to an incredulous Hutchinson that he had never seen a production of *King Lear*). Nor, seemingly, was he well up on human anatomy. Though Hutchinson had shown himself similarly confused at the committal proceedings, he was now able to inform Ross-Cornes that what he had taken to be an erect Roman penis was, in fact, the actor's cunningly protruded thumb. All in all, Hutchinson gave this single pillar of the prosecution case a rough shaking.

On the third day, the bit between his teeth, Hutchinson made a submission to the judge, Mr Justice Staughton, to the effect that there was really no case to answer. In return, the judge gave a controversial ruling. Taking Hutchinson's three main points he determined: (1) That the 1956 Sexual Offences Act could indeed apply to events on the theatrical stage – there was no special privilege for drama. (2) That a 'simulated' sexual act could still constitute gross indecency. (3) That the motive of 'sexual gratification' was not essential for the charge to stick. Altogether, the prosecution was 'specious, although technically correct'.

Thereafter, proceedings dissolved into what the next day's papers, in a fury of frustration, variously called a 'shambles . . . farce . . . débâcle'. Having secured the judge's go-ahead, the prosecuting counsel, Mr Ian Kennedy, announced that they no longer cared to pursue their case. Mrs Whitehouse, from her HQ in farthest Essex, insisted that she had nothing to do with this astounding turnabout. (Some commentators immediately surmised that her rustication was schemingly set up to pull just such a trick. She had been very prominent at the other trials she instigated.) Having gone on record to say that there was a case in law, the judge was understandably miffed at being left with nothing to preside over. The Attorney-General was reported (by the *Sunday Telegraph*) as being furious that his court had been used by Mrs Whitehouse for what looked like a publicity coup. He was obliged to intervene with a '*nolle prosequi*'. (This odd termination to a trial apparently occurs about half-a-dozen times a year when, for example, a key witness dies.)

In the confusion outside the court, both sides claimed victory. According to Hutchinson, the moral was 'You get your knickers in a twist if you launch a private prosecution.' The chaplain to the National Theatre expressed a quite pagan jubilation at his fellow-Christian's discomfiture (as he saw it): 'The spiritual fascism she advocates has got to be resisted. She has a good deal of egg on her face today and hallelujah.' But significantly, the principals were gloomy and frustrated. Brenton could 'see no justice of any kind'. Bogdanov was 'very angry that it finished without a conclusive decision. We were not able to put forward coherent and cogent arguments for a play that we had performed with absolute integrity.'

For her part, Mrs Whitehouse was radiant. She had, she

repeated time and again on television, radio and in the papers 'made her point'. Of course she didn't want to send a nice young man like Bogdanov to prison – and him with a wife and young family. As for the £20,000 estimated costs: 'the Lord wanted me to do this; I believe the Lord will provide.' (That very morning after the trial, she had received a 'heart-warming' £400 in the post.) If her knickers were twisted, and her face egg-spattered, she wasn't showing it.

There was conjecture that Mrs Whitehouse had lost her nerve, cut and run. But, with hindsight, it looks very much as if her decision was canny, and left her winner on points. For one thing, she probably would not have got a guilty verdict with nothing more than Ross-Cornes's honest simple-mindedness to sway the jury. Secondly, she had quite taken the wind out of the defence sails at the most tantalising moment for them. There they were at the Old Bailey with Sir Peter Hall and the Lords Goodman and Olivier all waiting outside with no witness stand to go to. Bogdanov and Brenton had been muzzled by *sub judice* for over a year, now they had been denied their great perorations – all they could do after the trial was ineffectually complain. Thirdly, the judge's ruling left Mrs Whitehouse, as Harold Hobson put it, with a half-nelson on the whole of London theatre. If Staughton's opinion were taken as a precedent, anyone might now bring a gross indecency charge against 'simulated' sexual activity on stage, secure in the knowledge that it was technically admissible. It all created a vague climate of fear for the British theatre, which after the 1968 Act had felt itself safe from the philistines. The dramatist David Edgar was inclined to see the whole thing as very sinister indeed – a harbinger of that imminent totalitarian *putsch* which haunts the imagination of the younger National Theatre dramatists:

> It is [Edgar wrote in the *Guardian* 20 March] at the very least symbolically significant that, in the same week as crime, race, hanging, corporal punishment and the decline of the family became neatly congealed in one reactionary package, a mucky and murky judgment lays the theatre open to arbitrary prosecution under statute law.

Of course, the efforts of the Theatre Defence Fund were now directed to blocking the loophole Mrs Whitehouse's ingenuity had found. (Briefly, the drafter of the 1968 Act overlooked the fact that private prosecutions might be brought under statute as well as common law.) But such

emendations take time. Anyway, who knew what other
loopholes for private action the wily Whitehouse might
discover? (Her range was already impressive; in 1974 she
turned up the vagrancy laws to persecute the film *Blow Out*;
in 1977 the supposedly defunct blasphemy laws for *Gay
News*; in 1980, the Sexual Offences Act for *Romans in
Britain*.)

Mrs Whitehouse, may well have decided the trial was going
nowhere, and never would. As usual with trials about literary
obscenity, issues were becoming totally fogged by the mis-
match of two discourses, the literary–critical and the
forensic. Take, for instance, a crucial exchange on the question of 'simulation' between Hutchinson and Ross-Cornes
(as reported in the *Telegraph* 17 March);

> Mr Ross-Cornes said he could not see any difference be-
> tween an act of gross indecency committed in the street
> and on the stage. 'I think gross indecency is gross in-
> decency no matter what context it is in.'
> LORD HUTCHINSON. If three young men walked about
> naked in the street would that be entirely different than
> walking about on the stage of the National Theatre?
> MR ROSS-CORNES. Yes it would. Clearly it would be an
> offence if it happened in the street. As far as the law is
> concerned it would appear not to be an offence in the
> theatre.
> LORD HUTCHINSON. Supposing a man and woman were
> making love on the stage or on film. It is a very different
> situation from them doing it on the pavement, is that
> not right?
> MR ROSS-CORNES. I think the degree of indecency would
> be the same wherever it takes place.

The central quarrel here returns to an aesthetic problem,
definitively worked over long before the Romans invaded
Britain. In the *Poetics*, Aristotle takes 'mimesis' as his starting point. Why do we 'enjoy' tragedy – a literary form
depicting such events as Oedipus blinding himself or Prome-
theus having his living liver torn out? Surely not because
we are sadists, but because we know, while responding with
a full range of emotion, that what is before us is an 'imitation'.

All this is basic stuff for English students. But there are irreconcilable differences between the procedures of law and the procedures of literary criticism in such matters. The law takes a different view of 'imitation'. In legal terminology the concept cohabits with 'counterfeit', 'forgery', 'fraud'. A more intractable problem than vocabulary is the monistic nature of legal discourse. For the literary critic, ambiguity is often a very good thing and its presence is taken to enrich a text. The process of the law is designed strenuously to eliminate ambiguity from its discussions and from the appearance of what it investigates. More directly to the point of the *Romans*, the law cannot tackle the literary–critical doublethink by which – as Dr Johnson put it – we can know quite consciously that we are in a theatre watching a performance of *Henry V*, yet respond with patriotic tears to the battle of Agincourt. For the law, it was *either* a penis (if so the worse for Bogdanov) *or* a thumb. For literary criticism, the thumb *was* a penis, insofar as a good imitation was achieved.

In the example quoted above, Hutchinson is turning his coat somewhat and discoursing like a literary critic the more effectively to bamboozle Ross-Cornes. In terms of legal theatre, it was a clever performance and made his victim look a clodhopping clown. But Mrs Whitehouse, conscious of her power to stage-manage, had a *coup de théàtre* of her own.

1982:

The Censorship of Enlightenment – Feminism and Pornography

In the struggle to get the 1959 Act passed, and in its defence from reactionary backlash in the 1960s, the liberal lobby had no more dedicated parliamentary ally than Tom Driberg. Towards the end of his life, Driberg took advantage of the freedoms he had helped to bring about and preserve in his candid autobiography, *Ruling Passions*. Published post-humously in 1977, the work attracted favourable reviews both for its stylistic elegance and its utterly frank confession of homosexuality. The following, for instance, describes the young Driberg's encounter with a hungry, unemployed man in the 1930s:

> Sodomy does not happen to be my favourite sexual pas-time, but I could hardly resist so unassuming a charmer . . . The actual entry was I fear I must say suspiciously easy; this meant either that the orifice had been coated with Vaseline (or the better class 'K.Y.') to facilitate previous entries or that my bed-mate was suffering from diarrhoea, a common by-product of dietary impoverish-ment. The latter, alas, proved to be the case as a saffron smear on the cheap cotton sheet testified.

There was general admiration for *Ruling Passions* (even a foreword by Michael Foot). But some socialists were slightly niggled by aspects of Driberg's cruising adventures, so honestly narrated. In the *New Statesman* (15 July 1977) Mervyn Jones (a prominent witness in the recent *Lovelace* trial) ruminated: 'I find it hard to make my mind up about the sexual passages . . . what bothers me is that the men who were Driberg's one-night stands are treated simply as sex objects.' This famous socialist never suffered 'dietary im-poverishment' nor lay on 'cheap cotton sheets' except in the way of fun. However one applauded the openness of his memoirs, did Driberg's candour amount to 'exploitation'?

Doubts of Jones's kind are symptomatic, and mark a second phase in decensorship. Once the principle of literary freedom was gained (effectively around 1977-79), did its supporters really approve of what was freely expressed? It was particularly the emergent women's movement who registered this anxiety. As Polly Toynbee, a member of the Williams Committee, recalled: 'women's groups testified uneasily . . . on the one hand they detested pornography for its exploitation of women. On the other, most of them did not want to ally themselves with the Festival of Light, or to demand tight censorship' (*Guardian*, 30 October 1981). Women fought and witnessed as fiercely as any for *Lady Chatterley*'s emancipation. But since 1960, things had become even muddier. Not that it was all bad news. In America, particularly, there had come up a very liberated generation of writers since 1959; if Henry Miller, for example, had any direct literary progeny they were of the opposite sex – Gael Greene, Erica Jong, Judy Blume. These women offered fiction with balls, as if to deny the imputation of Germaine Greer's eunuch thesis. And if Mr Griffith-Jones had cared to count the four-letter words in their work (as he fatuously and pedantically did for *Chatterley*) he would have needed a pocket calculator.

But such liberations were a marginal gain set against the huge volume of male chauvinism unleashed in the same period. It ranged from Norman Mailer's high literary piggism to the Naked Apism of the mass circulation girlie magazines. Some skin mags actually made sexism their gimmick: *Hustler* in the US, for instance, or *Rapier* launched in the UK in 1978 with promotion such as the following:

> Yes, monthly *Rapier* (the Magazine the Libbers hate) for Male Chauvinist Pigs is still on the loose . . . After all those threats from militant women libbers, more and more copies are selling of this large-size, picture-packed monthly devoted to putting women back where they belong [pre-Indecent Display Act covers show nude women, subserviently kneeling in front of a haughty, phallic male, his 'rapier' decently masked from view]. Men seem to leap at this new weapon in the hotting up sex war. Maybe it's no holds barred features like *Rapier*'s Womenhater's diary.

Rapier's sweaty provocation is so blatant as almost to be

innocent. Women were more concerned at subtler forms of ideological aggression. Orthodoxy had changed since 1960, when the pro-censorship lobby was held to comprise blimps, prudes and old-maids. In the late 1970s there emerged a coherent 'censorship of enlightenment'. It was not just women: librarians and teachers combined to form pressure-groups against racism and against sexism (typically, they demanded the withdrawal – censorship in old-fashioned terminology – of obnoxious texts, such as, notoriously, *Little Black Sambo*.) The gays who picketed Friedkin's film *Cruising* for its travesty of homosexuality were loosely part of the same 'progressive' forces of reaction as the women who picketed de Palma's *Dressed to Kill*.

For such protesters, 'obscenity' was redefined in sectarian terms as 'containing violence or condoning violence against women' (or gays, or blacks). Thus Anna Coote (the same who gave evidence that *Lovelace* was not obscene) began a *New Statesman* 'Londoner's Diary' in 1981 with the angry observation: 'Why won't Universal Pictures deny that they are making a film about Peter Sutcliffe? Rumours have been flying for some time now and women in Leeds have launched a campaign to try and pre-empt the *obscenity*.' In fact and in law, a film about the Ripper would be tasteless; libellous if it identified some victims as prostitutes; and even blasphemous if God were shown giving Sutcliffe orders. But it could not be 'obscene' by the now slackened terms of the 1959 Act. It is clear, however, that progressive formers of opinion, like the *New Statesman*, were strongly in favour of censorship of the doctrinaire kind that would have made them indignant some years earlier. (Indeed, there was still a residual tendency to such indignation; the literary editor, David Caute, was supposed to have resigned in 1981 because he could not take the journal's 'book-burning' campaign against racist-sexist children's literature.)

By 1980, a majority of thinking women manifested broad consensus about pornography. Like contact sports, it was a typically male pastime. It is true that the American Commission of 1970 had detected a potential feminine market for erotic material of the kind universally sought after by men; and there had been attempts by some British sex-shop chains to introduce gimmicky 'women's hours' (largely because women are major purchasers of sex aids like vibrators). Some magazines, like *Playgirl*, offered male centrefolds, and pornography certainly influenced modelling and mannequin styles in magazines directed solely at women. But in general, pornography remained obstinately an overwhelmingly male commodity which used women. It was almost entirely about one sex, and almost exclusively for another sex.

By 1980, one could go on to say that a lot of women actively loathed pornography, and saw it as a malign genie let out of the bottle in 1960. But how to act against it? Two courses suggested themselves. One was direct action. American 'Women Against Pornography', had, for instance, opened a storefront in Times Square offering guided tours of sex joints. They had marched to 'reclaim the night' and picketed tirelessly. The same methods had been used, less fiercely, in Britain. In some provincial towns, patrons had been threateningly photographed as they entered and left sex shops (the implication being that the picture would be published). Some sex shops were daubed, had superglue stuck in their locks, and even arsonised. London advertisements (the Bond *For Your Eyes Only* was a favourite target) were generously splattered with 'sexist crap' stickers. There had been marches and candlelight parades through Soho. But, on the whole, the direct action option was taken to be unEnglish and unwomanly.

A second course of action was to analyse pornography in order to integrate a critique of it into a larger ideological programme. For this, the facts on pornography must be got straight. It must be dismantled, to uncover how it constructed false female identity socially and politically. Once this secret was revealed, the correct mode of subsequent, decisive struggle would be clear.

Enthusiasm for feminist analysis of pornography as the essential prelude to combative action accounts for the huge publicity and urgent debate which accompanied the (English) Women's Press publication of two American books on the subject in 1981: Andrea Dworkin's *Pornography: Men Possessing Women* and Susan Griffin's *Pornography and Silence*. Of the two, Griffin's has the more philosophical approach. She takes pornography as the expression of a dominant, chauvinist 'mind', in terms of which women (together with Jews and blacks) are oppressed. With considerable eloquence, Griffin develops the Lawrentian, lapsarian view that pornography 'does dirt' on sex, extending his theory to the contemporary, post 1960s scene. (She gives, for example, an excellent description of the ubiquitous urban 'combat zone', a desolate sex-ghetto of boarded windows and seediness that varies astonishingly little from capital city to capital city.) As Griffin sees it, pornography incarcerates the psyche: 'its task is to chain and imprison the heart, to silence feeling'. The pornographer and his accomplice addict are a sick patriarch; 'like the church father he hates and denies a part of himself'. And this hated part he cuts away and exteriorises as the pornographic woman-object. Pornography plays out, obsessively and with Sisyphean futility an over-determined masculinity's futile attempt to deny its feminine component. Pornography's opposite is, according to Griffin, not puritanism, but 'eroticism' in which the male and female principles are harmoniously fused.

Dworkin's book is angrier both in its 'barbaric yawp' tone and in its thesis. Her analysis derives from Susan Brown-miller's. In that author's bestselling polemic, *Against Our Will*, rape is analysed not as 'crime', but as the apparatus by which men keep women in line; rape is a disciplinary measure – it bears the same relationship to feminism as hanging to murder. For Dworkin, pornography is systematic and ubiquitous; it too holds women in their subordinated place. Not for her is porn 'symbolic', 'fantasy' or 'wish fulfilment'; as she bluntly and transitively puts it: 'porno-graphy is what men *do* to women.' In this, her thesis actually hardens Brownmiller's much quoted maxim: 'pornography is to rape as theory is to practice.' For Dworkin, porno-graphy is tantamount to rape in itself. As she portrays it, pornography is the main constituent of 'male supremacist ideology', and is, therefore, as ubiquitous as is sexual oppres-sion. In a flight of commercial hyperbole, Dworkin goes on to assert that 'pornography is larger than the record and film industries combined.' (The 1970 American Commission on the subject convincingly demonstrates that porn is in fact small potatoes, compared with other media products.) More convincingly, Dworkin argues not just that pornography is a boom industry, but that it has changed its 'political' charac-ter radically since 1960:

The old pornography industry was a right-wing industry; secret money, secret sex, secret promiscuity, secret buying and selling of women, secret profit, secret pleasure not only from sex but also from the buying and selling. The new pornography industry is a left-wing industry: pro-moted especially by the boys of the sixties as simple pleasure, lusty fun, public fun, the whore brought out of the bourgeois home into the streets for the democratic consumption of all men . . . The new pornography is left wing; and the new pornography is a vast graveyard where

the Left has gone to die. The Left cannot have its whores
and its politics too.

Dworkin's most daring historical interpretation of porn, is to
link it directly to the holocaust:

> The concentration camp woman, a Jew – emaciated with
> bulging eyes and sagging breasts and bones sticking out all
> over and shaved head and covered in her own filth and cut
> up and whipped and stomped on and punched out and
> starved – became the hidden sexual secret of our time.
> The barely faded, easily accessible memory of her sexual
> degradations is at the heart of the sadism against all
> women that is now promoted in mainstream sexual propa-
> ganda . . . in fact, in creating a female degraded beyond
> human recognition, the Nazis set a new standard of mas-
> culinity.

(Dworkin, incidentally, seems to forget or ignore that there
were male inmates.)

Dworkin's *Men Possessing Women* is a powerful tract. Nevertheless, there are weaknesses in her case. These may be
described under three headings.

(1) Aesthetic   For Dworkin 'pornography *is* violence
against women'. At first, this formula seems clearer-cut than
the conventional 'pornography represents/symbolises/ex-
presses violence against women.' But Dworkin's direct equation lands one in difficulty if one removes it from the
certainty of sloganeering, and tries to apply it as an insight.
A visit to any Soho film 'club', strip joint or massage parlour
suggests that the clients (punters) are more pathetic than the
girls. This is particularly the case in strip shows, where female
contempt comes off in waves as astringent as anything
Dworkin could project. Minimal field work suggests that
pornography exploits a large class of purchasing men. The
men who organise the porn-industry do not clubbably *give*
their products to other men in a spirit of leering cameraderie.
They sell it at vast mark ups, as a pusher might exploit the
weakness of an addict.

(2) Historical   According to Dworkin 'we [i.e., women]
shall know that we are free when pornography no longer

exists.' When Khomeini came to power, one of the first things he did (after deporting Kate Millett) was to abolish 'pornography'. It was a term he defined narrowly, and for which the penalty would be death. The very next thing the Ayattolah did, was to return women to the Middle Ages by the reintroduction of polygamy, child marriage, limited education and the compulsory veil (naked faces being pornographic). In this up-to-the minute case, the abolition of pornography meant the enslavement of women.

(3) Tactical   The pornography issue brings the ultra-committed feminist, like Dworkin, into a position of Crusoe-like ideological isolation. 'Right-wing, backlash' feminism of course is shunned – even though Mrs Whitehouse is as passionately against filth as any enlightened woman. Right-wing men are, of course, the blackest of beasts, even though they too abhor (or publicly profess to abhor) pornography. But according to Dworkin 'right-wing men want pornography kept private and secret for their own use, their dirty little secret . . . They want to use it to maintain the distinction between 'good' and 'bad' women, even though they really believe *all* women are inferior.' So much for Longford, Holbrook and Muggeridge. On the other side of the political line, the 'Left' with its advocacy of 'no censorship' is hardly better: 'the male Left and Right . . . are one in their underlying hypocrisy and disregard for women . . . the Left cannot keep both its politics and its pornography. It must choose' (i.e., come out for the suppression of porn, the revocation of the first Amendment and the repeal of the 1959 Obscenity Act). Gay men are a particular disappointment to Dworkin: 'the schism between gay men and lesbian feminists caused by pornography is equalled only by the schism caused by paedophilia.' 'Gay men', observes Dworkin 'tend as a group to be active and passionate supporters of pornography' (indeed they do, as the advertisements in *Gay News* testify). Those time-serving women who 'believe in community with men – whether sexual or political' will similarly have no chance until the pornography issue is resolved. All of which leaves Dworkin and a few other enlightened feminists fighting a long, lonely battle. And opposed against massive apathy and an ever-more sophisticated pornography industry, it is hard to see how they could ever expect victory.

At least one could say that the consensus with which the whole process began in 1959-60 was well and truly fragmented. With the nicest of historical ironies, a new film of

Lady Chatterley's Lover was issued in 1981-82 (by the director of *Emmanuelle*) to violent objurgations from the women's movement. As one feminist wrote in the *Guardian* (9 December 1981):

> Twenty odd years ago the degree of sexual ignorance in this country was so appalling that it was an easy matter for the academic establishment to promote a sexually repressive fascist novelette such as *Lady Chatterley's Lover* as a beacon of enlightenment . . . Are we still prepared to accept this cheating obscenity?

Griffith-Jones could not have put it more forcibly.

Index

199